THE ETHICAL ORGANISATION

ETHICAL THEORY AND CORPORATE BEHAVIOUR

Alan Kitson and Robert Campbell

MACMILLAN
Business

First published 1996 by
MACMILLAN PRESS LTD
Houndmills, Basingstoke, Hampshire RG21 6XS
and London
Companies and representatives
throughout the world

ISBN 0–333–62565–X hardcover
ISBN 0–333–62566–8 paperback

A catalogue record for this book is available from the British Library.

Copy-edited and typeset by Povey–Edmondson
Okehampton and Rochdale, England

10   9   8   7   6   5   4
05   04   03   02   01

Printed & bound by Antony Rowe Ltd, Eastbourne

Contents

Contents vii

Acknowledgements

This book is concerned with the problems raised by collaborative enterprise. Fortunately, few of the problems it discusses were faced in its actual production even though the book itself was also a collaborative enterprise. Because we realised early on the value of including material which focused on specific areas of management and actual cases, we also realised we would need to draw on contributions from specialists in those areas. We would like to take this opportunity to record the extent and nature of those contributions and also our thanks to those who made them:

Peter Taylor, Senior Lecturer in Accountancy, Bolton Business School, for Chapter 4

Trevor Williamson, Principal Lecturer in Financial Services, Manchester Metropolitan University, for Chapter 5

Dr M. Teresa Lunati, Senior Lecturer in Economics, Bolton Business School, for Chapter 9

Peter W.F. Davies, Lecturer in Strategic Management, Buckinghamshire College, for Chapter 10

Professor Greta Richards, Assistant Director, Newcastle Business School, and Collette Blanchfield, National Provincial Bank, Leeds, for Chapter 11

Graham Wood, Head of School of Business, University College Salford, for Chapter 12

Brian Elliott, Senior Lecturer in Operations Management, Bolton Business School, for Chapter 13

Wes Haydock, Senior Lecturer in Human Resources Management, Bolton Business School, for Chapter 14

Margaret Leigh, Lecturer in Accountancy, and Richard Schofield, Lecturer in Law, Bolton Business School, for Chapter 15.

ALAN KITSON
ROBERT CAMPBELL

Notes on the Contributors

Collette Blanchfield works for the National Provincial Bank in Leeds.

Peter W. F. Davies teaches strategic management and business ethics at Buckinghamshire College (a college of Brunel University). He is a member of COPE (Centre for Organisational and Professional Ethics), a joint Buckingham/Brunel venture. He graduated in mining engineering from Newcastle University in 1977, and worked for several years as a mining and production engineer. He took a master's degree in robotics and manufacturing automation at Imperial College.

Brian Elliott is Senior Lecturer in Operations Management at Bolton Business School. He gained management experience leading functional areas like productivity services, industrial relations and planning in several large manufacturing companies in both the textile and engineering sectors.

Wes Haydock is Principal Lecturer in Human Resource Management at Bolton Business School. He is course leader for the BA (Hons) business administration and teaches on a range of undergraduate and postgraduate courses, including an MBA and MA in human resource management. He obtained a BSc in industrial engineering from Hatfield Polytechnic in 1972 and an MSc in industrial relations and personal management from the London School of Economics in 1983. He worked in the electronics industry as a production manager and production control manager before entering the teaching profession. He current interests include management development, teamwork and general human resource management issues.

Margaret Leigh is Lecturer in Accounting at Bolton Business School. Her major research interests are concerned with the interface between law and accountancy.

M. Teresa Lunati is Senior Lecturer in Economics at Bolton Business School. She has also lectured at the University of Turin, Italy, and at the University of Wales, Aberystwyth. She holds a Laurea con Lode in Economia e Commercio from the University of Turin, an MA in economics from Essex University, and a DPhil in economics from the University of York. Her areas of interest include macroeconomic aspects of public finance (the macro effects of financing the public sector formed the topic for her doctoral thesis), the economic beliefs and behaviour of individuals, and ethical issues in economics (especially concerning altruism, co-operation, commitment and equity).

Greta Richards is Professor and Assistant Director at Newcastle Business School, University of Northumbria at Newcastle. A chartered psychologist, she has experience over many years of market research for products and services with consumers and industry, largely in the private sector, and twenty years as consultant for the Civil Service Commission in management recruitment and selection. She has designed and directed portfolios of undergraduate and postgraduate degree programmes in business and marketing and is an assessor in business and management for the Higher Education Funding Council for England.

Richard Schofield is a Lecturer in Law at Bolton Business School. His major research interest is in the area of organisational accountability, in particular systems of self-regulation.

Peter Taylor is Senior Lecturer in Accountancy and Finance at Bolton Business School. After qualifying as a chartered accountant he spent several years employed in the tourism industry as a financial accountant. He currently lectures in management accounting and taxation.

Trevor Williamson is Principal Lecturer in Financial Services at Manchester Metropolitan University. A graduate in management science from the University of Manchester Institute of Science and Technology, he was appointed course leader for the BA (Honours) financial services degree at Manchester Metropolitan University in January 1992. This followed over ten years of senior management experience working in finance houses and banking organisations. His latest position was Advance Controller at Girobank plc, responsible for control and development of the bank's commercial lending activities.

Graham Wood is Head of School of Business Studies at University College Salford. He graduated with a first-class honours degree in economics from University College Cardiff and also has an MA in business analysis from Lancaster University. His research interests are in marketing and purchasing ethics and he has published papers in the *International Marketing Review* and *Business Ethics: A European Review*.

Introduction

Our reason for adding to the plethora of volumes on business ethics is that we hope we are contributing something new, something, moreover, that fills an important gap in what is currently available. The recent growth of interest in business ethics began in the US and the literature reflects this. We felt it was important to try to redress this balance by concentrating on European cases and the issues that matter in European business. We also wished to avoid the problems inherent in transposing discussions rooted in a very different business culture and legal system to the European context.

A problem in writing on business ethics is the risk of falling into one or another of two traps: of concentrating on theoretical (philosophical) material without grounding that material sufficiently in the real issues to which it should apply; or else of taking an overly pragmatic approach which ignores or minimises the theoretical difficulties such approaches should raise. We have tried to avoid both of these traps by placing at the heart of the book a sequence of case studies (Chapters 3, 4, 5 and 6) and sharply focused surveys of areas of management practice (Chapters 10, 11, 12, 13, 14 and 15) and surrounding them with the theoretical material which is designed to supply both introduction and commentary. We hope we have thereby achieved an appropriate balance between theorising about business ethics and describing actual ethical problems.

It is not just a matter of balance, of course. There needs to be an integration of theory with practice and that presupposes a methodology to achieve it. We have adopted a position that owes a good deal to John Rawles (1972, p. 20f).[1] A given ethical theory will have implications (obviously) about what is right and what wrong and these implications may or may not square with our moral intuitions ('gut feelings'). It would be naive to suppose that the first attempt to formulate a theory must be correct. But nor can we assume that our pre-theoretical moral feelings are defensible just as they stand. Rawles suggests that we should go through a process of reflectively considering how to adjust both our feelings and our theory until a stable balance is struck between them. He calls this position 'reflective equilibrium'. We do not claim to have achieved this here. But we do believe that the book provides material which will enable readers to achieve a 'reflective equilibrium' between their own instinctive reactions to the cases and vignettes we describe and a more considered, theoretically informed judgement. It is hopeless to suppose that theories can be formulated (or worse, taken off the philosophical shelf) in advance of considering the nature of the actual cases or problems to which they are meant to apply. But neither is it sensible to believe that simply working through cases, however thoroughly and assiduously, is enough to generate suffcient insight to generate realistic and principled responses to them. There is a halfway house which in our view is as bad as, or worse than, either of these, and this is to apply a limited number of simplified theoretical insights (usually loosely based on Kantianism and utilitarianism) and mechanically derive some stock conclusions which are often inconsistent with one another and which yield no insight into either the nature of the problems or of the merits and shortcomings of the theories themselves.

Quite apart from anything else, all of these ignore the question of how case studies are selected and formulated. What makes something a problem which is worth our attention? How much information is needed to convey what makes a situation problematic? What is important and significant in a case study and what inessential and incidental? Clearly without some kind of theoretical 'take' on an issue, none of these questions can be answered and examples, problems and case studies cannot even be put together. The belief that a pre-theoretical position is possible usually means that the most conservative view has prevailed and that, in itself, is something which ought to be questioned. Nonetheless, consideration of actual cases may lead one to wish to adjust the initial theoretical 'take' and then to reconsider the case in the light of that next move. Ultimately, what is being aimed at is a set of mutual adjustments which achieves the best possible 'fit' between example and theory.

Theory needs to be informed by actual cases in another sense, too. We need to be clear about what kinds of cases really are morally problematic for practitioners, and not just rely on theory to tell us what ought to be difficulties. We do not want to invent problems which are hardly ever confronted in practice but which are theoretically interesting, but nor do we want to swamp the reader with cases structured only by the most superficial or naive theoretical underpinnings. It has been our aim throughout to avoid both of these undesirable outcomes.

Finally, we hope that this volume will make a contribution through its stress on the importance of organisations to the study of business ethics. Whilst it is true that organisations are made up of people and that much depends on whether those people are equipped to make ethical decisions, to consider just those people and their decisons is to leave out something which is so important that, in its absence, the rest hardly makes any sense. Not only are organisations increasingly important influences on our lives, but most of us, for a significant portion of our lives, work within an organisation of one kind or another. Our ability to live an ethical life is profoundly affected by the ethics of the organisations with which we deal and within which we operate. For this reason we have chosen to focus on the extent to which it is possible for an organisation to be ethical and the impact that that will have on the actions of those who work for it.

ALAN KITSON
ROBERT CAMPBELL

Note

1. Rawles, J. (1972) *A Theory of Justice*, Oxford University Press.

PART I

ORGANISATIONS AND ETHICS

CHAPTER 1

Business Ethics

1 Introduction

There have always been those who have attempted to conduct their businesses according to their own high principles – religious or political. Robert Owen is one example (see Stuttard, 1992) and the Quaker Cadburys and Rowntrees are another. But, in many ways, their concern, and the concern of others like them, was to set an example. It was a practical rather than a theoretical concern. Thus, despite the undoubted fact that such people have existed through the centuries and that, for just as long, philosophers and ethicists have occasionally turned their attention to the ways in which business is conducted, we cannot say that the story of business ethics begins with them.

According to Norman Bowie (1986) 'One might date the birth of business ethics [in the USA] as November 1974 – the date of the first conference on business ethics at the University of Kansas .' Bowie lists the evolving concerns of business ethics in the US as beginning with the issue of whistle-blowing and extending to cover codes of ethics, employee rights, and the question of corporate social responsibility and the relationship between businesses and the civil and institutional environment in which they operate. Business ethics is now taught in most major US Business Schools and is a well-established and recognised subject area in its own right in the US.

The UK and mainland Europe have been slower to develop business ethics as an integral and distinct part of business education curricula, though several chairs in the subject exist, especially in Germany and two have recently been established in the UK (at the Manchester and London Business Schools). As in the US, the initial moves towards sketching out the topography of an area to be called 'business ethics' has come from philosophers specialising in applied ethics and working in related fields such as medicine, law, journalism and politics. However, these moves mirror growing concern in both business and business schools for the social responsibilities of businesses and managers which was surfacing in courses on business policy, corporate strategy, organisation theory and human resource management. (Mahoney, 1989, 1993; Harvey, 1992; and Schoenfeldt *et al.*, 1991).

It is difficult to be sure what sparked this growth of interest, but it can scarcely be coincidental that it happened at a time when Western society took the governmental brakes off the market and a brief period of economic growth was followed by a major recession. This left a nasty taste in most people's mouths and some pressing questions about the behaviour of some corporations and individuals. The list is lengthy, but includes Ivan Boesky, the Wall Street arbitrageur, Guinness, Maxwell and BCCI. Another factor, though whether cause or effect is hard to determine, is the steady growth of business ventures which make their pitch, avowedly or quietly, on the basis of an ethical approach in their dealings with their own staff, their customers and the general public. The Body Shop and the British Co-operative Bank are big players in this particular league, but many smaller companies are, for example, finding it desirable to emphasise their ecological policies or the fact that they are equal opportunity employers. In some cases, no doubt, this is pure cynicism. But cynicism of this kind, if it exists, can only make sense against the background of an increasingly vocal and influential public demand that corporations deal fairly and honestly with each other and the general population, that they seek not to exploit unduly third world suppliers or markets and that they do not make a bigger mess of the environment than they have to. As we write, the very first South African election to be held on the basis of a full franchise of the whole population is taking place. For many this proves that international companies can, if they allow principle as well as profit to guide their actions, change the world for the better. For it is obvious that increasingly stringent trade restrictions, brought about not by government intervention but by the weight of world opinion, i.e. by those companies' own customers and employees, was a decisive factor in the downfall of apartheid.

At the time, and perhaps since, there were those who felt that such pressures distorted business practice in an untoward way; that it simply was not the *business* of business to pursue political action. To do so was dangerous not just to business itself, but also, and equally, to those very ends at which the lobbyists and political activists were aiming. (This is substantially the same argument put forward in regard to sporting boycotts of South Africa, and summed up in the slogan 'Keep sport out of politics'.) Even now, it is not *obvious* that they were wrong. The damage done to the South African economy may well still jeopardise the political progress made. It certainly created problems which have still to be addressed and have not been resolved by the resumption of trading links.

Should a business organisation pass judgement on or seek to affect materially the political or social environment in which it operates? US and UK companies were certainly criticised for continuing to trade in South Africa and, thereby, it was alleged, offering support to the then apartheid regime. But equally, US companies have also been criticised for interfering politically (or soliciting the interference of the CIA and the US government) in South American countries such as Nicaragua and Chile. One of the most notorious examples of this was the case of the United Fruit Company (now called 'United Brands') who, effectively, organised an armed invasion of Honduras in 1910 in order to further its business interests in bananas and, in 1954, was allegedly implicated in the *coup d'état* which overthrew a Honduran president whose land reform programme threatened its profits. (see Donaldson, 1982, pp. 11–12.)

One obvious distinction between these two kinds of case is that between acting to protect or further the commercial interests of a company and acting to further the interests of a community even at the risk of commercial profits. This seems to imply two distinct and not always compatible sets of values – business values and community values. What, if anything, is wrong with a company acting in accordance with its own business values? Does the non-business community have a right to expect business to jeopardise its own values in order to realise those of the community? What exactly *are* business values?

Values are what makes it possible to choose between alternatives, and the values held by an individual or an organisation are revealed in those choices. To make a choice entails preferring one option over the other(s), i.e. *valuing* that option more than the other(s). Thus the *actual* values held by an individual or organisation can be shown by an analysis of the decisions she, he or it takes, though what is *not* chosen is as important to that analysis as what is. The result of such an analysis can be as much a surprise to the one whose values are revealed by it as to anyone else, and this is as true in the case of private individuals (in psychoanalysis, for example) as it is in the case of organisations (where the vehicle of analysis may well be an audit of one kind or another). Such analyses can reveal a marked discrepancy between the values we think we hold and those which our actions show that we actually do. They may also, and perhaps more importantly, show a difference between our actual values and those which we *ought* to be pursuing.

So, if choices reveal actual values, how can we determine what our values ought to be? What distinguishes the values a business might actually espouse from the ones it ought, ideally, to have? This is a question which is fiercely contended and some possible answers will be considered in the next section. For now, we will consider only the narrowest possible conception of business values as those which a business needs to pursue in order to survive and prosper, *as a business*. A business is a commercial enterprise which exists, in a capitalist society, in order to make a return on the capital invested in it. It needs, therefore, to make a profit on the bottom line if it is to survive as the kind of thing its creators intended it to be. It is this point which leads some to insist that profit is the only value that a business ought to pursue and that to insist that it pursue others is, at the least, to jeopardise its chances of realising that basic value and, at the worst, to distort its nature and unjustly subvert its owners' intentions and purposes. (See Friedman, 1962, 1980; and Hayek, 1982.) The South African example shows, however, that it is logically possible for a business to have values other than that of simply making a profit. The question must therefore be one of whether a business *should* or *ought* to have other values.

As soon as this question is pressed, it becomes clear that the answer must be 'yes'. For though offering a return on investment is a necessary condition of a business's survival,[1] clearly it is not sufficient. Failure to comply with the law has ended many an enterprising drug-dealer's otherwise entirely profitable career. Arguably, failure to comply with community values and standards could do exactly the same. In 1985, in Sale, Greater Manchester, a pornographic bookshop, licensed by the local authority in accordance with recently enacted legislation, was run out of town by a small but determined pressure group who picketed the premises, photographing all its customers and, on occasion, supergluing its locks. Together with a well-orchestrated campaign in the local press, this was sufficient to induce its proprietors to move elsewhere. It could be said that it was the threat to the shop's profits that caused its closure. But the decline in those profits was itself a measure not of the local market, the efficiency of the business or the quality of its products, but of the extent to which it was felt to undermine values strongly held by the community. It would therefore be tendentious to claim that that pornographer's business failed because it did not make a profit, or failed to provide a product for which people were willing to pay. It failed because the community objected, on moral grounds, to the product itself.[2]

It is necessary for a business's survival, therefore, not just that it make a profit, but that it comply with the state's legal regulations and also with society's moral values (or, at the least, must not violate them too grossly or frequently). These are necessary because failure at any one of them will prevent the business from continuing to trade. (Though, as we have suggested – see note 1 – the timeframe is a problematic factor here.)

But presumably most businesses, like most people, do not wish simply to survive, but to prosper. What values does a business need if it is to flourish and grow? Clearly a short answer to such a question simply is not possible, and there is a vast literature devoted to the attempt to identify just those factors which distinguish success in business. What is interesting, from the point of view of business ethics, however, is that values which in other contexts would be seen as indisputably moral ones are evidently important (see Clutterbuck *et al.*, 1992, pp. 17–19). They might include equity and responsibility in dealings with employees, customers and suppliers, community involvement, environmental concern, openness, integrity and responsiveness to criticism and complaint. These are not just the qualities we might wish for in businesses if things were ideal but are increasingly being recognised as qualities actually possessed (to a degree, at least) by some of the world's most successful business corporations.

2 Ethics

2.1 Utilitarianism

To see why values such as these matter and how they might plausibly be held to contribute to an organisation's success involves an excursion into moral theory. One of the most initially plausible moral theories (or, rather, family of theories, since it comes in nearly as many varieties as tinned soup) is utilitarianism. It says that when we have a choice the right thing to do is that which brings about the 'greatest happiness of the greatest number'. Nothing is wrong which does this, and nothing is right which fails to do it. The first, most obvious, difficulty with this is what counts as happiness. Bentham dealt with that by equating happiness with simple pleasure or the avoidance of pain (see Bentham, 1789). Mill complicated the issue by distinguishing different kinds and degrees of happiness (see Mill, 1862). Modern economists tend to look either to preference satisfaction or economic gain (which, given the model of 'rational economic man' comes to the same thing, but see also Sen, 1987). But for our purposes, we can simply state that utilitarianism advocates the view that to act morally is to attempt to secure the most good for the most people, and stay agnostic about what that good might consist in.

From your own point of view, then, you must choose to do that which it seems to you will benefit most people most. But what that is will clearly depend, in most cases, on what other people do as well. Let us suppose that you work for the marketing section of a medium-sized national company and you have been asked by a colleague to think about helping her draw up, publicise and attempt to have implemented an environmental awareness policy for the company. There is no opposition to such a policy within the company, but no great enthusiasm either and, for a variety of reasons familiar to anyone involved in anything similar, everyone else has cried off, leaving you and her, should you decide to join her, to get the thing started.

Becoming involved will carry certain personal costs. There will be much hard work in the initial stages. The policy must not only be formulated, but formulated in such a way that the maximum number of people are consulted and involved. Only then will it stand some chance of being implemented and not simply acknowledged as a good idea which is promptly ignored. Such problems will be well known to those who have been involved in the management of change within any organisation. There is also the risk of being associated with a project which, should it fail, could damage your own reputation and career prospects within the company. However, should the project succeed, your reputation would be considerably enhanced, the company should save money (you have done the figures) and its image in the market will be much improved. It could, in fact, be just the kind of factor to give you an edge over the competition and make you finally the market leaders you have been so close to being for such a long time. There will also be genuine environmental improvements to be gained from such a policy.

Perhaps you decide that the benefits do not sufficiently outweigh the costs and that you will plead pressure of other work and decline to help your colleague. She, on the other hand, may decide to see how much she can get done by herself. But in fact it really does need two people to get it going, and if she does decide this she will get nowhere. The same would be true if you did decide to help her but, for reasons we need not worry about, she dropped out. By yourself you would get nowhere. Only if you both commit ourselves to the project does it seem likely that it would succeed.

Let us assume that the extra time needed for the project would cost you five points each in effort, lost opportunities, etc. Either of you acting individually and without the benefit of the other would generate nothing in compensation. Acting together, however, you will probably generate outcomes worth fifteen points each in terms of enhanced reputation, promotion, bonuses etc. (We will disregard, for the moment, losses and benefits that might accrue to other people.) The choices open to each of you, together with their outcomes, are shown in Figure 1.1. (Helping costs five points. Helping by oneself yields no returns. Helping co-operatively yields fifteen points each which, less the cost of helping, gives a net return of ten points each. The idea of 'points' should not be taken too seriously. It is only a way of clarifying the relative value of the various outcomes.)

Whether you are concerned only for your own benefit, or for that of both of you (or, indeed, for the overall good, measures of which are not included in Figure 1.1), it is clear that box no. 4 represents the optimum outcome. You

		SHE		SHE	
		DOES NOT HELP		DOES HELP	
YOU	DO NOT HELP	1. You She Total	5 5 10	2. You She Total	5 −5 0
	DO HELP	3. You She Total	−5 5 0	4. You She Total	10 10 20

FIGURE 1.1   The collaborator's dilemma

cannot secure no.4 by yourself, however. So, as long as you are sure that your colleague will stay the course, collaborating with her in this project makes sense for you. But if you have reasons to think that she will not, then collaborating does not make sense, for you would lose out and there would be no compensating gain for anyone. (So it does not make sense even if you are a serious altruist and are prepared to invest your loss for the sake of others' gain.)

If you were reasonably sure that you knew what your colleague would do, then it is clear what would make sense for you to do. But suppose you were not. (You do not know her terribly well and you are not in a position to judge her sincerity, or her determination with any great degree of confidence.) Suppose, too, that your colleague is waiting for your decision before she finally makes her mind up. If you take the thing on but she backs out, then your loss and her gain will balance each other out and nothing will have been achieved overall. But if you decline then she has no reason for pursuing the matter (for, let us suppose, she knows the possible costs and benefits as well as you do). So if you choose to collaborate, you gamble on securing 10 points for yourself and a total of 20 overall, but you risk achieving nothing and suffering a personal loss of 5. But if you decide not to then there is no risk to you at all. You will save the time which you can invest in something else, and that will be true whatever your colleague decides to do. But, probably, she will be sensible too, and there will, overall, be a net gain to you both compared to what you might have lost.

Being sensible, and weighing risks and benefits will, then, unless you are an inveterate gambler or constitutionally reckless, lead you inexorably to, if not the worst outcome, then what is clearly a second-best for all concerned. You may realise this and wish, a little regretfully, that it were possible to lessen the risks and improve the chances of securing the best outcome. How is that to be done? Perhaps the situation might be changed by your exchanging reciprocal promises: 'I will promise to help if you will also promise.' And so you do. But what now? For what this does is to change the superficial form of the dilemma whilst leaving its structure as it was. Instead of a collaborator's dilemma, we now have a promise-keeper's dilemma (see Figure 1.2).

The reason for this is that you are seeking that action which will do most good and so you must decide whether keeping the promise you have just made will do more good than breaking it. And since you know, or can guess, that your collaborator is faced with exactly the same decision, then you also know that she, like you, will have realised that the safest decision is to break the promise rather than keep it, just as, before, the safest decision was not to help rather than help.

The paradoxical conclusion that must be drawn from this is that, in dilemmas of this kind, a strategy of seeking rationally to opt for the best outcome (whether it is simply the best for oneself or the best for all) will fail to bring about just that outcome. The best we can hope for is second-best and in

		SHE			
		DOES NOT KEEP PROMISE TO HELP		DOES KEEP PROMISE TO HELP	
YOU	DO NOT KEEP PROMISE TO HELP	**1.** You	5	**2.** You	5
		She	5	She	-5
		Total	**10**	Total	**0**
	DO KEEP PROMISE TO HELP	**3.** You	-5	**4.** You	10
		She	5	She	10
		Total	**0**	Total	**20**

FIGURE 1.2   **The promise-keeper's dilemma**

some dilemmas it will be the worst. Consider a rapidly falling stock market as seen by someone with a large portfolio. It is the worst possible time to sell, yet that is the only rational thing to do so long as you have every reason to believe that the market still has a way to fall and is unlikely to recover rapidly. But not only do you lose on your shares, you do the very thing that is making the market fall, i.e. putting yet more shares on the market at a time when people are reluctant to buy because share values are falling. It is a vicious and self-fuelling spiral. But that does not mean that it would make any sense not to sell. It would make sense for everyone to refuse to sell, but since everyone is selling for precisely the same reasons as you will, you have no rational alternative to selling. Actions which are individually rational and sensible are creating a situation which is collectively irrational.[3]

Such dilemmas are not uncommon. Voting poses another version of this problem. Should you turn out to vote on a cold and wet night when you have many other, more enjoyable, things you might be doing and you would, in any case, rather just sit by the fire? Your vote is unlikely to make any difference. So you have very little to lose and much to gain by staying at home. But this is likely to be true of a lot of potential voters. What if they all looked at it like this? (Labour and Liberal Democrat voters, it is sometimes said, often do. Conservative voters, again according to canvassers' lore, tend to vote simply because they feel they should. We shall see shortly that this is an important point.) Well, if enough of them looked at it like this, and especially if the tendency to do so was reflected in party political allegiance, it would, of course, make a considerable difference. Donating to charity, despoiling the environment, fiddling income-tax returns, parking on double-yellow lines, over-fishing, conscientious objection to military service in times of war, eating factory-farmed chicken or buying goods from morally objectionable régimes – all of these potentially are versions of the collaborator's dilemma. An imaginative reader will be able to multiply such examples indefinitely.

The version of utilitarianism we have been considering so far is known as 'Act Utilitarianism'. Act Utilitarianism says that, for every action, we should choose that which will, or which seems most likely to, bring about the maximum good for the maximum number of people. But doing that generates just the kind of dilemmas we have been examining. It also gives rise to other important problems. Firstly, it may well be that pausing to calculate possible consequences and estimate their relative utility will actually affect one's ability to bring them about. Suppose whilst walking by a river I see someone apparently drowning. If I were a good Act Utilitarian then I could well be working out what to do whilst they drowned. In many situations *not* calculating consequences may well bring about the best results. Secondly, it is often pointed out that good Act Utilitarians are at best unpredictable and, at worst, unreliable. They cannot, for example, be trusted to keep their promises or tell the truth, show loyalty or uphold justice because they will only do any of these things when, it seems to them, doing so will bring about the best consequences (which it sometimes will not, of course).

But looking closely at what Bentham and Mill actually proposed has led many theorists to suggest that, rather than Act Utilitarianism, we should be considering 'Rule Utilitarianism'. Rule Utilitarianism looks at the utility not of individual actions but at the rules by which we ordinarily guide those actions. Rule Utilitarianism says that we should choose a set of rules following which, on average and overall, will produce the best consequences. That promises should be kept is a rule which, if followed by most people, will produce better consequences than not following it would, even though in some circumstances it would be better (would yield better consequences) if a promise was broken. So a Rule Utilitarian would not, or so it would seem, have to face the promise-keeping dilemma. For a Rule Utilitarian the utility of having promise-keeping as a rule and social norm is more important than the utility of keeping or breaking a promise on a particular occasion. Rule Utilitarianism says nothing about waiting to see what others do, or cutting your losses if you find yourself on your own. The rule, subject only to the general principle that following it has greater utility than not following it, enjoins unconditional compliance.

Not only does Rule Utilitarianism resolve the promise-keeping dilemma, it also accords with our pre-philosophical intuitions about what moral obligation is rather better than Act Utilitarianism does. If it is right to vote, to donate to charity, to fill in one's income-tax returns correctly, to park legally, etc., then it is right whatever anyone else does. But Rule Utilitarianism resolves these dilemmas only on the assumption that everyone believes in it

and acts on it. Only if you and she both adhere to Rule Utilitarianism do you
get the best result. If she is just plain selfish then your duty impels you to act
in a way which secures the worst outcome – zero gain. Rule Utilitarianism
says you should follow those rules which, if everyone followed them, would
produce the best outcome ('the greatest happiness of the greatest number'). It
does not say what you should do if not everyone does follow those rules.
Suppose you *know* that not everyone will follow those rules, so that you also
know that your following them will not produce the best outcome, but
something less (perhaps very much less) than that. Should you, in that case,
continue to be a Rule Utilitarian or not? Posing that question, interestingly,
yields a dilemma of a familiar form (see Figure 1.3).

The problem is that, confronted with such a dilemma, there are two options
for the Rule Utilitarian. He or she can accept the dilemma; in which case, it
becomes clear that at this point Rule Utilitarianism has collapsed into Act
Utilitarianism; there is nothing to choose between them. Or, he or she can
refuse the dilemma by declining to consider the possibility of abandoning
Rule Utilitarianism. This second option, if chosen, creates a curious state of
affairs. The Rule Utilitarian has refused to consider abandoning Rule
Utilitarianism when persisting with it may well not maximise the greatest
happiness of the greatest number, and may even cause greater harm than any
available alternatives. The Rule Utilitarian is saying, in effect, that adhering to
principles (rules) of certain kinds is more important morally than trying to
bring about good consequences. This, second, version of Utilitarianism is not,
therefore, a Utilitarian theory at all, but something else. Rule Utilitarianism

		SHE	
		DOES NOT ADOPT RULE UTILITARIANISM	DOES ADOPT RULE UTILITARIANISM
YOU	DO NOT ADOPT RULE UTILITARIANISM	**1.** You 5 / She 5 / Total **10**	**2.** You 5 / She −5 / Total **0**
	DO ADOPT RULE UTILITARIANISM	**3.** You −5 / She 5 / Total **0**	**4.** You 10 / She 10 / Total **20**

FIGURE 1.3   **The Rule Utilitarian's dilemma**

cannot solve the problems inherent in Act Utilitarianism. It either collapses back into something which is indistinguishable from Act Utilitarianism and the problems resurface, or else it avoids the problems by turning itself into something other than a Utilitarian theory, something which looks far more like the kind of moral theory we will consider in a moment.[4]

What goes wrong in such cases is that utilitarianism fails to generate obligations strong enough to produce the very outcomes that it enjoins. It would be better, on utilitarian grounds, if utilitarianism was a theory no one believed[5] in, but thought, instead, that there were some things you should do, or not do, irrespective of outcome. If both of the collaborators had given their word and both simply took it for granted that you should not break it, except for the morally weightiest of reasons, then that would give both of them the best possible chance of securing the best possible outcome. This is one example of something which is in fact quite common – *trying* to bring something about actually interferes with your chances of achieving it. (For an illuminating discussion of this kind of moral dilemma, see Parfitt, 1984.)

2.2 Deontology

One solution to this problem is Kant's. He maintained that doing your duty is the only thing which ethics requires, but it requires that it be done because it is your duty, and not because it coincidentally happens to be what you wanted to do anyway. (Hence 'deontology' from the Greek δεον: duty.) It also requires that it always be done. There are no exceptions. 'Let duty be done, though the heavens fall', to paraphrase a famous quotation. (The connection with the second form of Rule Utilitarianism should be clear; what should be done should be done regardless of consequences. This makes this form of Rule Utilitarianism more deontological than utilitarian.) Your duty is to do what you would expect anyone else to do in the situation in which you find yourself.[6] You cannot, in other words, allow yourself to pick and choose which bills you will settle this month (if any) unless you would also be happy for those who owe you money to do exactly the same. Kant's assumption is that you wouldn't. But there's more than just an assumption involved here. The kind of reason you might give for defaulting on your payments might be that it suited you to. Logically, you then must allow that suiting them must also be a sufficient reason for anyone else to default (or else it couldn't be a reason for you to). But business simply could not be conducted, would cease to exist as such, if people only paid bills when it suited them to and everyone was completely happy about that. So paying bills on time, even when it hurts, is simply being consistent about tying together reasons, excuses and actions. Two Kantians, faced with the kind of dilemma we have been discussing, would probably keep any promises they had made to each other, simply because it was their duty to. We say 'probably' because, although they certainly would if they were being consistent, logical and rational, we know that people are not consistent, logical and rational all the time. In particular, we know that the appeal of consistency and rationality is not a psychologically very strong motivating factor for people under stress, in a tight spot, under pressure or without the time or resources fully to think through what they are doing and why. Consider this example:

X is the production manager of a plant which produces cast-iron components for the automotive industry. The industry as a whole is in difficulties and the plant is struggling to compete both with overseas suppliers of iron castings and also competitors urging the merits of pressed steel alternatives, which are cheaper to produce. The Managing Director of the parent company which owns the plant is urging X, in face of declining sales, to cut overhead costs in an effort to produce their product more cheaply. X realises that probably her present job and certainly her chances of promotion depend on her achieving the MD's indicated target.

X knows that, in the long term, the only real hope of survival for the plant lies in conversion to the production of pressed-steel components. This would be exceedingly costly, requiring, as it does, massive capital expenditure on new plant, a certain amount of rebuilding and retraining and/or replacement of labour. Slightly less costly, but correspondingly less certain of success, would be automation of the existing production line which would enable the workforce to be 'downsized', reduce the incidence of 'scrapped' (because faulty) components and increase production capacity. Neither of these two options is likely to meet the MD's approval because both would raise costs in the short term, rather than cutting them.

A third option is to pare overheads wherever this is possible. It means, for example, not replacing workers and sharing the additional work out amongst those who remain, repairing and patching up plant and buildings rather than replacing or properly refurbishing them, running down stock levels, not just of raw materials but of tools and protective clothing, just short of violating health and safety legislation. Other measures X contemplates include filling and machining cracks and flaws in faulty castings rather than scrapping and remaking them, relaxing quality control in the inspection department and slowing down the production line (thereby making it impossible for piece-workers to earn full bonuses whilst hoping that the production shortfall would be made up for by the smaller number of components rejected as scrap by quality control procedures).

These 'other measures' X contemplates with some hesitation, for she knows they clearly cross the line between what might (just) be called 'good housekeeping' or 'prudent management of resources' and what is clearly imprudent and, in some ways, dishonest. For, in the long term, this third option may (and if the 'other measures' are included, certainly will) cause grave problems. Because next to nothing is being reinvested in the plant then, sooner or later, there will come a crisis point at which either huge capital expenditure will be needed simply to keep going, or the plant will fold. Overworked, underpaid and imperfectly protected workers will either leave (to be replaced, if at all, by less conscientious, less skilled and less reliable staff who will be all the company can get to work for that money in those conditions), or strike, unless a sufficiently serious industrial accident closes the plant first. And finally, the deteriorating quality standards of the product will eventually lose the plant those customers it has managed to hang on to by cutting its costs. The faulty products – trailer couplings, transmission housings and wheel hubs – may well even be dangerous to the public. How the third option is managed may well hasten or postpone such consequences, but they are inevitable, once that road has been taken.

There are two problems raised in considering this (invented but not fanciful) example from a Kantian perspective. The first is that, as we have already suggested, an appeal to Kantian rational principles is unlikely to lessen the pressure on X to consider her own job first, and those of the workforce second, if at all. It is also unlikely to provide her with the right kind of excuses and defences she will need if she decides to defend the plant against the MD's apparent wish for a short-term profit.[7] The second problem is that Kant's insistence on duty does hardly anything to resolve X's dilemma, even if she is perfectly able to resist the pressure to protect her own job, to please the MD, be a model employee, etc. For what does one's duty consist in here? As plant manager X certainly has a duty to the plant itself and to those it employs and serves. But as an employee of the company she works for, she also has a duty to comply with company policy as formulated by, for example, the MD and also a duty to abide by the MD's requests and instructions. These duties were probably spelt out or implied in the contract of employment she agreed to when she accepted the job.

The problem with utilitarianism is that, if not formally inconsistent, it is self-defeating when applied to certain very common kinds of dilemma which involve co-operative action (and 'co-operative' needs no particularly high-minded gloss in this context: it means any action directed at an outcome whose realisation also depends on how someone else acts). Kantianism, potentially, at least, supplies obligations sufficiently strong to avoid this self-defeatingness, but does so at the cost of psychological realism and also of being indeterminate in the face of complex and intricate real life situations.

2.3   Virtue theory

Two things are wrong about these approaches to the morality of choice in difficult and complex situations. The first is that the nature of the agent is assumed not to be important or, at least, to be determined by the outcome of the choice and not as determining it. The same may be said of the culture (in an unpretentious sense) in which the choice is to be made – the expectations of others, the values embedded in the institutional arrangements and so on. The second thing that is wrong is the implicit assumption that what we are looking for is a rule, a mechanistic decision procedure, something to which we can appeal to resolve our moral difficulties for us. This cannot work because life and people are much too complicated and various for a general rule ever to give us a clear and determinate answer. We do use general rules, of course, and one way of approaching a moral problem is to generalise it in order to try and achieve a rough fit with some rule ('do not tell lies'; 'treat people with respect'; 'practise what you preach'; and so on). But the fit will only ever be a rough one, and doing as much as we can with the rules will always still leave many things open. Even when the rules, and the procedures for applying them, are made as explicit and detailed as possible, this still happens. The law on theft, for example, defines stealing as dishonestly taking someone else's property with intent to permanently deprive them of it. ('Dishonestly' here means knowing full well it is not yours.) Does this cover receiving a service and then making off without paying for it? It ought to, because this is a kind of theft, but it does not say so. The law, therefore, has added (by the Theft Act, 1978) a separate offence called 'making off' which is committed when you benefit from a service for which payment is normally expected on the spot and you dishonestly 'make off' without paying with the intention of avoiding paying. Examples might include leaving a restaurant without settling the bill, or jumping out of a taxi to avoid paying the fare. This seems explicit and detailed enough, but a case arose in 1985 (*R* v. *Allen* (1985), 1 All ER 641) which did not quite fit. A man stayed in an expensive London hotel for several days, conducting a business deal which he expected to cover his expenses. The deal fell through and he left the hotel hurriedly, intending, he said, to raise the money to meet the hotel bill. He never intended to avoid paying the bill, only to avoid paying it there and then.[8] Was that dishonest? Does it fall under the rule or not? It took several judges some time to come to a conclusion on that, not because the rule was a difficult and complicated one which needed interpreting, but because the conclusion had to go beyond the rule. The judges had to do what they are paid for and use their judgement, based on public policy, existing law, precedent cases, morality and their experience of the world. They could not *discover* whether the rule applied, they had to *decide* whether it did or not; that is, whether to *make* it apply.

Moral rules are just like this. No matter how detailed or explicit they are, judgement is always required to decide how the general rule fits the individual case. In the legal case, judgement is based on a mixture of legal training, professional experience and general knowledge of the world. Aristotle maintained that moral judgement is formed in a very similar way. There is moral training and education, experience of actual situations and knowledge about how things and people in the world generally work.

Just as a carpenter learns how to make furniture which not only looks right but also does the job, partly from theory but mainly from the experience of making furniture, so we learn what the right thing to do is, partly from our moral education, but mainly from the experience of doing it. There is no specific faculty we could call moral judgement. It is just our judgement (practical wisdom, *phronesis*) applied to moral problems and dilemmas.[9]

Moral virtues are not rules but personal characteristics, tendencies to behave in one kind of way rather than another. Initially they are acquired by training and education, but the mature person will learn to scrutinise and adjust his or her behaviour on the basis of experience of the world and the exercise of reason. We do not and cannot, however, make every decision a fresh start and, as it were, rebuild ourselves from scratch. We often simply do not have time, but also, and more important, many virtues will not do their job unless they are quite deeply engrained. If temptations were easily resisted they would not be temptations.

As examples of virtues, Aristotle lists, amongst others, courage, temperance, liberality, a sense of self-worth, gentleness, modesty, justice and wisdom. These are qualities he felt were necessary to live well, to prosper and to flourish. We might dispute whether they are all equally necessary, or whether, to succeed in modern business, we might not have to add one or two others ('firmness of purpose' perhaps, or 'persistence'?), but that some such list would describe the kind the person (or organisation?) one would have to be to survive, prosper and sleep soundly at nights is probably beyond dispute. Such qualities are exhibited in action, in how one behaves, and if you wish to know what they imply for a particular situation you must look at how a virtuous person behaves (or imagine how they would behave) in that situation. There is no theoretical way of reading off from the nature of virtue what the right thing to do is. The right thing is what a virtuous person does.[10]

There is a lesson here, and also, perhaps, an explanation, for all the volumes produced on how to succeed in business, which have tried to produce a recipe or a series of rules for success.[11] (Or, to be fair to many of them, they have been so successful because of the hope that that is what they would yield; probably many of the authors knew that it was not possible.) Such books never work, in the sense that there are always successes which do not conform to the rules and failures which do. Success in business is a matter of a certain amount of luck, but also of skills and expertise and judgement acquired through practice and experience, and it cannot be reduced to a set of rules which anyone could follow mechanically without that practice and experience. Not everyone is equally good at it; we value the expertise and judgement of those who are. The same is true of morality. How is expertise and judgement, whether in business or morality, to be acquired? By training and education, certainly, but also, and most importantly, by experience and practice supplemented by reflection. This is why the Case Study approach is so valued in Business education. It supplies real examples in their full complexity and difficulty, but does so in a situation where there is space to reflect on one's judgement about them. And this is exactly the reason why case studies are also important in educating moral judgement.

This is not to say that rules and reasons have no place in morality any more than that they have no place in business. But it is to say that they can only take us so far, and once that point is reached then wisdom, experience, imagination, flair, practical intelligence – good judgement acquired by experience in practice – must take over. All, in fact, are needed. For without the rules and the reasons, judgement has very little to go. But without judgement, rules and reasons go nowhere.

Notes

1. Though even that point is more complicated than it seems. TML, the channel tunnel operating company, estimates that it will be able to pay dividends to its investors no earlier than the turn of the century. Nonetheless, those investors probably have little option but to put up still more capital to keep TML going (hundreds of millions of pounds are needed) if they are not to see what money they have already put in disappear. It is conceivable that TML could function as a corporate business organisation for many years and still, in the end, fail to produce any net returns at all. The 'truism' that a business needs to make a profit to survive only stays true if the timeframe within which it applies can be adjusted indefinitely.

2. There were those who argued, at the time, that what people really objected to was the threat to house prices. And this may have been true of some. But it cannot explain both the sheer persistence of the lobby group or the widespread local support for its stand.

3. Critics of this line of argument may wish to suggest that precisely the opposite is true: that irrational decisions by buyers and sellers, especially brokers and most especially computerised brokers are, in a situation like this, being corrected by the 'invisible hand' of the market moving towards an equilibrium which reflects a more rational evaluation of the worth of companies and shares. But such a 'correction' only occurs when shares are over-valued, and that occurs when a situation exactly parallel but opposite to the one we described occurs. The market 'corrects' its own irrationalities, but it is the collectivity which behaves erratically and is irrational, not the decisions of individual participants who are, for the most part, rational people making sensible decisions. This analysis only applies to those movements in the market for which no obvious or complete explanation can be found, not to those which are clearly reactions to genuine changes in the external world which really affect share values, like wars or earthquakes.

4. For a more detailed discussion of this point, see Lyons (1965) and Regan (1980).

5. For interesting arguments as to why utilitarians should not advocate utilitarianism, see Don Locke's (1976) paper 'Why the Utilitarians Shot President Kennedy', and also Smart (1986) 'Utilitarianism and Its Applications'. Interestingly, Locke suggests that this point is, and Smart that it is not, an objection to utilitarianism.

6. This is a rather informal paraphrase of Kant's 'I ought never to act except in such a way *that I can also will that my maxim should become a universal law*' (which is, admittedly, somewhat stronger than my version). I. Kant (1948), p. 67.

7. 'It is an old theme of tragedy that we will be responsible for our actions beyond anything we bargain for, and it is the prudence of morality to have provided us with excuses and virtues against that time.' Stanley Cavell (1969), p. 196.

8. Or so he said at the subsequent trial. Fortunately we are not concerned with whether what he said was true, or even likely, but with whether, if it was true, he had committed an offence.
9. For a longer discussion of *phronesis* and its role in applied ethics, see B. Flyvbjorg, (1993).
10. For an extended discussion of Aristotelian virtue theory as applied to business ethics, see Robert Soloman (1992 and 1993).
11. The best known of these, and probably the most interesting, is still Peters and Waterman (1982). But even it apparently falls into the trap of supposing that there are rules or maxims for success which can be generalised from one case to another.

References

Bentham, J. (1789) 'Introduction to the Principles of Morals and Legislation', in Warnock (1962).
Bowie, N. (1986) 'Business Ethics', in J. P. Demarco and R. M. Fox (eds), *New Directions in Ethics*, Routledge & Kegan Paul, London.
Cavell, S. (1969) 'Music Discomposed', in Cavell, *Must We Mean What We Say?*, Cambridge University Press, Cambridge.
Clutterbuck, D., Dearlove, D. and Snow, D. (1992) *Actions Speak Louder*, Kogan Page in association with Kingfisher, London.
Donaldson, T. (1982) *Corporations and Morality*, Prentice-Hall, New Jersey, pp. 11–12.
Flyvbjorg, B. (1993) 'Science, Ethics and Rationality', in Winkler and Coombs (1993).
Friedman, M. and Friedman, R. (1962) *Capitalism and Freedom*, University of Chicago Press, Chicago.
Friedman, M. and Friedman, R. (1980) *Free to Choose*, Avon.
Harvey, B. (1992) 'Market Morality', *Times Higher Education Supplement*, 11 September 1992.
Hayek, Fv. (1982) *Law, Legislation and Liberty*, Routledge & Kegan Paul.
Kant, I. (1948) *The Moral Law* (ed. and trans. H. J. Paton), Hutchinson (first published 1785).
Locke, D. (1976) 'Why the Utilitarians Shot President Kennedy', *Analysis*, 36.
Lyons, J. (1965) *The Forms and Limits of Utilitarianism*, Oxford University Press, Oxford.
Mahoney, J. (1989) 'Morality at the Boardroom Level', *Times Higher Education Supplement*, 5 May 1989.
Mahoney, J. (1993) 'Teaching Business Ethics', *Professional Manager*, March.
Mill, J. S. (1861) *Utilitarianism*, in Warnock (1962).
Parfitt, D. (1984) *Reasons and Persons*, Oxford University Press, Oxford.
Peters, T. J. and Waterman, R. H. (1982) *In Search of Excellence: Lessons from America's Best-Run Companies*, Harper & Row.
Regan, D. (1980) *Utilitarianism and Co-operation*, Oxford University Press, Oxford.
Schoenfeldt, L. F. *et al.* (1991) 'The Teaching of Business Ethics: A Survey of AACSB Member Schools', *Journal of Business Ethics*, vol. 10: pp. 237–41.
Sen, A. (1987) *On Ethics and Economics*, Blackwell, Oxford.
Smart, J. J. C. (1986) 'Utilitarianism and Its Applications', in Demarco, J. P. and R. M. Fox (eds), *New Directions in Ethics*, Routledge & Kegan Paul, London.
Soloman R, (1992, *Ethics and Excellence: Co-operation and Integrity in Business*, Oxford University Press.
Soloman, R. (1993) 'Corporate Roles, Personal Virtues: An Aristotelian Approach to Business Ethics', in Winkler and Coombs (1993).

Stuttard, G. (1992) 'Robert Owen, 1771–1858; A 19th Century Pilgrim's Progress in the World of European Business Ethics', in J. Mahoney and E. Vallance, *Business Ethics in A New Europe*, Kluwer Academic Publisher, Dordrecht, pp. 49–58.
Warnock, M. (ed.) (1962) *Utilitarianism*, Fontana, London.
Winkler, E. R. and Coombs, J. R. (eds) (1993) *Applied Ethics: A Reader*, Blackwell, Oxford.

CHAPTER 2

Case Studies in Business Ethics

1 The Use of Cases in the Study of Business Ethics

Business and management education has the purpose of improving business practice. Many other claims are made for it but none is as intuitively or philosophically appealing as this. Employers and practitioners may sometimes take the view that business and management education exists to serve their needs for competent employees who can carry out the tasks necessary for successful operation. Therefore, education should aim to provide people with the requisite skills and appropiate attitudes as well as knowledge of business practice. Others take the view that an education should enrich the mind and develop critical faculties. Therefore, a good critical and theoretical understanding is central to the process of business education and skills and attitudes can be acquired during the early stages of employment.

We take neither of these positions. Our view is that both business education and business practice are enriched by the synergy of theory and practice. The best practice is theoretically informed. It is based on a clear and firm grasp of concepts and principles. These are not developed as independent, free-standing intellectual products. They are developed within the context of theory. Good theory reflects a sound grasp of practice. Just as it is the case that theory can often be challenged on the basis of non-compliance with reality, so business practice can be criticised because it is not in accordance with best practice. The notion of best practice is that of practice which is theoretically informed.

Case studies can help students of business ethics to refine theory by referring the application of theory to instances and by illustrating the deficiencies of or inadequacies of theory. One argument against the use of cases might be that since ethical issues are essentially unresolvable dilemmas there is little point in trying to resolve them. An introduction to ethical reasoning would help the student to analyse situations and cases rationally. Furthermore, even if some dilemmas are not totally resolvable, they may be partially resolvable. Dilemmas may also be avoided or minimised in their force by skilful management. The use of cases can help to sensitise current and future managers to the situations likely to lead to ethical dilemmas and to ways in which they might avoid, minimise or otherwise cope with such situations.

2   Aims of the Case Study Approach

Mathews *et al.* (1991) identify three purposes for the study of cases in business and management education. First, it is to develop the sort of understanding, independent thinking, judgement and communication which are needed in the business world. It is the stubborn facts embedded within a chunk of reality which require us to face up to the thorny issues faced by business people. Second, the study of cases develops confidence in the exercise of judgement and the willingness to give regard to other viewpoints. Third, analysing cases in ethics helps to develop moral judgement. Cases in business ethics are usually difficult to resolve and require a moral understanding on the part of the analyst.

The cases presented in the next four chapters are intended to help you to develop confidence and skill in the analysis of complex issues in business ethics. In analysing these cases, you will develop the ability to recognise the complexities of ethical issues in business, to relate those complexities to the relevant theories and principles and to form your own judgements. The cases are intended for classroom discussion and it is in the process of challenging others' conclusions and defending your own that you will be able to refine your ideas and produce more sustainable conclusions.

Beyond this, you will also develop greater sensitivity to others' views and greater awareness of the different perspectives which can be brought to bear on ethical problems in business.

3   Approaches to the Analysis of Cases

There is no 'one best way' of analysing cases. There is, however, a well-established and widely used approach. This is often labelled the 'rational' approach. This approach to analysis owes much to the belief in systematic and positivistic explanations of organisational behaviour. It is a powerful, explanatory approach, derived substantially from Benthamite utilitarianism.

Jeremy Bentham's 'felicific calculus' was based on the view that the consequences of any social, economic or political action could be divided into pains (costs) or pleasures (benefits) and that it was possible to calculate with some precision the balance of cost and benefit for any such action. It has been developed into the dominant, almost unquestioned method of problem-solving within business.

The rational approach consists of the following five steps:

- identify the problem
- generate alternative solutions
- evaluate the alternatives, using cost–benefit approaches
- select the solution
- implement the chosen solution.

Each step can require detailed investigation and some very hard thinking and the process may become iterative, i.e. the analyst may need to think again about an earlier stage as a result of the work carried out in later stages.

It may also be the case that instead of seeking to identify and implement the optimal solution, the analyst may be satisfied with a sub-optimal solution. This may be because of pressures of time, lack of analytical capacity, the inability to obtain all the necessary information or basic human faults such as laziness or lack of interest (see Simon, 1947).

An alternative, less widely used but equally powerful approach, is Aristotelian in origin. Malloy and Lang (1993) present this method as a 'transrational' approach. The transrational approach to analysis is more comprehensive than the merely rational.

In his *Metaphysics* (1947), Aristotle explores the causes of things in existence. He proposes that things exist because of the First Principle and Four Causes. The First Principle is the cause of all causes or the prime mover – Aristotle's equivalent of the Judeo-Christian God. The Four Causes are the material cause, the formal cause, the efficient cause and the final cause. The material cause is that from which something is made. The formal cause is that into which something is made. The efficient cause is that by which something is made. The final cause is that for the sake of which something is made.

The Prime Mover in relation to business organisations is the person who creates the organisation. The final cause for an organisation could be described as its *raison d'etre* – it is the organisation's philosophy or ideology. It can be seen in mission statements and ethical policies. The formal cause is the organisation's culture or its way of doing what it does. The culture is shaped by the climate of the organisation and this is a product of the leadership process. Leadership is therefore the efficient cause of the organisation. The material cause of the organisation is its membership.

Malloy and Lang offer the following questions, based upon the four causes, as an aide to case analysis:

Final Cause
1. What is the stated purpose of the organisation?
2. What is the unstated purpose of the organisation?
3. What are the organisation's official goals?
4. What are the organisation's operative goals?
5. Is there a stated organisational philosophy?
6. Is there an unstated organisational philosophy?
7. How do employees, management, clientele, and society perceive the organisation's purpose, goals and philosophy?

Formal Cause
8. How does the organisation socialise new members?
9. What are the organisation's rituals, myths, unique language and slogans?
10. What are the explicit standards of organisational behaviour?

Efficient Cause
11. What is the style of leadership?
12. What is the perceived style of leadership within the organisation? By superiors? By subordinates?
13. What is the preferred style of leadership in the organisation? By superiors? By subordinates?

Material Cause
14. How do employees perceive the organisation?
15. What are the employees' value orientations towards work?

Malloy and Lang claim that their approach to the analysis of managerial dilemmas is holistic in nature and they contrast this with the limited perspective on organisational reality provide by the rational approach.

A third approach to the analysis of cases is provided by Goodpaster (1983). He begins by describing several frameworks for analysis of ethical issues. First, he distinguishes between issues relating to the external environment of the organisation as a whole and those relating to the internal environment. Within the context of the external environment, the manager sees the organisation as a moral agent in the wider society. The internal environment is to be managed with a view to maintaining the freedom and well-being of the organisation's members.

He goes on to distinguish between descriptive ethics, normative ethics and metaethics. Descriptive ethics is aimed at an empirical or neutral description of the values of individuals and groups. Normative ethics seeks to develop and defend judgements of right and wrong, good and bad, virtue and vice. Metaethics is concerned with examining questions about the meaning and provability of ethical judgements or of comparing one ethical theory with another.

He then divides approaches to ethics into three categories. These are, utiltarianism, contractarianism and pluralism. The first asks, 'what actions or policy maximises the ratio of benefits to costs?'. The second asks 'what action or policy most fairly repects rights?'. The third asks 'what action or policy reflects the stronger duty?'.

Goodpaster, on the basis of these frameworks, then offers a list of questions which may be asked in relation to a case study. They are:

1. Are there ethical issues involved in this case? Centrally or peripherally? Is a decision required?
2. If there are ethical issues involved do they relate to the eternal environment or the internal environment? Or are both involved? How? What precisely are the ethical issues involved in each category?
3. From a descriptive ethical perspective, what appear to be the critical ethical assumptions or values shown by the persons or organisations in the case?
4. From the point of view of maximising utility for those affected, what is the best course of action? What facts in the case support this conclusion?
5. From the point of view of fairness or individual rights, what is the best course of action? Again, what facts support this conclusion?
6. From the point of view of setting priorities among duties and obligations what should be done? Why ?
7. Do the three avenues (utilitarianism, contractarianism and pluralism) converge on a course of action or do they diverge ?
8. If they diverge which avenue should override?
9. Are there ethically relevant considerations in the case that are not captured by any of the three avenues? What are they?
10. What is the decision or action plan?

The three approaches to the analysis of cases all offer useful guidance. We suggest that, for cases designed to encourage identification of and deliberation about ethical issues, the approaches of Malloy and Lang or Goodpaster may be more helpful than the rational approach.

4 The Cases

The case studies in the next four chapters are intended to present well-grounded material to which you may return or upon which you may reflect during the later parts of the book. They are lengthy and detailed examinations of actual events and problems. They offer a rich background from which to draw and against which to test understanding of the models and theories introduced later.

These case studies are not vignettes. They are not short, stylised stories of incidents. They provide considerable contextual material and are complex. Vignettes, of which there are several in later chapters, provide an opportunity to focus sharply on issues and to identify dilemmas. Complex and detailed case studies present a different challenge. There is the need to clarify the issues, to relate them to the body of information and to place onself within the culture and structure of the organisation.

The case of British Airways and Virgin Atlantic, in describing a complex set of events, alerts us to the impact of organisational structure, culture and circumstances on behaviour. The case of Queens Moat provides opportunities to review the relationship between shareholders and directors within the context of business regulation and control.

There are two substantial case studies dealing with the British Co-operative Bank. The first demonstrates the process of development of the Bank's Ethical Policy and offers an example of its implementation. The second examines the impact of the ethical policy on a significant group of managers within the Bank.

References

Aristotle (1947) *Metaphysics* (W. D. Ross trans.) in T. L. Beauchamp, *Case Studies in Business Society and Ethics*, Prentice-Hall, New Jersey, 1989.

Goodpaster, K. E. (1983) 'Some Avenues for Ethical Analysis in General Management', Harvard Business School, case 9-383-007.

Malloy, D. C. and Lang, D. L. (1993) 'An Aristotelian Approach to Case Study Analysis', *Journal of Business Ethics*, vol. 12, 5pp. 11–516.

Mathews, J. B. *et al.* (1994) *Policies and Persons: A Case-book in Business Ethics* (2nd edn), McGraw-Hill, New York.

Simon, H. A. (1947) *Administrative Behaviour: A Study of Decision-Making Processes in Administrative Organisations*, Macmillan, New York.

CHAPTER 3

Virgin Atlantic and British Airways

1 Introduction

In January 1993 British Airways ended a libel case brought against them by Richard Branson's company, Virgin Atlantic, by apologising unreservedly for any 'injury caused to the reputation and feelings of Richard Branson and Virgin Atlantic' and particularly for questioning the good faith and integrity of Mr Branson. The judge ordered BA to pay legal costs (approximately £3,000,000) and Mr Branson was awarded £610,000 in damages.

This case was widely seen as a humiliating climbdown for BA, especially for Lord King, the Chairman of the Board, and Sir Colin Marshall, Chief Executive of the company. BA were labelled as a company which would stoop to any level of dirty trickery to get rid of competition. The shock-waves from this case will reverberate around the halls of big business and government for some time.

The case involves several strands of interest to students of business ethics. The clash between BA's carefully crafted image as the world's favourite airline and its publicly pronounced customer culture and its actions in this case is one such theme. The avoidance of responsibility by senior executives and board members is another. The logic of free-market competition and its effects on business behaviour is a third. The consequences of unethical behaviour is a fourth.

This case study examines the background to the case, the details of BA's behaviour and the consequences which flowed from the discovery of unethical business behaviour.

2 Background

Competition between airline companies is fierce. Much of the competitive action revolves around pricing, flexibility of flight arrangements, customer convenience, quality of service at airports and on the plane. There is another side to the battle between airlines of which most air-travellers are not aware. It relates to 'slots'. A slot represents the right of an airline to take off or land at a given airport. Slots can be 'arrival' or 'departure' slots. They are allocated by the hour so that a slot in the 0800 hour may be from 0800 to 0855.

Each airport has an Airport Coordinator responsible for allocating slots. This can be either an individual or a group or committee consisting of airline representatives. Airlines make seasonal submissions to the coordinator at each airport which they wish to use. This is a submission for a whole season – summer (April to October) or winter (November to March). Clearly, the greater the congestion at an airport and the greater the demand for slots, the more difficult the role of the coordinator becomes.

Airlines compete for the most lucrative slots and the process of slot allocation can be crucial for the success or failure of the competitive strategies of individual airlines. From one season to the next, airlines are able to rely on their historical allocation. Any planned growth in activity requires new slots.

Slot planning is affected by some unpredictability in the environment. This might consist of announcements about enhanced runway capacity by the British Airports Authority (as happened in 1992) or changes in the Traffic Distribution Rules by the Department of Transport (as happened in 1991 enabling 17 new airlines to operate in and out of Heathrow). Virgin Atlantic has long been campaigning to be allowed more slots (i.e. take-off and landing times). Their longstanding ambition is to fly to the world's 12 largest cities from Heathrow. In 1993 Virgin had 3,000 slots per year and had been offered a further 1,000 slots. This gave Virgin a 1% share of total available slots. This can be compared with 5% for Lufthansa which was Heathrow's third largest carrier (*The Guardian*, 18 January 1993).

The relative sizes of the two protagonists in this case were remarkably disparate. Virgin Atlantic employed 2,400 people whereas BA employed 48,450; Virgin had 8 aircraft, BA had 227; Virgin carried approximately 1 million passengers a year, BA carried 25 million; Virgin made a loss of £3 million in 1991, BA made over £300 million profit; BA had a turnover approximately 14 times greater than that of Virgin (*The Guardian*, 12 January 1993).

The Virgin Atlantic case is the latest in a series of controversial cases involving British Airways and smaller competitors.

In 1985 Freddie Laker alleged that BA had conspired with a group of other airlines to put Laker out of business and to remove the threat created by the novel and popular Skytrain operation which made air travel more convenient for the regular traveller. The case against BA was settled out of court with significant payments being made to the Laker organisation, its creditors, pension fund and staff.

Sir Michael Bishop, the chairman of British Midland, also considers his company to have been the victim of sharp practice by BA. British Midland has a small sister airline, Loganair. Sir Michael claims that he was approached during 1992 by Liam Strong, then BA's marketing director. BA was interested in a joint venture serving the Scottish highlands and islands. They had some problems with their own service in this area and approached Sir Michael because of the Loganair connection. Loganair was involved in this area also.

Sir Michael states that letters of confidentiality were drafted and had to be signed by both companies. These letters were designed to protect the commercial secrets of both organisations and to prevent either side using any confidential information to its advantage. Sir Michael signed his, BA management did not sign theirs. Sir Michael trusted them and proceeded with the exchange of information about passenger numbers and began negotiations. As the time approached to sign a final deal, Sir Colin Marshall, BA's Chief Executive, called the whole thing off.

Six months later BA had established new flights from Manchester to Edinburgh which happened to be Loganair's most profitable route. Sir Michael took the view that BA extracted useful commercial information from him and then withdrew from a possible agreement to take commercial advantage of the information which they had been given in confidence (*The Independent on Sunday*, 17 January 1993).

BA is clearly the dominant player in the British civil aviation industry. It also makes strenuous attempts to maintain strong links with important political and governmental decision-makers.

The House of Commons publishes annually a list of members' interests. This is a list, declared by MPs themselves, of any outside interest they have with external bodies including trade unions, charitable organisations, pressure groups and businesses. It is common for MPs to indicate the financial aspects of any relationship which may exist. The list of members' interests published in early January 1993 indicates that BA appears as a donor more often than any other company. At least 14 MPs received free flights or other benefits during 1992. Angela Rumbold, Deputy-Chairman of the Conservative Party and Alan Haselhurst, a member of the House of Commons Select Committee on Transport were among the beneficiaries. (Select Committees can exert some influence on government policy and the practices of the departments which they scrutinise.) Two Members of Parliament registered that they had received free flights from Virgin.

BA decided to stop making payments to the Conservative Party in 1991, after Mrs Thatcher was ousted as party leader.

BA was privatised in 1985. It had been prepared for privatisation by Sir John (now Lord) King and Colin (now Sir Colin) Marshall who launched a series of major training events and reorganisations within the business to enhance the quality of customer service.

There is considerable evidence to show that the changes brought about by BA management have led to a clear customer service focus. BA's Annual Report for 1991/92 describes the company as being 'Committed to quality with everyone of its 50,000 staff participating in its new customer service programme, Winning with Customers'. David Young (1989), in a report for the Ashridge Management Centre, indicates that employees generally recognise that considerable changes had taken place between 1983 and 1989. BA managers interviewed in 1988 saw the organisation as being more professional, customer-led, adapting, innovative and more purposive. This change is further underlined by customer reaction. The airline has regularly won awards for good customer service voted by the customers themselves.

The BA Mission Statement (*British Airways Reports and Accounts, 1991–92*) contains a series of value-statements which are meant to guide the operations of the company. The Mission Statement declares that the overall mission is 'To be the best and most successful company in the airline industry' and the goals which stem from this mission are:

to be a safe and secure airline

to deliver a strong and consistent financial performance

to secúre a leading share of air travel business worldwide with a significant presence in all major geographical markets

to provide overall superior service and good value for money in every market segment in which we compete

to excel in anticipating and quickly responding to customer needs and competitor activity

to sustain a working environment that attracts retains and develops committed employees who share in the success of the company

to be a good neighbour concerned for the community and the environment

In addition to introducing a strong customer culture within the company, Sir Colin Marshall also made fundamental changes to the management style within BA. The emphasis has shifted from decision by committees and the avoidance of individual responsibility to an approach which stresses urgency, the need for individual managers to take decisions and to accept responsibility. There is also an expectation that managers will be visible. David Young describes the style thus: 'At all levels it is clearly about "putting the customer first", the customer service focus established by Marshall back in 1983. At a management level it appears to be about getting things done, responding to the business challenges, and not standing on ceremony in doing it' (Young, 1989, p. 13; see also Bruce, 1987, and Höpfl et al., 1992).

In discussing the reasons for BA's success in creating a sense of mission within the organisation, Young (1989, pp. 14–15) identifies the following 'keys to this success':

the selection of simple and appropriate themes encouraging care for people and personal accountability

a context of uncertainty to make change possible

consistent, persistent, courageous, visible and open leadership

focus on the practicalities

formal programmes which reinforced the messages of the new management style

Sir Colin Marshall, according to a former BA manager Michael Levin, is recognised by the staff as a decent human being who projects caring, concern and moral probity and Young asserts that this is an important factor in BA's success. Michael Levin reappears below.

3 The Story

The activities of BA which came to light as a result of the court case brought by Mr Branson could be taken straight from any novel about big business. All it appears to lack is a sex theme. Searching through journalists' rubbish, phone-tapping, people attending meetings with hidden microphones secreted about their person, attempts to hide trails and shuffle off responsibilities to others are all aspects of this bizarre case.

There are three main components to BA's campaign against Virgin Atlantic. First, there is the attack on Virgin's Atlantic operations. This consisted of persuading Virgin passengers at airports to switch to BA, cold-calling Virgin customers and alleged hacking into computers to discover sensitive commercial information. Secondly, there was a report on Virgin produced by Brian Basham, a public relations consultant hired by BA. This cost BA £40,000 and was presented to the chief executive in the form of a slide show. Finally, there was operation Covent Garden which began in 1991 as a response to worries within BA that it had a mole in its midst.

The first campaign, the so-called switch-selling campaign, was allegedly backed up by hacking into Virgin's computers. Former BA employees reported on television in January 1992 that they had accessed Virgin's computerised reservations service. They had subsequently telephoned passengers to tell them that their flights had been cancelled and offered them flights with BA.

This may be in breach of the Data Protection Act which seeks to establish certain basic principles about the fairness and legality with which personal information is obtained. The Computer Misuse Act 1990 makes it a crime to access other people's computers.

The second component consisted of the report produced by the external consultant. This component was known as Operation Barbara. Estimates as to its costs vary from £40,000 to £50,000. That it was sanctioned by the Chief Executive, Sir Colin Marshall, seems not to be in doubt. This report was selectively leaked to parts of the press and resulted in items appearing which were critical of Richard Branson personally and made allegations about the weaknesses of Virgin as a company. The report was produced in April 1991 and authorisation for the project was needed from the chief executive's office because it cost more than the Director of Public Relations, Mr David Burnside, was able to approve.

The report summarises financial, personal and operational aspects of Mr Branson's businesses. It identifies popular misconceptions about Virgin, and draws attention to Mr Branson's personal style of management and his highly experimental strategy. It also comments on the fact that he owns a nightclub about which there have been allegations of crime, drug-peddling and homosexuality. The report states that this ownership 'seems to be high risk in terms of his all-important image' (*The Guardian*, 15 January 1993).

The third component is known as Operation Covent Garden. The court case made it clear that Mr Branson had not attempted to discredit BA or its business but BA executives became convinced during their attempts to undermine Virgin that Virgin was organising industrial espionage against BA.

It was towards the end of 1991 that BA became worried about possible spying by Virgin. Ian Johnson Associates were hired by Sir Colin Marshall and David Hyde, BA's head of security (*The Independent on Sunday*, 17 January 1993). Such was the paranoia at this time that when Mr David Burnside, BA's head of Public Relations, went for dinner with a mutual friend of Mr Branson he was wired for sound and the conversation was recorded. Staff from Ian Johnson's organisation were also keeping watch. As it happened, this meeting had been arranged by the mutual friend so that Mr Burnside could meet with the person who had indeed been hired by an organisation other than Virgin to investigate Mr Burnside.

The report produced by Mr Johnson details phone-tapping of BA's senior executives. An executive's car was broken into and details of BA's UK management were taken. Informants told BA senior staff that informants had been planted at one of their offices and that a secretary at headquarters was feeding information to Virgin.

The report strung together a series of unconnected events to support a claim that Virgin was spying on BA. However, it concluded that the investigators were not able to substantiate the claim. The report also recommended that senior executives should be very cautious when using mobile telephones, fax machines and engaging in conversations which could be heard (*The Guardian*, 15 January 1993). But the court case showed conclusively that Virgin had not been investigating BA.

4   The Consequences

The consequences flowing from the court case and judgement made can be divided between consequences for BA as a business; consequences for individuals within BA and consequences for Virgin.

Clearly BA's image has been tarnished. Press and other media coverage was generally unfavourable to BA. What effect this will have on customer loyalty and confidence in BA is difficult to identify clearly.

The Opposition spokesman on Transport, Mr John Prescott, called for resignations from Lord King and Sir Colin Marshall for what he labelled their 'disreputable campaign of deceit, lies and illegal activities' (letter to John MacGregor, Minister of Transport). He refused to accept the attempt made by BA to dissociate the Board from the actions taken.

Following the court case, Mr Branson demanded a concrete expression of good faith from BA and negotiations began between the two companies focusing on slot allocation and financial compensation for Virgin.

On 27 January 1993, Mr Prescott wrote again to Mr McGregor protesting at the way in which airline slots were being traded by BA as part of the negotiations between BA and Virgin. His criticism was that such private deals should not be the way in which slot allocation is made and he urged the minister to intervene.

Other airlines have watched with some apprehension as negotiations between BA and Virgin have proceeded. These negotiations have been seen as an attempt by BA to buy off Virgin and to encourage them not to take the threatened legal action against BA in the US courts. On 15 February 1993, Sir Michael Bishop, Chairman of British Midland, said 'It has to be nipped in the bud that BA has the power to pass over slots other than the ones that they own. If BA want to settle their dispute with Virgin by trading slots they can only trade the ones they already have' (*The Guardian*, 16 January 1993).

Further political pressure was brought to bear when Peter Mandelson, MP for Hartlepool, urged the Transport Secretary to arrange for the Office of Fair Trading to investigate the 'commercial bullying and political manipulation' allegedly practised at British Airways (*The Guardian*, 8 February 1993). The Data Protection Registrar, established by the Data Protection Act, began investigations into possibilities of breaches of the law by BA and asked for details of allegations and information from Virgin. If a case is brought and proven against BA then this will further damage their reputation as a business.

The outcome of the libel case could have serious implications for BA's activities in the USA. Shortly after the court case BA acquired a 19.9% shareholding in US AIR which is America's sixth largest carrier. On 1 February 1993 the three biggest US airlines formally lodged a petition with the US Department of Transportation in an attempt to overturn this arrangement. Previous bids by BA had been received with hostility by the US authorities and the three US airlines were now arguing that the deal between BA and US Air was substantially the same as an earlier plan from which BA had been forced to withdraw. Much will depend on the reaction of American politicians and media. Mr Branson has appeared on US TV and is very widely admired as an entrepreneur. President Clinton may adopt a more protectionist approach to industrial policy than his predecessor and the three airlines are pressing the administration to form a definitive policy regarding foreign investment in the US airline industry.

Press coverage in Britain has been generally damning of BA. Jeremy Warner, in the *The Independent on Sunday* (17 January 1993), writes of a company driven by deep paranoia operating a no-holds barred approach to business. Will Hutton, writing in the *The Guardian* (12 January 1993), says 'Competition British Airways style seems to include personalised attacks, systematic campaigns of denigration and even abusing commercial privacy – not what the enterprise culture was supposed to be about.'

The boardroom changes which took place on 5 February 1993 were unsympathetically covered by the media with prime time news broadcasts showing an angry and somewhat harassed Lord King responding aggressively to loud press questioning.

Further image and public relations difficulties for BA arose from the awards of the *Executive Travel* magazine. Its readers voted Virgin Atlantic 'Airline of the Year' and best transatlantic carrier, best business class, cabin staff, food and wine, in-flight entertainment and airport lounges.

Despite the generally unsympathetic media coverage, BA's customers show no signs of deserting them as a result of the 'dirty tricks' case. The *Financial Times* reviewed customer reaction (22 January 1993) and found that factors other than BA's guilt in conducting 'dirty tricks' were foremost in travellers' minds. The quality of customer service on BA flights and its safety record were important factors in retaining customer loyalty. Even customers of Virgin stated that BA's behaviour would not stop them using BA in future.

Shareholders (see Appendix 2) were reported in the press to be alarmed at the extent of the 'dirty tricks' campaign and the prospects of Sir Colin Marshall taking over as Chairman and retaining his Chief Executive position, contrary to the recommendations of the Cadbury Committee. They were, however, unwilling to press Sir Colin too hard on this issue as he had let it be known that he would resign if he were not made Chairman, and they were impressed by his performance as Chief Executive.

Some shareholders were concerned that the board had not tried hard enough to get to the bottom of the case. BA's solicitors had conducted an investigation a year before and found nothing. Sir Michael Angus, non-executive deputy chairman, emerged as a pivotal figure during January and February. He ordered a second full investigation, the report of which was highly critical of aspects of the 'dirty tricks' campaign. The *Financial Times* stated (21 January 1993) that this report 'confirmed that the campaign was carried out by a few individual employees and did not involve the highest levels of management'.

Shortly after the court case was closed BA published a new code of business conduct for all its staff (see Appendix 4). Mr Branson is still considering whether to bring any further action against BA under the competition laws of the United States or European Community law. The outcome of negotiations between the two companies will determine whether or not such legal action is taken.

Calls for the resignations of Lord King and Sir Colin Marshall quickly followed in the wake of the outcome of the court case. BA insisted that no director was involved in the case. The claim by the company is that no director – including Lord King and Sir Colin – knew anything about the case despite the fact that substantial sums were spent and the case lasted for almost a year. Also, Richard Branson claims that a member of the Board, Mr Michael Davies, who is also a friend of Mr Branson's father, was sent as an emissary from the board of BA to ask Virgin to drop their libel case.

Mr Basham, the public relations consultant who produced the report on Virgin Atlantic which was selectively leaked to the press, has signed a sworn statement insisting that everything he did was with the full approval of the board (*The Guardian*, 12 January 1993).

It had been planned that Lord King would take up the position of President, an honorary position, during the summer of 1993 and that Sir Colin Marshall would take on the role of Chairman and Chief Executive. There was much media speculation about boardroom manoeuvrings during January and February 1993. Finally, after strong intervention from non-executive directors on the BA board, Lord King became President on 5 February and Sir Colin became Executive Chairman. Robert Ayling was appointed as Group Managing Director.

Lord King's remuneration package as President was the subject of a number of press articles. He was said to be receiving £200,000 per year, plus a contribution to his pension, a central London office and secretary, use of a limousine and chauffeur, free first-class air travel for himself and his family, and free air travel for his staff. This could amount to £600,000 per year for life. Lord King is also Chairman of Babcock International.

Sir Colin will be responsible for corporate strategy, finance, legal and company secretary affairs, safety, security, public relations, the environment, health and medical matters. Mr Ayling will add to his previous portfolio of marketing and operations, responsibility for engineering, flight crews, information services, and human resources (*The Independent*, 6 February 1993). The changes in the boardroom also resulted in Sir Michael Angus agreeing to give more time to his role as deputy chairman of the board. In addition two further non-executive board members were to be appointed. Mr Basham's public relations contract has not been renewed. Mr Burnside resigned on the day the board changes were announced.

Michael Levin, who was quoted above (p. 31), provides a curious postscript to the discussion of consequences for individuals in BA. *The Guardian* reported on 28 January 1993 that confidential papers collected by a former aide of Sir Colin Marshall had been offered for auction by a New York lawyer. This former aide was Michael Levin who had acted as a management consultant for BA between 1983 and 1989 when he was dismissed. He died in 1991. The contents of the papers have yet to be revealed.

The winning of the case and the positive publicity for Virgin Atlantic resulting from it should help Virgin in its campaign to open up competition in the civil aviation industry.

Mr Branson divided up the damages paid by BA amongst his workforce at Virgin Atlantic in an action which received widespread press coverage. In a letter to his staff he wrote 'Thank you all for your help in our defence. After all, a Virgin's honour is her most prized possession.' Mr Branson also indicated that he expected an expression of good faith from BA and made the case to the Secretary of State for Transport that more slots should be released at Heathrow generally. The official government view is that the court case and the slots issue are unconnected. Slots are agreed by an independent committee made up of the airlines.

Clearly, the outcome of the case has opened up some possibilities for Virgin. Their ability to exploit whatever commercial advantage might accrue is however limited by the structure of the industry and by the system of public regulation and control.

5   Postscript

Protracted negotiations between Virgin and BA aimed at settling the dispute between them came to halt on 19 March 1993. They had started in January immediately after the court case. They focused on demands by Virgin for compensation from BA for business lost by Virgin during the 'dirty tricks' period.

Mr Branson claimed that BA had insisted on demanding a commitment from Virgin not to refer again to the dirty tricks campaign. He was prepared to accept the £9 million financial compensation but not to accept a clause in the draft agreement which he claimed would 'gag' Virgin and restrict 'its ability to refer to the case in any further actions or to provide information to anyone else in a similar dispute' (*The Guardian*, 18 January 1993).

BA's Group Managing Director, Mr Robert Ayling, said 'We have simply asked them not to rake over the events of the past. The fundamental point on which we cannot agree with Virgin is their requirement to reopen past events, (*The Guardian*, 18 January 1993).

BA published the controversial clause. It reads 'British Airways and Virgin Atlantic agree that they shall each use their best endeavours to discourage media coverage or comment about the past relationship between BA and VA and the matters covered by this agreement' (*The Independent*, 20 March 1993).

Virgin instructed its lawyers to consider all the remedies available to it including UK legislation concerning the misuse of computer information (the

Data Protection Act and the Computer Misuse Act), US anti-trust laws and the competition rules of the Treaty of Rome through the European Commission.

Whichever route was finally chosen by Virgin, it was likely to be a very costly and prolonged business with no certainty of a successful outcome for Mr Branson.

The British government was said to be unhappy about the prolonged dispute. Adverse publicity, especially in American courts, would damage its position in discussions with the US government about aviation deregulation (*Financial Times*, 20 March 1993).

References

British Airways Report and Accounts, 1991–92.
Bruce, M. (1987) 'Managing People First – Bringing the Service Concept to British Airways', *Industrial and Commercial Training*, Mar/April.
Höpfl, H., Smith, S. and Spencer, S. (1992) 'Values and Valuations: The Conflicts between Culture Change and Job Cuts', *Personnel Review*, vol. 21, no. 1, pp. 24–38.
Young, D. (1989) *British Airways – Putting the Customer First*, for Ashridge Strategic Management Centre, July 1989.

Appendix 1   Chairman's Statement

I BEGAN my annual report to you a year ago by describing the preceding 12 months as among the most volatile in the history of our industry. Times since then have been little, if any, easier. The effects of the Gulf war persisted well into the financial year ended 31 March 1992.

In fact, 1991 has been described as the most difficult year since records began. ICAO, the International Civil Aviation Organisation, has reported the first ever annual fall in international scheduled passenger traffic, down over-all by six per cent, with IATA, the industry association, estimating combined losses on international scheduled services alone of some $4 billion.

Against this background, I think we may fairly describe British Airways' performance as highly creditable.

Profits are up 119 per cent to £285 million at the pre-tax level and turnover up six per cent, leading the Board to recommend a final dividend of 7.24 pence a share, against the 6.05 pence in each of the past two years. This would give dividends for the full year of 10.18 pence a share, a rise of 15 per cent.

To accomplish this, your company had to call upon its considerable store of talent, skill, ingenuity and sheer determination as never before. The World's Biggest Offer, our imaginative and bold promotion, which took off on 23 April last year, jumpstarted the world travel market after the slump caused by the Gulf war. Besides creating immense goodwill towards British Airways, this daring promotion attracted publicity worth tens of millions of pounds. More importantly, it ensured that we recovered from the downturn faster than our rivals. Meanwhile we have had to contend with economic recession in our main markets, which has meant that a return to more normal trading conditions has not happened as speedily as we would have wished.

As expected, we have also faced increasingly tough competition, particularly at our Heathrow home base. Following changes in the Government's traffic distribution rules controlling access to the airport, the number of carriers competing with us there last summer increased by 17, to 87. They include some of the largest and most competitive airlines in the world. We have responded strongly, with a whole host of marketing initiatives and product enhancements. The result has been an increase in our market share at London.

Within the company, we have acted energetically in the past 12 months to reduce our costs, with the support of our employees and trade unions. The contraction in the size of our workforce has been achieved through early retirement, voluntary severance and the disposal of certain activities, with a consequent increase in productivity of almost 12 per cent.

We have made some important changes in the structure of our business. In order to liberate resources for the development of the airline, we sold the business formerly carried on by British Airways Engine Overhaul Limited to a subsidiary company of General Electric Company of the USA. We believe that the new owners, as engine manufacturers, will be able to invest further resources in the development of this excellent business, while allowing us to get on with what we do best. We also contracted out our property maintenance and parts of our security functions.

We have carried out in-depth reviews of our operations at Gatwick and in the UK regions, to ensure that these activities have the best opportunities to reach adequate levels of profitability.

We exceeded our initial targeted savings of £200 million in the initial phase of our three-year Gap Closure programme by £65 million. We are aiming to trim a further £150 million from our costs in the 1992-93 financial year.

What we shall not trim, however, is the quality of our customer service. In our determination to build on this principal underlying strength of British Airways, we recently launched 'Winning for Customers', the latest and most extensive in our series of customer service development initiatives. Every employee will take part in its corporate event, called 'Winners'. Our intention is that this programme should gain us as much of a competitive edge in the 1990s as did our original 'Putting People First' initiative in the 1980s.

There has been a great deal of media speculation in the past year regarding British Airways' globalisation plans. Although we remain committed to the concept of a global airline, and while we believe our long-term future may be bound up with worldwide alliances, we are still in a position of strength which many would envy. We will not act in haste and repent at leisure. Finding the right partner remains high on our agenda, but there is much else besides. Until the right deal presents itself, we will continue to operate a highly successful, profitable business achieving exceptional levels of customer satisfaction.

Growth prospects for this industry remain sound. British Airways is in a good position to take advantage of the opportunities afforded by the liberalisation of the industry, provided the playing field is level and 'competition' is not misinterpreted to mean 'substitution'. We are encouraged by the support of the UK's newly-elected Government for opening the skies of Europe and for examining the role of state subsidies enjoyed by some continental carriers – particularly as the United Kingdom holds the presidency of the European Community in the six months leading up to 1993 and the dawning of the single European market.

We now have our own first platform on the continent, with the establishment of the new German airline Deutsche BA, in which we hold a 49 per cent stake. We are also progressing the development of Air Russia, working with our partners in Russia.

The Company's Directors have for many years benefited from the counsel of Robert Ayling, in his capacity as Company Secretary, Legal Director and Director of Human Resources. Following his appointment as Director of Marketing and Operations, we were pleased to welcome him in December as a full member of the Board.

British Airways is now firmly on its flightpath to recovery after the turbulence caused by the Gulf conflict and recession in many countries. We have demonstrated our ability to manage this business effectively during the most severe downturn it has experienced. In doing so, we have earned the admiration of the industry.

For this, the employees of your Company deserve a substantial vote of thanks, reflected by my Board's decision to increase the level of their profit sharing bonus from the formula driven 1.4 weeks to a full two weeks' basic pay. Their contribution in a trying, often unsettling and constantly challenging 12 months cannot be overstated.

Nonetheless, they and I are only too well aware that there is still much to achieve if we are to accomplish our mission of becoming the undisputed best and most successful company in the industry – to which we remain committed.

King

Lord King of Wartnaby *Chairman*

BOARD MEMBERS AND EXECUTIVE MANAGEMENT

BOARD MEMBERS

Lord King of Wartnaby (74) *Chairman*
Chairman since 1981. Chairman. Babcock International PLC since 1972. Director. Daily Telegraph plc. (B)

Sir Colin Marshall (58) *Deputy Chairman and Chief Executive*
Chief Executive since 1983. Director, Grand Metropolitan PLC. IBM United Kingdom Holdings Limited, Midland Group plc and British Tourist Authority. (B)

Sir Michael Angus (62) *Deputy Chairman and Chairman of the Audit and Remuneration Committees*
Deputy Chairman, Whitbread PLC and National Westminster Bank PLC. Director, Thorn EMI plc. President, Confederation of British Industry. (A.C)

Robert Ayling (45) *Director of Marketing and Operations*
Joined the Board of British Airways in December 1991 after his appointment as Director of Marketing and Operations in September. Joined the airline as Legal Director in 1985 and subsequently took on the duties of Company Secretary and, later, Director of Human Resources. Formerly Under Secretary at the Department of Trade.

Derek Stevens (53) *Chief Financial Officer*
Chief Financial Officer since 1989. Formerly Finance Director, TSB Group plc.

Captain Colin Barnes (58) *Chairman of the Air Safety Review Committee*
Joined the Board of British Airways in 1991 after 36 years flying with the airline as a pilot, the last ten as Chief Pilot and the final five as Director of flight Crew. (A.B)

Michael Davies (57)
Chairman, Calor Group PLC, Wiltshier PLC
and Perkins Foods PLC. Deputy Chairman, TI
Group Plc. (A.B.C)

Sir Francis Kennedy KCMG CBE (66) *Special
Advisor to Chairman and Board*
Diplomatic Service, 1964–86. Director. Fluor
Daniel Corp. and Smith and Nephew plc. (B)

The Hon Charles H. Price II (61)
Former United States Ambassador to the UK.
Chairman, Mercantile Bank of Kansas City.
Director. Hanson Plc, Texaco Inc. Sprint
Corporation and New York Times Company
Inc. (A.B.C)

Lord White of Hull KBE (69)
Chairman. Hanson Industries (A.C)

The letters in brackets indicate membership of
the following committees of the Board:

(A) Audit Committee, (B) Air Safety Review
Committee, (C) Remuneration Committee

EXECUTIVE MANAGEMENT

David Burnside (40) *Director of Public Affairs*

Alistair Cumming (57) *Director of Engineering*

Dr Michael Davies (54) *Director of Health
Services*

Tony Galbraith (53) *Treasurer*

David Holmes (57) *Director of Government and
Industry Affairs*

David Hyde (55) *Director of Safety, Security and
the Environment*

Captain Jock Lowe (48) *Director of Flight Crew*

Clive Mason (48) *Director of Purchasing and
Supply*

Roger Maynard (49) *Director of Corporate
Strategy*

Gail Redwood (43) *Company Secretary*

Mervyn Walker (33) *Legal Director*

John Watson (48) *Director of Human Resources
and Information Management*

Membership as at the time of publication.

Appendix 2   Shareholder Information and Directors' Interests

SHAREHOLDERS
As at 15 May there were 265,819 shareholders.
An analysis is given below.

Size of shareholding	Percentage of shareholders	Percentage of shares
1 – 1,000	95.59	9.11
1,001 – 5,000	3.77	2.70
5,001 – 10,000	0.24	0.61
10,001 – 50,000	0.18	1.57
50,001 – 100,000	0.05	1.43
100,001 – 250,000	0.07	4.47
250,001 – 500,000	0.05	6.36
500,001 – 750,000	0.01	2.99
750,001 – 1,000,000	0.01	3.06
Over 1,000,000	0.03	67.70
	100,00	100,00

Classification of shareholding	Percentage of shareholders	Percentage of shares
Individuals	98.33	12.21
Nominee companies	1.02	77.15
Insurance companies	0.03	3.72
Banks	0.14	1.52
Pension Funds	0.02	0.90
Other corporate holders	0.46	4.50
	100,000	100,000

The following have holdings in the company in excess of 3 per cent of the total shares issued:

	Percentage of shareholding
Templeton Investment Management Limited	5.53
Fidelity Investments	4.52
Schroder Investment Management	3.96

Morgan Guaranty Trust Company of New York, the Company's ADR Depositary, has a non-beneficial interest in 17.68 per cent of the shares in the name of Guaranty Nominees Limited. British Airways is not aware of any other interest in its shares of three per cent or more.

DIRECTORS' INTERESTS

At 31 March 1992   British Airways Plc   British Airways Capital Ltd

	Ordinary Shares subject to no restrictions		Ordinary Shares subject to restrictions		Options Executive and SAYE Share Schemes		Options exercised during year	Convertible Capital Bonds	
	31 March 1992	1 April 1991	31 March 1992	1 April 1991	31 March 1992	1 April 1991		31 March 1992	1 April 1991
Lord King	105,000	35,084	-	316	296,809	853,330	556,521	13,332	13,332
Sir Colin Marshall	25,836	25,520	-	316	485,436	710,155	224,719	11,304	11,304
Sir Michael Angus	3,000	3,000	-	-	-	-	-	1,333	1,333
R J Ayling**	4,459	3,485	744	1,718	215,261	334,224	187,938	-	-
D M Stevens	5,050	5,050	3,403	3,403	337,254	337,254	-	109	1)9
A M Davies	5,060	5060	-	-	-	-	-	2,221	2,221
Captain C A Barnes	7,983	831	4,723	6,875	69,976	208,334	135,692	644	644
Sir Francis Kennedy	5,250	5,250	1,860	1,860	166,666	166,666	-	1,421	1,333
Hon Charles Price II	10,000*	10,000*	-	-	-	-	-	-	-
Lord white	-	-	-	-	-	-	-	-	-
	171,638	93,280	10,730	14,488	1,571,402	2,609,963	1,104,870	30,364	30,2'6

*Held in American Depositary Receipts.
**R J Ayling was appointed to the Board on 16 December 1991.

The Directors interests set out above are in each case beneficial. The options under the Executive Share Option and Savings Related Share Option Schemes are at prices varying between 135p and 210p per share. No Director has any beneficial interest in shares in any subsidiaries of the Company other than those shown above in the 9.75 per cent Convertible Capital Bonds 2005 in British Airways Capital Limited. There have been no changes in the interests set out above between the end of the financial year and 18 May 1992.

Appendix 3   Principal Investments

At 31 March 1992

SUBSIDIARY UNDERTAKINGS
Principal subsidiary undertakings are all wholly-owned direct subsidiaries except where indicated

	Principal activities	Country of incorporation and principal operations
Air Miles Travel Promotions Ltd	Airline Marketing	England
(51 per cent of ordinary shares owned)		
Bedford Associates Inc	Specialist computer reservations software	USA
(a subsidiary undertaking of BritAir Acquisition Corp Inc)		
BritAir Acquisition Corp Inc	Holding company	USA
British Airways Associated Companies Ltd	Airline management services	England
British Airways Australia (Holdings) Pty Ltd	Holding company	Australia
British Airways Capital Ltd	Airline finance	Jersey
(89 per cent of founders' shares owned)		
British Airways Finance BV	Airline finance	Netherlands
British Airways Holidays Ltd	Package holidays	England
Caledonian Airways Ltd	Airline operations	England
Chartridge Centre Ltd	Airline training services	England
Speedbird Insurance Co Ltd	Airline insurance	Bermuda
Travel Automation Services Ltd (trading as Galileo UK)	Computer reservations systems	England

ASSOCIATED UNDERTAKINGS

	Percentage of equity owned	Principle activities	Country of incorporation and principal operations
Air Russia	31	Airline operations	Russia
Concorde International Travel Pty Ltd	50	Airline marketing	Australia
Deutsche BA Luftfahrtgesellschaft mbH	49	Airline operations	Germany
Euro-Hub (Birmingham) Ltd	21	Airport terminal services	England
G B Airways (Holdings) Ltd	49	Airline holding company	Jersey
The Galileo Company Ltd	24	Computer reservations systems	England
World Aviation Systems (Australia) Pty Ltd	50	Airline marketing	Australia

TRADE INVESTMENTS

	Percentage of equity owned	Principal activities	Country of incorporation and principal operations
Covia Partnership	11.0	Computer reservations systems	USA
Hogg Robinson plc	12.4	Travel, transport and financial services	England
Ruby Aircraft Leasing and Trading Ltd	19.3	Aircraft leasing	England
Sapphire Aircraft Leasing and Trading Ltd	19.3	Aircraft leasing	England
The Plimsoll Line Limited	49.9	Airline holding company	England

(Holding company of Brymon Aviation Ltd and Birmingham European
Airways Ltd. The investment is equivalent to 14 per cent of the voting rights).

Appendix 4　BA's Code of Business Conduct

This is the text of BA's code of business conduct:

The success of British Airways is dependent on the quality of the decisions and the behaviour of individuals at all levels throughout the organisation. The code has been developed to provide guidance and assistance to both managers and staff in their dealings with all those with whom we do business, with our customers and suppliers, and with each other.

Adherence to the principles will help ensure that our reputation and success that has been built up over the years through the dedicated hard work of you and your colleagues will continue to grow.

Judgment and discretion will need to be exercised in applying the principles where, at first sight, they appear to be at variance with local custom and practice or commercial common sense.

It is the intent of the code to anticipate and provide a framework of governing values and advice on how to proceed when making difficult decisions namely to establish the norms of business behaviour throughout the company.

General Standards

Compliance: Comply with all the laws that regulate and apply to the company, its systems and the conduct of its business.

Fairness: Treat all groups and individuals with whom we have a business relationship in a fair, open and respectful manner.

Integrity: Show respect for the individual, treating each in a consistent way and honouring commitments made.

Openness: Share and declare information on personal and corporate conflicts of interest (political, financial, relationship) including the offer or acceptance of gifts or hospitality of significant value. Seek guidance and where appropriate confirmation from a higher authority before acting.

Honesty: This goes beyond simply telling the truth to ensuring that any misrepresentation is quickly corrected. Do not allow people to be misled. Where there are valid reasons for withholding information, be clear about the motives and if possible explain why you are doing so.

Fair Competition: Ensure comparisons drawn with competitors and working partners are based on fact and avoid innuendo. Competition should be based on the quality, value and integrity of British Airways' service and products.

Determination: Demonstrate a sense of purpose and commitment to achieving the optimum even in adversity.

Responsiveness: Recognise changes in the business environment and use a creative flexible style to respond to them.

Enablement: Provide sufficient guidance to enable individuals to act upon their own initiative to solve problems and grow in their role.

Conformity: Promote corporate values and competitive edge through the established performance systems of performance and appraisal.

Through employing these practices and behaviours, staff should:

- Use British Airways' stated goals and objectives as guidance, using your values and judgment to interpret against the principles of this code.
- Treat others as you would like to be treated.
- Be prepared to solicit views as to whether something would be appropriate before action, rather than after.
- Discuss difficult decisions with those whose values and judgment you respect. Use company process to earn respect.
- Ask whether you would feel comfortable explaining your decision or behaviour to your boss, your family or the media.
- Be prepared to challenge if you believe others are acting in an unethical way. Create the climate and opportunities for people to voice genuinely held concerns about behaviour or decisions that they perceive to be unprofessional or inappropriate.
- Do not tolerate any form of retribution against those who do speak up. Protect individuals' careers and anonymity if necessary. Encourage an environment of learning from mistakes and mutual trust in each others' motives and judgments.
- Treat the assets and property of British Airways and its customers and its suppliers with the same respect as you would your own. Apart from tangible assets this would include company information as well as the name, image and reputation of British Airways.

CHAPTER 4

Queens Moat Houses Plc

1 Introduction

In April 1982 Queens Moat Houses raised £30 million, including a first rights issue, and proceeded to buy 26 hotels from Grandmet, followed by a second rights issue of £10.6 million. This was the start of a ten-year period of expansion culminating in one of the largest corporate losses in history, a complete change of the Board of Directors and of protracted negotiations with lenders to restructure the finances of the company. John Bairstow was the founder of the group and remained the driving force until he left the company in August 1993. Jeff Randall (1993) commented that 'the impression of reality created by the Bairstow regime deserves membership of the magic circle'.

During this period the reported results and financial statements gave little indication of the troubles ahead. Expansion was the mood of the time. In November 1983 the group purchased the Hilton International Hotel and was confirmed as the UK's largest provincial hotel chain (Randall and Olins, 1993). This was followed by a continental acquisition of the Dutch Belderberg Hotel group for £15.5 million, plus a further 24 hotels on the continent, and in February 1990 the group gained control of Norfolk Capital for £157 million.

This growth was funded in part by a number of rights issues as follows (in £ millions):

12 Apr 82	1st rights issue	(part of £30 raised)
10 May 83	2nd rights issue	10.60
1 Apr 85	3rd rights issue	25.00
20 Aug 87	4th rights issue	83.00
13 Oct 88	5th rights issue	57.50
16 Aug 89	6th rights issue	141.00
4 Oct 89	7th rights issue	1.26
29 May 91	8th rights issue	184.00

All this would appear to indicate that the shareholders had faith in the long-term future of the group. This faith was perhaps founded on the chairman's statements, which as late as April 1991, reporting on the results for the year to 31 December 1990, gave little indication of impending disaster:

> Despite the economic set-back in the UK, and more moderately on the continent and less favourable trading in the early months of this year in some of the large inner-city hotels, they remain cautiously optimistic. Current trading has been more encouraging and they therefore believe that shareholders can reasonably expect modest progress in 1991 and further improvements in 1992 as the UK economy recovers. A series of re-financing moves have brought the borrowing ratio down to 45%. (*Micro View Plus Report*, 10 April 1991)

A statement on the results for the year to 31 December 1991, was again up-beat:

> On the continent a strong progress was continued and a good start was made to 1992, with profitability in the first 3 months of this year at new high levels. There is still no sign of a sustained recovery in the UK though some UK hotels also made good headway. The company is strategically well-positioned and the Board antici-pates a satisfactory outcome in 1992 and a positive return of growth thereafter. Trading results were close to the record-breaking performances of 1990, and re-financing during the year reduced gearing from 69% to 55%.
>
> Also the reduction in the net asset value of the group was mainly due to a sensible and prudent reduction by independent valuers of the value of certain UK hotels, which to a large extent was offset by an overall increase in the valuation of continental assets. (*Micro View Plus Report*, 8 April 1992)

How, therefore, could the hoped for profits of £85–90 million for 1992 turn out to be a £1 billion plus loss, the shares suspended at 47½p and effectively worthless, with the net liabilities amounting to £338 million, plus debts of £1.1 billion? A new assessment of the property portfolio by Jones, Long, Wootton put their value at £861 million.

Jeff Randall (1993) commented, 'the assets and profits seem to have vanished like cards up a sleeve', and proceeded to highlight the following facts:

1. Reported profits of £90 million in 1991, widely expected by analysts to be repeated in 1992.
2. Earlier in the year when its shares were trading at 59p, its stock-market worth was more than £500 million.
3. In December 1992, Weatherall Green and Smith, the property valuers, said Queens Moats' 200-strong hotels estate was worth £2 billion.

2 Tale of Two Valuers

A major issue in the Queens Moat saga has been the valuation of the property portfolio of the group, which in the first instance was valued in December 1992 by Weatherall Green and Smith at £1.86 billion and then subsequently revised downwards to £1.35 billion. These valuations were followed by a figure of £861 million from Jones, Long, Wootton. This led to shareholders asking for an explanation for the difference in the figures.

The Royal Institution of Chartered Surveyors, reacting to a call from the former chairman John Bairstow, agreed to consider the matter, but promptly dropped out of the discussions subsequent to the appointment of the DTI inspectors.

Kirstie Hamilton (1993) reported that 'on the 26 November 1993, Andrew Coppel, Chief Executive of Queens Moat said the restructuring proposals will include a full new valuation, but he emphasised that no valuation, however high, could solve the company's problems, which stemmed from an inability to generate enough cash to service its debt'.

3 Department of Trade Investigation

On 12 November 1993 the Secretary of State for Trade and Industry, Michael Heseltine, appointed inspectors to look into various matters which were drawn to the department's notice by the new board of Queens Moat. The inspectors were appointed under Section 432 of the Companies Act 1984, which gives them wide powers to obtain documents and summon past and present directors, officers and agents of the company.

4 Corporate Governance in Action

A major recommendation of the Cadbury Committee which produced a report on Corporate Governance was the need to emphasise the role of the non-executive directors in the management of a company.

A comment in *Accountancy Age* (11 November 1993) on the Queens Moat saga questioned the position of the last non-executive directors to resign: 'In the case of Queens Moat, these watch-dogs are, however, in the doghouse. David Howell and John Gale were the last of the company's non-executives to resign, and with hindsight, any belief that their credibility with investors would have survived the revelations regarding Queens Moat and its management looks optimistic.'

Melvyn Marckus (1993a) quotes David Howell as saying 'I have sought to perform my non-executive duties conscientiously throughout my appointment and I believe the non-executives were clearly misled.' This is in contrast with an earlier statement attributed to Howell by the *The Sunday Times*: 'I am definitely staying, Queens Moat is a company with a very good future.' (Marckus (1993a))

5   Debenture Holders and Capital Reorganisation

At the AGM held on 29 November 1993 (*Micro View Plus Report*, 29 November 1993) the chairman stated that 'the group had over £1.2 billion of net borrowing and an annual net interest bill in excess of £100 million to service and that the group's borrowing facilities had been capped at their outstanding level at 31 March 1993 and no new money was available to the company from its lenders. The group was not paying some 60% of its interest bill, but was continuing to pay its trade creditors as they fall due to enable the business to continue to trade'.

A further issue of concern to the board was the Debenture Trust Deeds which required that the value of the secured properties must not be less than 150% of the nominal value of the debenture stocks. Unfortunately the Jones, Long, Wootton valuation valued the secured properties at 67% of the principal owed. As a result, default under the Trust deed had occurred and consequently the trustee was entitled to take control of the secured properties which could have resulted in Queens Moat having to cease trading.

It was therefore necessary for a request to be made to the debenture holders via the Trustee not to enforce the security so that directors had time to prepare proposals as part of the overall restructuring. This was agreed at a meeting held on the 30 November 1993.

Reporting on 2 February 1994 the company announced that 'progress has been made towards financial restructuring of the group and that a steering committee of the group's lenders had recommended a continuation of the present arrangements for lender support for a further 2 months' (*Micro View Plus Report* 2 February 1994).

6   Past Dividend Payments and Shareholders' Interests

The investigations undertaken by the new management revealed that the company had paid dividends to both Ordinary and Convertible Preference shareholders which under the Companies Acts it was not legally entitled to do, because the company had insufficient distributable reserves. The total amount involved was approximately £33 million, but the board stated it would attempt to reclaim the dividends paid to the directors.

On the 19 November 1994 the board reported that 'it had been advised that resolutions passed at meetings, amending the borrowing limit in the company's articles were not valid because recognition was not given to a right to attend and vote, at such meetings incorporated in the company's 7% Convertible Accumulative Redeemable Preference shares. The Company had therefore appointed Freshfields and leading Counsel to assist the directors in resolving these issues' (*Micro View Plus Report*, 19 January 1994).

Concern was growing amongst the shareholders as to their position after any capital reorganisation, and a Shareholder Action Group was formed to represent their case at the annual meeting on 29th November 1993. Denis Woodhams, a shareholder in Queens Moat, issued a petition asking the High Court to declare that the group's affairs are being conducted in a manner unfairly prejudiced to the shareholders (Pangalos, 1993).

Mr Beaumont-Dark, supporting the case of the shareholders, was quoted in the *Financial Times*: 'The banks, and one understands it, are protecting their own situation. But people feel other interests ought to be looked at as well. The banks have a certain responsibility. How well did they check before lending money? They're not just innocent victims. The people who are the most innocent are the shareholders' (Skapinker, 1993).

7 The New Management

The new Board of Directors soon became embroiled in the battle between the various interested parties and were themselves criticised by the shareholders on the question of their remuneration packages. The annual general meeting held to adopt the company's 1992 accounts (including the £861 million property valuation) (Marckus, 1993b) was a stormy three-hour debate and the chairman Stanley Metcalfe was obliged to call for a poll to secure adoption of the 1992 accounts.

The new board, Metcalfe, Coppel and Le Poideven, were criticised by the shareholders who questioned the validity of the £861 million valuation and attacked their salaries and incentive arrangements. The chairman, Metcalfe, warned shareholders that the vote to be taken by debenture holders, on whether or not to enforce their security, could threaten Queens Moat's survival. Adoption of the 1992 accounts was defeated by 158 to 80 on a show of hands. In the subsequent poll 256,719,019 votes were cast in favour of adoption and 52,527,297 against adoption.

References

Anon (1993) 'Corporate governance reform hit by QMH affair', *Accounting Age*, 11 Nov 93.
Hamilton, K. (1993) 'Queens calls in valuers again', *The Times*, 27 Nov 93.
Marckus, M. (1993a) 'Time for QMH to publish Assets in Wonderland', *The Times*, 6 Nov 93.
Marckus, M. (1993b) 'QMH chiefs face a gale of criticism', *The Times*, 29 Nov 93.
Pangalos, P. (1993) 'QMH investor issue petition', *The Sunday Times*, 28 Nov 93.

Randall, J. (1993) 'Queens Moat: now you see it, now you don't', *The Sunday Times*, 31 October 93.

Randall, J. and Olins, R. (1993) 'Queens Moat: City anger turns on Howell as new horrors emerge', *The Sunday Times*, 31 October 93.

Skapinker, M. 1993, 'Queens Moat shareholders establish fighting fund', *Financial Times*, 16 Nov 93.

Appendix 1   News Report Results for Year to 2 January 1994

News Report (Microview Plus Report)

QUEENS MOAT HOUSES PLC [Suspended]

8 March 94: Balance Sheet

At meetings held today resolutions amending the borrowing limit of Co and its Subs were passed.

31 March 94: Balance Sheet

At meetings held today holders of 10% First Mort Deb Stock 2020 and 12% First Mort Deb Stock 2013, Extraordinary Resolutions to extend, until 30-6-94, directions to Trustees not to enforce security were duly passed. Steering Committee of Group's lenders has indicated to Co that it has recommended a continuation of present arrangements for lender support for a further 2 months.

8 Apr 94: Dividend

No dividend (1.395p per share) for year to 2-1-94.

8 Apr 94: Results

■ Result for year to 2-1-94, figs in £m: Turnover 381.3 (387.4). Operating profit 18.4 (loss 0.7). Exceptional items – net surplus on revaluation of tangible assets 26.0 (Dr 803.9) restructuring costs nil (32.0) loss on disposal or closure of businesses nil (69.2) and amounts written-off investments 0.3 (17.2) foreign currency gains 13.9 (nil) and interest payable nil (16.7). Interest payable 110.1 (112.6). Loss before tax 46.4 (1,040.5). Tax credit 2.0 (Dr 7.0). Net loss 44.4 (1,047.5). Loss per share 6.4 (116.9p) and excluding exceptional items 10.7p (13.6p).

■ Analysis of turnover and operating profit in £m: Continuing operations – hotels – UK 134.8 (115.1) and 18.5 (8.0), Germany 91.4 (88.2) and loss 0.9 (loss 10.3), The Netherlands 51.9 (45.5) and 8.0 (8.3), France 24.4(26.1) and loss 0.3 (profit 0.9), Belgium 16.8 (16.8) and 0.7 (1.1), elsewhere 10.3 (9.6) and loss 1.7 (profit 2.2), discontinuing operations – property – UK 24.8 (52.1) and loss 3.8 (profit 4.3), discontinued operations – property – UK 14.2 (21.1) and 1.3 (3.1) and leisure – UK 12.7 (12.9) and 2.4 (1.6), less central costs and provisions nil (nil) and 5.8 (15.5), totals 381.3 (387.4) and 18.4 (loss 0.7).

■ Consolidated balance sheet as at 2-1-94, shows in £m: Tangible assets 927.0 (891.1). Add investments 0.6 (1.1) and deduct net current liabilities 1253,2 (1,208.0), creditors due after more than one year 2.0 (4.4) and provisions 49.4 (68.7), giving net liabilities 377.0 (388.9), represented by shareholders deficit.

■ Accounts have been prepared on going concern basis which assumes that Co and all its Subs will continue in operational existence for foreseeable future, having adequate funds to meet their obligations as they fall due.

■ Validity of this assumption depends on: Successful completion of financial restructuring; continued provision of adequate facilities by Group's banks and other lenders pending completion of financial restructuring; and holders of Co's Fist Mortgage Deb Stocks not seeking to enforce their security over assets of certain Subs of Co.

■ Board reports that a satisfactory start to current financial year has been made by Group in UK, which has seen increased occupancy rates but lower than projected average room rates. Overheads have benefited significantly from a reduction in wage costs at unit level. In Continental Europe, difficult trading conditions experienced in 1993 have continued into current financial year. However, measures have been taken to reduce Group's cost base in line with current market conditions.

Board has appointed Cazenove & Co as stockbrokers to Co.

Appendix 2 Queens Moat House Plc Annual Report 1992

(i) Chairman's Statement

I was appointed a director of your company and elected Chairman of your board on 26 August 1993. The results for the year ended 31 December 1992 show that the group incurred losses before taxation of £1,040.5 million (1991 – £56.3 million loss – restated) on turnover of £387.4 million (1991 – £314.7 million – restated). Exceptional losses, which accounted for £939.0 million of the pre-tax losses in 1992, included £803.9 million arising from the reduction below historical cost in the value of the group's properties since 31 December 1991. Losses per ordinary share were 116.4p (1991 – 8.5p loss – restated). No final ordinary dividend in respect of the year has been declared.

As a result of these losses, the group's consolidated balance sheet as at 31 December 1992 showed net liabilities of £388.9 million, compared to net assets of £1,192.6 million as restated as at 31 December 1991. Borrowings as at 31 December 1992 stood at £1,165.9 million (1991 – £860.4 million – restated). These figures include the full liabilities associated with finance leases (1992 – £173.8 million; 1991 – £149.5 million – restated) which, in 1991, were partly treated as operating leases and therefore, as off-balance sheet liabilities.

In common with the experience of other hotel groups in Europe, the operating performance of the group was disappointing in 1992, reflecting difficult trading conditions. The group made an operating loss of £0.7 million in 1992 (1991 – £22.4 million profit – restated). A discussion of the trading performance of the group's businesses is contained in the Chief Executive's Review which follows this statement.

The group's consolidated profit and loss account and balance sheet for 1991 have been restated as a result of adjustments necessary to reflect the more prudent accounting policies and treatments used for the 1992 accounts. The effects of such restatements are that the 1991 pre-tax profit has been reduced from £90.4 million to a pre-tax loss of £56.3 million and the 1991 net assets have been reduced by £105.3 million to £1,192.6 million.

You will find enclosed within this Annual Report and Accounts the unaudited interim results for the six months ended 4 July 1993, which show that the group made an operating profit of £9.1 million over the period. The group incurred net interest charges of £57.5 million during the period resulting in a net los before tax of £48.4 million. The interim results for the period ended 12 July 1992 were based on the previous board's application of accounting policies and treatments which have now been changed. Your board believes that it is not appropriate to compare the 1993 interim results with the 1992 interim results and, for the reasons indicated below, the latter have not been restated.

Background to the 1992 results and reasons for the delay in publications

These results demonstrate a substantially different financial position of your company from that indicated by the Report and Accounts dated 30 April 1992 and the Interim Results dated 12 August 1992. Whilst neither I nor any of the current executive directors were members of your board during the period under review, it is nevertheless necessary for me to explain the background as I understand it. Inevitably, many of the comments made in this statement are based on information available to me and my board colleagues at this time. Accordingly, I have summarised below the principal factors responsible for the changes in the financial position of the group. On pages 19 to 21 is set out a Report by the Finance Director explaining the steps taken to introduce an effective system of financial and management controls, summarising the principal changes in accounting policies which have been made and commenting on the liabilities of the group.

The delay in the production of the 1992 Report and Accounts has been due to a number of factors. The gravity of the group's financial position was first brought to the attention of the group's banks by the former chairman on 31 March 1993, when it was indicated that the group's 1992 results were likely to fall seriously short of expectations and that the preference dividend due on 1 April 1993 could not be paid. Grant Thornton were appointed to investigate the financial position of the group on behalf of the group's banks and Andrew Coppel and Andrew Le Poidevin were appointed as consultants to the group in April 1993. Coopers & Lybrand were appointed as auditors and Morgan Grenfell were appointed as financial advisers in May 1993. It became clear to the board and its advisers at an early stage that a thorough review of the financial position of the group was imperative. As a result, the group's accounting policies were reviewed and appropriate changes made, a rigorous review of the group's contingent liabilities was conducted and Jones Lang Wootton ('JLW') were appointed to value the group's properties.

Given the background to the present situation, the preparation of the 1992 accounts, including the substantial restatement of the 1991 accounts, has taken a considerable period of time. I am confident that the accounting policies on which we have based the 1992 results, and therefore those for 1991 as restated, are entirely appropriate and are the result of considerable deliberation with our auditors and other financial advisers. Certain of those policies were, in fact, accepted by the previous board following recommendations by Andrew Coppel, now the Chief Executive, and Andrew Le

Poidevin, now the Finance Director, when they were consultants to the company. The new accounting policies are set out on pages 36 to 39 and detailed effects of the changes on the 1991 results and financial position are set out in note 1 to the accounts.

Contingent liabilities have been rigorously reviewed in order to ascertain whether they are in fact actual liabilities, for which provision should be made in the accounts, and your board has endeavoured to provide as appropriate for all known liabilities and potential losses. Whilst the new management team has focused on the stabilisation and recovery of the group, a number of issues have surfaced as the problems of the group have been identified. We have ensured that both the auditors and our legal advisers have, as appropriate, carried out proper investigations into known matters affecting the group. These issues include the payment of unlawful dividends in 1991, 1992 and 1993, other breaches of the Companies Act and the infringement of Stock Exchange regulations and have been referred to, where appropriate, in these accounts. Your board has brought these issues to the attention of the Department of Trade and Industry and the London Stock Exchange.

The Finance Director's Report describes certain serious shortcomings which existed in the group's management and financial controls. In view of these shortcomings, your board regarded it as essential to subject the 1992 accounts to particularly detailed scrutiny. The group's 1991 consolidated profit and loss account and balance sheet have been restated in order to make them comparable with 1992.

Reduction in the value of the group's properties

The principal reason for the exceptional losses in 1992 was the reduction in property values resulting from an independent valuation of the groups's portfolio of properties as at 31 December 1992.

At 31 December 1991, the group's properties were valued by Weatherall Green & Smith ('WGS') at £2.0 billion, a valuation which was incorporated in the 1991 audited balance sheet. WGS also presented a draft valuation in respect of 31 December 1992 to the previous board as well as a draft valuation as at 31 March 1993 to the group's bankers in May 1993. Both of these valuations reflected a substantial diminution in value compared to the 31 December 1991 valuation.

In June the previous board appointed Jones Lang Wootton ('JLW') to value the group's hotel portfolio in place of WGS. They have valued the portfolio of properties as at 31 December 1992 at £861 million.

The JLW valuation as at 31 December 1992 differed substantially from WGS's valuation as at 31 December 1991 and also materially from the values presented to the banks on 27 May 1993. The board subjected the JLW valuation to lengthy and detailed examination. Attention was focused on the methodology used, including adjustments made to net operating income, the use of income capitalisation and discounted cash flows in arriving at the actual valuations and deductions relating to capital expenditure.

After careful consideration the board accepted the JLW valuation and the valuation has been incorporated into the group's balance sheet at 31 December 1992. In the UK and Continental Europe there was considerable hotel expansion in the late 1980's fuelled by abundant availability of capital. Circumstances have changed materially over the past few years and the recent market place for hotels in the UK has been dominated by distressed sale values. On the continent, the declining profitability has lagged the UK but the market place for hotels has shown similar adverse developments. It is this adverse context of declining profitability and limited purchasers' interest in hotels in which the valuation has been prepared. However, the board is optimistic about the long term recovery potential of the group's asset values.

Further exceptional losses in 1992

The group made further exceptional losses in 1992 of £135.1 million, comprising restructuring costs, the write down of certain investments, provisions for losses on the termination of financial contracts and losses on disposals.

The accounts have been prepared on a going concern basis, which assumes that a financial restructuring will be successfully completed. Accordingly, your board has considered it appropriate to make provisions in these accounts for the costs incurred to date and the estimated further costs which may arise in 1993 and 1994 in connection with the envisaged financial restructuring, totalling £32.0 million.

In addition, the group has provided fully against certain of the group's investments in associated undertakings, some of which are in financial difficulties, and certain other investments. These provisions amounted to £17.2 million.

In the light of the group's financial position, your board has reviewed and continues to review its actual and contingent liabilities very carefully. In particular, full provision has been made for liabilities resulting from exposure on contracts taken out in the past with the intent of limiting the effect of interest and exchange rate movements. These contracts were terminated at a cost of £16.7 million as there was no longer any commercial or financial rationale for retaining them.

Finally, in accordance with best accounting practice, your board believes it appropriate to provide against the diminution in the book value of certain subsidiaries which it has now sold or is in the process of selling. We are also required to write off through the profit and loss account associated goodwill which was previously written off to reserves on acquisition. This has been treated as an exceptional item although it has no impact on consolidated net assets. The aggregate exceptional loss provided for in the 1992 accounts for book value adjustments and goodwill write-offs was £69.2 million, which has created a reduction in net assets of £40.7 million.

Relationship of the group with its bankers and other creditors

On 31 March 1993, the then chairman of the group met with the group's principal bankers. At the request of Barclays Bank PLC, on behalf of the group's banks, Grant Thornton, reporting accountants, commenced an investigation into the group's financial position. A meeting of the group's lenders was held on 7 April 1993 to give them the background to the situation. Subsequently, Andrew Coppel joined the group as a consultant on 8 April 1993 followed by Andrew Le Poidevin on 9 April 1993.

At this meeting the banks were asked to agreed to a standstill arrangement whereby the group's bank facilities were capped at the amounts outstanding as at 31 March 1993, payments of certain interest were deferred and strict limits were imposed on capital expenditure by the group. This agreement was to remain in place until Grant Thornton had completed their report. Further, a steering committee was formed, comprising eight banks, led by Barclays Bank PLC and National Westminster Bank PLC, to represent the interests of all the 65 lenders which provide facilities to the group.

The group and Grant Thornton made a presentation to the banks on 27 May 1993 and Grant Thornton's report was made available to all the banks at that time. At that meeting, the group sought an extension to an amended standstill arrangement until 31 October 1993 to enable management to prepare a strategic plan for the group as a basis for going forward beyond the short term. The basis of the extension provided operational terms more favourable to the group than the previous agreement. All the group's banks either signed the extended standstill agreement or have acted in accordance with its principles.

The group presented its plans and outline restructuring proposals at a meeting of banks on 28 October 1993 and has sought an extension of its interim banking arrangements in order to allow time for the detail of its outline proposals to be put in place.

Some of the group's creditors, particularly certain Continental European banks whose borrowings are well secured, are now receiving interest. We have paid particularly close attention to the banking relationships both in the UK and elsewhere in Europe and we have successfully resolved a series of problems and stabilised a number of difficult with individual banks.

In addition to liaising closely with the banks, we have also had discussions with the trustee of the company's £215 million First Mortgage Debenture Stocks and, latterly, with a steering committee of the Association of British Insurers. There are two debenture stocks, totalling £215 million, which were issued between 1983 and 1991 and which rank pari passu. The stocks are secured by a fixed charge over 27 UK hotel properties, floating charges over four UK hotel properties and the stockholders also have the benefit of a floating charge over certain UK subsidiary undertakings and assets. Interest on the stocks has continued to be paid. However, following the completion of the JLW valuation as at 31 December 1992, it is clear that there is a material shortfall (relative to the requirements of the Trust Deed) in the value of the property on which the Debenture Stocks are secured and this security no longer covers the nominal value of the Stock outstanding. Interim proposals to seek the support of stockholders are being considered pending the formulation of further proposals to stockholders in connection with the restructuring of the group. A meeting of stockholders is being convened to consider the interim proposals.

At the trading level, the news of the group's financial problems initially had a noticeable impact on suppliers and customers, particularly in the UK, where the publicity was more widespread than in Continental Europe. However, within a relatively short period, the position stabilised.

Financial restructuring

In 1992 the group's consolidated operating loss of £0.7 million compared with the net interest payable, including finance lease charges, of £100.9 million. Your board believes that the level of cashflow generated from the group's operations will be insufficient for the foreseeable future to service the current level of the group's indebtedness on the basis of the financial arrangements which existed as a 31 March 1993. In addition, the group's consolidated balance sheet shows net liabilities of £388.9 million as at 31

December 1992, which should be viewed against net borrowings (including finances leases) of £1,165.9 million. It has become evident to the board that a financial restructuring is essential for the group including, inevitably, a debt for equity swap which will dilute shareholders interests. Once proposals have been formulated, we shall communicate with shareholders.

Following the presentation of the group's plans and outline proposals on 28 October 1993, the Steering Committee of the group's lenders issued the following statement:

> 'The plan presented to the banks today demonstrates that Queens Moat Houses can be reconstructed to give it a viable future, despite the group's results for the year ended 31 December 1992 and for the six months ended 4 July 1993. It was stressed at the meeting that the best way forward for all the banks is to continue to support the group and maintain its stability.
>
> To this end, the steering committee, led by Barclays and National Westminster, recommended approval of the group's proposal for additional time to allow detailed negotiations to be completed with lenders on the final from of the reconstruction'.

These circumstances have closely focused the attention of your board on the issue of solvency and the position of the individual directors of the parent company and each subsidiary in the context of possible wrongful trading. We continue to take appropriate advice on this serious issue on a regular basis.

The costs of the enormous amount of work required to get the business back onto a sound footing will be considerable. To date, these principally relate to professional advice to the group and the group's bankers. Your board at all times seeks to minimise these costs but it must be recognised that the severity of the group's financial position demands proper advice and that the complexity of the group's financing arrangements has required a particularly large commitment of resources by the professional advisers concerned. However, as soon as the reconstruction of the group has been completed, the board is confident that professional costs will be reduced significantly.

Board of Directors

There have been major changes in the company's board and senior management since the group's problems become apparent. Between 26 May 1993 and 26 August 1993, all the previous board members, with two exceptions, either resigned or did not seek re-election at the annual general meeting held on 26 August 1993. Andrew Coppel joined the board as Chief Executive on 2 July 1993 and he has since been joined by myself, as non-executive Chairman, Andrew Le Poidevin as Finance Director and Michael Cairns as Chief Operating Officer – Hotels. Michael Cairns has extensive experience in the international hotel industry, having spent 25 years with Inter-Continental Hotels. Before joining your company he was responsible for the management of Inter-Continental's European, Middle Eastern and African properties. I am confident that the new management team, combining financial, hotel and general management experience, is sufficiently broadly based to attack the group's problems. John Gale and David Howell continue as non-executive directors, and further non-executive directors will be appointed in due course.

In line with the Cadbury Report on Corporate Governance, a remuneration committee has been formed, comprising the non-executive directors, and on the appointment of additional non-executive directors, and, on the appointment of additional non-executive directors, an audit committee will be reconstituted, to whom a group internal auditors will report.

Previous directors and advisers

All previous executive directors resigned without prejudice to any contractual rights they may have had. Shareholders should be aware that Mr Bairstow, the former chairman, and Mr Marcus, the former deputy chairman have made claims for wrongful termination of their respective service contracts. Mr Marcus and two other former executive directors, Mr Hersey and Mr Porter are also seeking compensation for unfair dismissal. All these claims are being strongly resisted.

Your board is aware that, in the light of the issues referred to in this statement and otherwise, your company may have rights of action against previous directors or advisers. Such matters are being kept under close review to ensure that the interests of the company are protected.

Listing of the company's securities

The possible relisting of the company's securities is an issue which has been raised by many shareholders and is a matter which is subject to regular review by your board. The board has liaised closely with the London Stock Exchange since the beginning of April 1993. However, it is not appropriate to seek the relisting of the company's securities until such time as shareholders and investors have sufficient information to use as a basis for trading the company's securities. Whilst the availability of this Report and Accounts for 1992 and the unaudited 1993 half-year results is certainly helpful in this context, it is also important for shareholders and investors to be aware of the level of support the group has from its bankers and mortgage debenture stockholders and the form of the anticipated financial reconstruction. As soon as we are in a position to clarity this matter we will review the situation again with the London Stock Exchange and our advisers.

Group pension schemes

Of some concern to our employees and pensioners will be the status of the group's final salary pension schemes. There are two main schemes – the UK Executive Pension Scheme and the UK Staff Pension Scheme. The results of recently received valuations show that the assets of the UK Executive Pension Scheme were valued at £5.8 million, a shortfall to liabilities of some £1.1 million. The principal reason for the shortfall was that the salary growth experience since the previous valuation in 1989 was considerably ahead of the assumed growth rate, but with the departure in 1993 of several high earning executives, the shortfall has been reduced substantially since the valuation date. The latest results of the UK Staff Pension Scheme show that the assets had a value of £4.2 million and there was an actuarial surplus of £1.4 million.

Interim results and current trading

In the six months ended 4 July 1993 the group incurred losses before taxation of £48 4 million on a turnover of £167.2 million. Your board does not have available meaningful consolidated financial information for the 1992 interim period with which these results can be compared. The interim results of the period ended 12 July 1992, which were published in August 1992, were based on the previous board's application of accounting policies which have now been changed. Your board has been unable to find the working papers which were used to construct the 1992 interim results. The absence of these papers, together with the time which would be required to prepare revised comparative figures has caused your board to conclude that it would be inappropriate to delay further the publication of the 1993 unaudited interim results.

At the operating level, the group's UK hotels in the first half of 1993 continued to suffer from the difficult trading conditions present in 1992. However, from the latter part of the second quarter there has been a modest recovery in the performance of this division led by an upturn in occupancy rates. Your board is encouraged by prospects in the UK although no material improvement in room rates is expected in the short term. The trading conditions for the group's Continental hotels have deteriorated throughout 1993 as a result of the general recessionary climate in a number of European economies. We continue to manage our European businesses to limit the impact of this downturn.

Further details of the trading performance of the group's businesses are contained in the Chief Executive's Review.

Serious loss of capital

On 27 September 1993, directors of the company became aware that the net assets of the company had fallen to one half or less of the called up share capital of the company. On 25 October 1993, notice of an extraordinary general meeting, convened in accordance with Section 142 of the Companies Act, was sent to shareholders. The meeting has been convened for Monday, 22 Nov 1993 to consider whether any, and is so what, steps should be taken in view of the fact that the net assets of the company have fallen beneath the relevant threshold. As it is proposed that the annual general meeting of the company will be reconvened for Monday, 29 Nov 1993, it will be proposed that the extraordinary general meeting be adjourned until immediately following the reconvened annual general meeting.

Support of banks and employees

The support of our banks has been particularly encouraging during a most difficult period. We have continued to work closely with the joint co-ordinators throughout and we are grateful to them, and the steering committee in particular, for their efforts in a difficult situation. Morgan Grenfell's advice has been particularly valuable.

I would like to conclude by thanking our employees throughout the group for their help in our endeavours to restore stability and to ensure the group's continued viability. The hotel business is very much a people business and the new management team can only be successful if it has their continued commitment, loyalty and determination.

Stanley Metcalfe

Chairman
29 October 1993

(ii) Report of the Auditors

to the members of Queens Moat Houses Plc
We have audited the accounts on pages 30 to 72 in accordance with Auditing Standards except that the scope of our work was limited by the matter referred to in paragraph 2 below.

1. As explained in the accounting policies, the accounts have been prepared on a going concern basis and the validity of this depends on the group's bankers and other lenders continuing their support by providing adequate facilities pending the successful completion of a financial restructuring, on the successful completion of such a restructuring, and on the company's first mortgage debenture stockholders not seeking to enforce their security. The outcome of these matters is currently uncertain. Should continuing support from the group's bankers and other lenders not be available, a successful restructuring not be completed, or if the company's first mortgage debenture stockholders were to seek to enforce their security, the group might be unable to continue trading. In this event the going concern basis would be invalid and adjustments would have to be made to reduce the value of assets to their recoverable amount, to provide for further liabilities which might arise and to reclassify fixed assets and long term liabilities as current assets and current liabilities.

2. The Chairman and executive members of the current board were not directors of the company at the time that the 31 December 1991 property valuation was obtained in May 1992. The current directors consider that they do not have a sufficient understanding of the 1991 property valuation to enable them to provide a full explanation for the decline in the property values from 31 December 1991 to 31 December 1992 of £1,341.5 million, of which £537.6 million has been charged to revaluation reserve and £803.9 million charged as an exceptional item in the profit and loss account. For this reason and in this respect alone, not all of the information and explanations we considered necessary for the purpose of our audit have been available.

3. Comparative figures for the cash flow statement have not been presented for the reasons set out in note (b) of the accounting policies.

    Subject to continuing support of the group's bankers and other lenders, to the successful completion of a financial restructuring and to the company's first mortgage debenture stockholders not seeking to enforce their security, in our opinion the accounts give a true and fair view of the state of affairs of the company and of the group at 31 December 1992 and, subject to any adjustments that might have been necessary in respect of the decline in property values referred to in paragraph 2 above, of the loss of the group for the year then ended and have been properly prepared in accordance with the Companies Act 1985. In our opinion the cash flow statement gives a true and fair view of the cash flows of the group for the year ended 31 December 1992.

    Without further qualifying our opinion above, we draw attention to note 10 which explains that during the year and prior year certain dividend payments were made by the company which were in breach of the Companies Act 1985 as the company did not have sufficient distributable reserves at the time of payment.

Coopers & Lybrand
Chartered Accountants and Registered Auditors
London
29 October 1993

(iii) Finance Director's Report

This report discusses the problems of financial management controls faced by the group and the changes in accounting policies and treatments which have been adopted in preparing the 1992 accounts. The report also comments on the indebtedness of the group and certain other off-balance sheet liabilities.

Financial control procedures

Shareholders will be aware of the group's rapid expansion in recent years, much of which was financed by the issue of shares and debt. The structure of the group had become extremely complicated, with nearly 200 subsidiaries, which, together with minimal group financial and management reporting systems, contributed to a scarcity of management information at group level capable of being used as a forecasting or management tool. There were no monthly consolidated management accounts to enable the board to monitor the progress of the group. In particular there were minimal group cash forecasts and no clearly defined treasury function.

Since early April 1993, a system of financial and management controls across the group has been introduced. A number of critical group financial functions have been established, including group financial control and group treasury. The first set of monthly consolidated group management accounts was produced in July of this year, and their quality and reliability continue to improve. The monitoring of cash flow has been of the utmost importance in recent months. Indebtedness reporting and cash flow forecasting have been put in place so as to ensure strict control. The increase in resources in this important area has been vital to ensure that the head office finance team is capable of exercising proper and effective financial controls in view of the tight financial constraints now imposed on the group. We have also reviewed the complicated corporate structure and web of complex cross-guarantees governing the banking arrangements.

Prior year adjustments

The 1991 accounts have been extensively restated to reflect changes in accounting policies and treatments which have been adopted in preparing the 1992 accounts. Without such changes, the board believes the 1991 and 1992 accounts would not give a true and fair view of the financial position and performance of the group. The principal changes can be summarised as follows, although shareholders are referred to more detailed explanations in note 1 to the accounts:

Licence fees The group had previously recognised the full fees to be earned in respect of so-called 'incentive fee' or licence arrangements with its hoteliers, regardless of the fact that the fee had only been partially paid and the contract covered a period beyond the end of the accounting period. These accounts are prepared on the basis that incentive fees are time apportioned and only that part of the fee relating to the accounting year in question is recognised as income. Your board believes this change is prudent and appropriate to the business. It has resulted, among other things, in a reduction in net assets in 1991 by £48.6 million and pre-tax profits by £13.5 million.

Sale and leaseback transactions The group had entered into a number of 'sale and leaseback' transactions in 1991 relating to two office developments and eight UK hotels under which the group retains the right to repurchase the assets during the lease and pays rents equivalent to the interest on and amortisation of a loan. Your board considers that such transactions should be treated as finance leases. The effect of this change is to recognise the value of these properties as assets, as well as the full liability of the outstanding lease obligations. Moreover, these transactions, in some cases, were structured to provide initial low rentals. The revised policy leads to the underlying interest expense being recognised in the profit and loss account, rather than the initial rent. The impact of these changes have been to reduce the 1991 net assets by £41.2 million and pre-tax profits by £18.3 million.

Depreciation and repairs and maintenance The group had previously not depreciated its fixtures, fittings, plant and equipment. Your board consider this to have been inappropriate. Moreover, certain repairs and maintenance expenditures were also being capitalised. Provision has now been made in the profit and loss account for depreciation of fixtures, fittings, plant and equipment and relevant repairs and maintenance expenditure is being expensed. This policy change has reduced net assets in 1991 by £2.5 million and reduced 1991 pre-tax profits by £50.9 million.

Acquisition of Globana In the 1991 accounts a fee of £10.3 million credited to the group as part of the acquisition of the balance of QMH France from Globana was included in turnover whereas your board considers that it was in fact a reduction in the cost of the acquisition. Restatement of the 1991 accounts leads to a reduction in pre-tax profits of £10.3 million.

Capitalised expenses The group had previously capitalised certain expenses in connection with certain hotels including interest, pre-opening marketing expenses, professional fees and maintenance wages. Your board considers that such expenditure should not be capitalised. Accordingly, the assets have been written off, with the result that pre-tax profits have been reduced in 1991 by £21.9 million.

Profit on disposals of fixed assets

Previously, profits and losses arising on the disposal of fixed assets carried at valuation were included in the profit and loss account based on the difference between the sale proceeds and depreciated historical cost. In accordance with the requirements of FRS 3, this policy has been changed and such profits and losses are now included based on the difference between the sales proceeds and net carrying amount, whether at valuation or at depreciated historical cost. This restatement reduces pre-tax profits in 1991 by £24.2 million.

These accounts also reflect the reclassification of certain profit and loss account and balance sheet items.

In aggregate, the prior year adjustments reduced the group's net assets in 1991 by £105.3 million to £1,192.6 million and reduced the group's pre-tax profits in 1991 by £146.7 million to a pre-tax loss of £56.3 million.

Borrowings, finance leases and operating leases

As at 31 December 1992, the group had net borrowings of £992.1 million (1991 – £710.9 million – restated). In addition, finance lease obligations amounted to £173.8 million (1991 – £149.5 million – restated), bringing the total net indebtedness to £1,165.9 million as at 31 December 1992 (1991 – £860.4 million – restated). The 1991 figures are restated to include finance lease obligations of £30.5 million which were previously classified as 'other creditors', as well as to include obligations arising out of certain sale and leaseback transactions which the board considers should be treated as finance leases. The group had net interest expense before exceptional items of £100.9 million in 1992 (1991 – £79.0 million – restated).

In addition, the group entered into sale and leaseback transactions in respect of seven hotels in Germany in 1991 and 1992 as referred to in note 25 to the accounts. Under these complex arrangements, the group has entered into 20 year operating leases. The group is in preliminary discussion with the owners of the hotels to consider ways in which these sale and leaseback arrangements may be amended in a manner which may lead to these leases being treated as on-balance sheet obligations. At this time the group is not able to quantify any losses which may arise as a result.

The group had rental expense of £12.1 million in 1992 (1991 – £6.3 million – restated). This rental expense increases significantly in 1993 owing to sale and leaseback transactions in late 1992. We are concerned at the onerous terms of certain leases, particularly in France, Germany and Austria, and are examining ways to reduce this burden on ongoing profitability.

Andrew D. Le Poidevin

Finance Director

29 October 1993

CHAPTER 5

The *Co-operative Bank 1*

1 Introduction

Research commissioned by *The* Co-operative Bank in 1993 revealed an increasingly high ethical awareness of British businessmen engaged in the pursuit of corporate profits, but a reluctance to sacrifice personal comfort for certain moral principles.

This case study examines the development, promotion and institutionalisation of the bank's own ethical policy, with particular reference to a profitable business connection it terminated because of a concern for the environment. An important question to be considered is whether implementation of the policy represents an opportunistic marketing initiative, or the manifestation of a deeply rooted belief that business ethics and financial services sector profits are mutually dependent rather than mutually exclusive phenomena.

2 Brief History of the Development of *The* Co-operative Bank

The development of *The* Co-operative Bank and its ethical approach to business can be traced back to a resolution put before the board of its parent company, The Co-operative Wholesale Society Limited, on the 8 July 1872 and the principles of Owenite socialism which underpinned the development of the Co-operative Wholesale Society movement in the early nineteenth century.

Robert Owen (1771–1858) has been described as the father of the modern social movement. At the age of 18, he became a partner in a Manchester cotton-spinning factory, living in Cooper Street, opposite to where the Co-operative Wholesale Society ultimately had its first offices. Writing in 1814, Owen expressed the view:

If there be one duty therefore more imperative than another on the government of every country, it is, that it should adopt, without delay, the proper means to form those sentiments and habits in the people which shall give the most permanent and substantial advantages to the individuals and the community.

It was 49 years later, on 11 August 1863, that the Co-operative Wholesale Society was legally enrolled. The economic principle of mutual effort for common gain, upon which the cooperative movement was built, was not new. It did, however, depart from the business principles of the Rochdale Pioneers, who lived at that time in a world where men, on the one hand, were bidden to love their neighbours as themselves, but on the other were led in all economic matters to pursue self-interest first. This contradiction was too much for the Co-operative Wholesale Society members to endure; hence, while they sought to advance themselves, it was with the difference of taking their neighbours and the community along with them. Their business principles were principally economic in nature, but also reflected a desire to conduct business in a socially and morally upright manner. In these respects their principles were more faithful to the ideals of the Owenites, which were stated as:

The acquisition of a common capital for the mutual protection of its members against poverty; the attainment of a greater share in the comforts of life; and the diffusion of useful knowledge and moral improvement.

The need for a central bank for the cooperative movement grew steadily from the first. Many small societies in the early years were slow to open accounts with private banks and the need to effectively manage and deploy surplus cash resources for the benefit of the movement as a whole, became increasingly recognised as a worthwhile and necessary business development opportunity. On 18 May 1872, the following resolution was put before the board of the Co-operative Wholesale Society Limited and gained full support:

That as a means to commence and gradually develop a banking business, authority be given to the Committee to receive loans from members, on withdrawal at call, and subject to interest at 1% below the minimum Bank of England rate of interest, the same to be used in our business, or lent out on approved security.

On 8 July 1872, The Co-operative Bank was formed as the Loan and Deposit Department of the Co-operative Wholesale Society. Its subsequent development retained the closest possible connection with the Co-operative Wholesale Society movement and its business principles.

The Co-operative Bank plc became a full clearing bank in 1975 and offers a full range of banking services to approximately 1.25 million personal and 0.25 million business customers, from 114 branches situated throughout the country. Its head office and administrative centre is in Manchester. It employs approximately 3,700 people.

3 Evolution of Business Ethics in the Financial Services Sector

There has been an enormous amount of interest recently in business ethics in the financial services sector. Almost every day there is some reference in the financial press to company value systems, regulation and self-regulation, codes of practice, social responsibility, corporate governance and so on. While banking has always had an image problem, particularly in respect of its money lending activities, the recent growth in media attention has contributed to a substantial increase in negative comment. This in turn has prompted increased effort by banks and the regulatory authorities to address this image problem and improve the reputation of the sector.

The poor image of bankers has not been helped by widespread publicity surrounding scandals at Barlow Clowes, BCCI, Saloman Brothers and Lloyd's, to name but a few of the financial service sector organisations that have hit the headlines in the press for their apparently unethical behaviour. Media coverage has focused on various issues, such as claims of insider dealing, fraudulent mismanagement of depositors' monies, conflicts of interest between insurance agents and underwriters, and bankers' insensitivity and high-handedness towards small business customers. The poor treatment of personal customers has also not escaped the attention of the Press. Aggressive cross-selling of services not suited to individual needs, poor investment advice and claims of overcharging of accounts to compensate for imprudent corporate lending in the late 1980s, are some of the image-damaging, headline issues, seen in the press over the past few years.

The intangibility of the services on offer, where what is for sale is largely trust and confidence in an organisation's ability to honour its obligations, makes it difficult, yet of paramount importance for a firm to portray an image of integrity and high moral behaviour in all its dealings. The integrity of banking is something which was taken for granted in the past, but the misdemeanours of a minority of individuals, coupled with greater general awareness of financial matters and the growth of pressure groups, has highlighted activity which suggests that this faith was, at times, misplaced. Regulatory authorities, government bodies and individual banks have responded with a number of initiatives in an attempt to restore this faith.

The Jack Committee Report of 1989 gave rise to the Code of Banking Practice. This led a number of banks to issue their own customer charters for both personal and business customers: some banks have published internal codes of conduct: others, like *The* Co-operative Bank plc, have made public pronouncements about their business practices. Without doubt, the code of ethics movement, rather like the cooperative movement in the early twentieth century, is alive and gathering momentum. John Donaldson (1992) draws attention to 'the increasing enthusiasm with which codes of ethics and codes of practice are being advocated and adopted by industry. . . . The enthusiasm continues, and each day sees the publication or advocacy of a new code in one context or another.'

This trend is reflected in statistics gathered by Simon Webley (1992), undertaking research on behalf of the Institute of Business Ethics, which showed that in samples of the 300/400 largest companies operating in the United Kingdom, the number of companies with codes of conduct increased from 55% (34% response rate) in 1987 to 71% (41% response rate) in 1991, respectively. It is likely that the percentage of large UK companies with codes is now much closer to the 93% of 229 Fortune 1000 American companies which responded to a survey conducted by the Center for Business Ethics in 1992.

Current British thinking with reference to corporate social responsibility is becoming increasingly strategic. Howard Davies, present director of the Confederation of Business Industry (CBI) notes that 'just as a company must have a clear idea of where to position itself in the market, so it must develop a guiding concept of social responsibility'.

Clutterbuck, Dearlove and Snow (1992) reported:

> Our research uncovered a number of companies, which had . . . instituted environmental audits, customer service audits and audits of special issues . . . We did not find any company, however, which undertook a comprehensive audit of all activities which would be grouped under the heading of social responsibility.

It is possible that the actions taken by *The* Co-operative Bank plc represent as comprehensive an audit of activities of any financial services sector company operating in the United Kingdom.

4   Development of Ethical Policy at *The* Co-operative Bank plc

Simon Williams joined the bank as Head of Marketing in 1988. The debate within the bank, at that time, was whether or not the bank should change its name and marketing strategy to overcome its traditional, down-market, old-fashioned image, which stemmed from its long-standing links with the Co-operative Wholesale Society. In the words of Simon Williams, the bank needed a 'charm offensive'. The bank's marketing approach needed re-vamping to increase public awareness of the bank's products and services and to improve its image. The key issue was how could the bank position itself in the market place, to secure and sustain a competitive advantage, particularly bearing in mind the increased level of competition in the financial services sector in the late 1980s?

A name change was seriously considered, but rejected. The growing pressure on financial institutions to become more socially accountable suggested there was merit in retaining 'co-operative' in the bank's title, in the sense that it portrayed an image of the coming-together of bank and customer in a mutually rewarding business relationship. It was felt that a new entrant to the market would probably consider such a name and it seemed foolish, therefore, to discard it. The bank had to decide on the best way to re-package and promote its name.

The first step was to change the corporate logo. The Co-operative Bank became *The* Co-operative Bank to highlight co-operative as an adjective rather than a noun. Also, the use of the full title was emphasised to distance itself from the abbreviation 'The Co-op', a term which was synonymous with Co-operative retail stores and which was partly responsible for its poor image.

The next step was to produce a new corporate mission statement for internal consumption by employees. In early 1989, a document was produced which outlined the bank's corporate aims and objectives and explained the bank's desire to remain true to the values of the cooperative movement, upon which its success had been based, but also explained the reasons behind adoption of the new corporate house style and marketing approach. Seminars and staff training sessions were held throughout the bank to reinforce the message and ensure compliance.

An analysis of the bank's customer base, which formed part of the initial research, indicated that 10–20% of customers banked with *The* Co-operative Bank as a direct consequence of the principles on which they perceived its business conduct was based. It was particularly pleasing that these customers, who were apparently attracted by such high moral principles, were precisely the type of customer with whom most banks would wish to do business. They tended to be well-educated individuals, earning above average incomes in professional occupations, and who adopted a responsible approach to the management of their personal finances. This finding reinforced the belief that there might be a sizeable market niche which could be targeted to gain profitable new business and at the same time provide an opportunity for the bank to differentiate itself from its competitors.

The next step was to undertake extensive market research to determine whether the target market niche displayed the necessary characteristics of being identifiable, measurable, profitable, and accessible by development of a differentiated marketing strategy to gain a worthwhile and sustainable competitive advantage.

5 Market Research

Five market research projects were undertaken during 1991 and June 1992. Three projects were qualitative – talking to small numbers of people in some detail about the subject of ethical banking – and two quantitative – obtaining numbers behind the ideas.

The qualitative research pointed the way to the bank's new policy statement and advertising theme which focused on the nature of the bank's investments, funded by its depositors. 'You can't bank with someone and say "Oh well, my money goes into this and I don't care"' (non Co-operative Bank customer).

Further research was undertaken into the subjects that mattered to bank customers and the public at large. This showed a split between:

(a) rather narrow, more straightforward issues such as animal testing, the fur trade and South Africa; and
(b) the broader, more global issues such as oppression, nuclear power, armaments and the environment.

The first quantitative survey followed, with a random sample of customers interviewed by telephone. The results suggested that the 'big' issues of human rights and armaments were the ones that customers wanted the bank to take a stand on, well ahead of the more specific issues.

Research subsequently undertaken amongst non-customers indicated that the proposed issue of an ethical policy would be powerful and motivating, not just to those who adopt a high moral stance, but to anyone who is relatively altruistic or concerned about moral issues in general. A subsequent survey provided evidence that while British business was trying to clean up its act, actual performance lagged behind good intentions. Business executives were ethically aware, but the closer they became to responsibility for company profit, the sooner they were more likely to jettison ethical constraints.

Collectively the research findings encouraged the bank to draw up a draft ethical policy statement to help it gauge the likely reaction to a more public pronouncement of an ethical policy to existing and potential customers.

The drafting of the policy statement was completed with the help of appropriate 'expert' organisations, such as the Royal Society for the Prevention of Cruelty to Animals, The National Council for Civil Liberties, Amnesty International, and Greenpeace. Expert help was needed to assist the bank to weave its way through complex issues such as factory farming. It was also conscious of the need not to project a 'holier than thou' image and to avoid possible accusations of attempting to play God. The bank acknowledged the fact that as a provider of finance in which subjective assessment of proposals is an essential part, it was not possible to be entirely neutral in affairs, but it was keen to promote the idea that it saw its role as implementing policy as determined by its customers and guided by leading authorities on the issues in question.

In November 1991, 30,000 of the bank's customers, chosen at random and including both personal and corporates, were polled with a copy of the draft policy statement (see below for the actual policy statement). The majority (84%) believed it was a good idea for the bank to have a clear ethical policy; only 5% felt that ethical issues had nothing to do with banking.

The types of customers who felt most strongly that the bank should take an ethical stance tended to be the young/middle age ranges (88%) of those aged

25–44, women (86%), those who had gone on to higher education (92%), and employees of Health and/or Local Authorities (88%).

Respondents indicated a high level of concern over most of the ethical issues listed in the draft policy. The issues that mattered most were:

Human rights	90%
Armaments exports to oppressive regimes	87%
Animal exploitation	80%
Environmental damage	70%
Fur trade	66%
Manufacture of tobacco products	60%

The individual issues which were included in the final policy statement were all supported by more than 60% of the bank's customers. The policy statement as a whole was endorsed by 78% of the customers and with this level of support the bank considered that it had a mandate to proceed.

6 Ethical Audit of Existing Customer Relationships

In the run-up to the launch of the ethical policy in May 1992, all employees were required to attend half-day training seminars. Directors and senior managers attended the first sessions. The policy and its implementation was discussed at length at managers' conferences, before being disseminated throughout the organisation using the already established Total Quality Management communication and staff briefing networks.

Final preparations for the launch of the new policy statement included a thorough review of all existing banking relationships, to ensure that retention of any business connection did not conflict with the ethical policy of the bank. Fortunately the vast majority of accounts complied with the policy statement. Less than ten accounts contravened the policy. The hard decision was then taken to terminate the bank's relationship with these accounts, subject to reasonable notice being given to allow the firms sufficient time to arrange alternative banking facilities elsewhere. The notice to terminate the banking relationship provoked a strong adverse reaction from customers in only two cases. The bank was therefore able to move forward without any significant loss of business.

Managing Director, Terry Thomas, was able to say, without impunity:

> This policy is all about how we do business and indeed who we will do business with. It is a policy only adopted after extensive research of our customers' views and a re-examination of co-operative custom and practice over 120 years.

> Given our origins as a part of the cooperative movement and its basic values, it is not surprising that we should be the first bank to respond to peoples' growing concerns about the quality of life here and in the rest of the world.

7   The Bank's Ethical Policy

Under the terms of its ethical policy the bank claims to be the only bank which offers its customers the right to know how their money is being invested, and a right to influence these decisions. The bank's position is that:

1   **It will not invest** in or supply financial services to any regime or organisation which oppresses the human spirit, takes away the rights of individuals or manufactures any instrument of torture.
2   **It will not finance** or in any way facilitate the manufacture or sale of weapons to any country which has an oppressive regime.
3   **It will encourage** business customers to take a proactive stance of the environmental impact of their own activities.
4   **It will actively** seek out individuals, commercial enterprises and non-commercial organisations which have a complementary ethical stance.
5   **It will not speculate** against the pound using either its own money or that of its customers. It believes it is inappropriate for a British clearing bank to speculate against the British currency and the British economy using deposits provided by their British customers and at the expense of the British taxpayer.
6   **It will try to ensure** its financial services are not exploited for the purpose of money laundering, drug trafficking or tax evasion by the continued application and development of its successful internal monitoring and control procedures.
7   **It will not provide** financial services to tobacco product manufacturers.
8   **It will continue** to extend and strengthen its Customer Charter, which has already established new standards of banking practice through adopting innovative procedures on status enquiries and customer confidentiality, ahead of any other British Bank.
9   **It will not invest** in any business involved in animal experimentation for cosmetic purposes.
10   **It will not support** any person or company using exploitative factory farming methods.
11   **It will not engage** in business with any farm or other organisation engaged in the production of animal fur.
12   **It will not support** any organisation involved in blood sports, which it defines as sports which involve the training of animals or birds to catch and destroy, or to fight and kill, other animals or birds.

The bank has committed itself to a regular review of its ethical policy to take account of new developments and the views of its customers.

The values which guide the way the bank operates on a day-to-day basis are outlined in its Mission Statement.

8 The Bank's Mission Statement

The bank's Mission Statement can be broken down into two halves; to be successful, innovative and profitable on the one hand, whilst on the other, ensuring that the bank's aspirations and plans are coupled with socially desirable objectives. The statement reads in full:

We, *The* Co-operative Bank Group, will continue to develop a successful and innovative financial institution by providing our customers with high quality financial and related services whilst promoting the underlying principles of co-operation which are . . .

1. **Quality and Excellence**
   To offer all our customers consistent high quality and good value services and strive for excellence in all that we do.
2. **Participation**
   To introduce and promote the concept of full participation by welcoming the views and concerns of our customers and by encouraging our staff to take an active role in within the local community.
3. **Freedom of Association**
   To be non-partisan in all social, political, racial and religious matters.
4. **Education and Training**
   To act as a caring and responsible employer, encouraging the development and training of all our staff and encouraging commitment and pride in each other and the Group.
5. **Co-operation**
   To develop a close affinity with organisations which promote fellowship between workers, customers, members and employers.
6. **Quality of Life**
   To be a responsible member of society by promoting an environment where the needs of the local communities can be met now and in the future.
7. **Retentions**
   To manage the business effectively and efficiently, attracting investment and maintaining sufficient surplus funds within the business to ensure the continued development of the Group.
8. **Integrity**
   To act at all times with honesty and integrity and within legislative and regulatory requirements.

9 *The* Co-operative Bank plc – Trading Performance 1992/3

In an address delivered at York University Campus on 11 July 1993, to the Christian Ethical Investment Group, during the Sessions of The Church of

England General Synod, Terry Thomas related to his experiences early in his banking career at the National Provincial Bank in Bristol, which brought to his attention the relationship between ethics, good business, longevity (corporate longevity) and profits. He expressed the view that good profitable and sustainable business is only possible against an ethical background of trust and integrity.

While research commissioned by *The* Co-operative Bank in April 1992 failed to provide conclusive proof that ethical principles and profits in British business were either mutually dependent or mutually exclusive, it is clear that the profitability of *The* Co-operative Bank has improved (see Table 5.1).

TABLE 5.1   *The* **Co-operative Bank, Consolidated Profit and Loss Account**

	Year ended 11 Jan 1992 £000	28 weeks to 25 July 1992 £000	Year ended 9 Jan 1993 £000	28 weeks to 23 July 1993 £000
Profit (Loss) before taxation	(5,972)	4,464	9,845	8,073
Taxation	3,343	(1,571)	(3,575)	(3,078)
Profit (Loss) after taxation	(2,629)	2,893	6,270	4,995
Minority interest	955	(54)	(113)	192
Dividend	(5,535)	(2,982)	(5,535)	(2,982)
Profit (Loss) retained	(7,209)	(143)	622	2,205

Announcing the much improved half-year figures, Terry Thomas said:

> The bank's ethical policy has been widely promoted . . . it highlights the bank's principles of high integrity and social responsibility and is clearly attractive to well-defined sections of the populace. The ethical policy has heightened awareness of the bank and its considerable strengths.

An 8% improvement in operating income was reported. This was partly because of the bank's other head-line grabbing move, the 'free for life' gold card and Robert Owen card. Both credit card products had showed solid growth.

Bad debt provision was down 14% because of reduced exposure to commercial lending and fewer bad debts from the personal banking side, particularly on credit cards.

To substantiate and ensure that the bank's claim to be 'as sound ethically as it is financially' is justified requires strict adherence to the ethical policy. Institutionalisation of the policy manifests itself in a number of ways, as we now show.

10　Institutionalisation of the Ethical Policy

The strong commitment to ethical behaviour starts at the very top of the organisation in Terry Thomas, the Managing Director, whose leadership and direction permeates the bank. He is regularly called on to write articles for banking journals and the financial press and to speak at an increasing number of conferences which have business ethics as their theme.

At all levels in the bank, every effort is made to contribute to and support environmental initiatives from the government, local authorities, industry associations and other bodies. For example, the bank supports the Department of the Environment's Energy Efficiency campaign and is a member of British Industry's Environment Business Forum. In addition, each division within the bank has appointed an environmental coordinator to identify opportunities to support and protect the local environment.

The Co-operative Bank has also sponsored a Chair in Corporate Responsibility at Manchester Business School, the first such appointment in the UK. It is hoped that this initiative will complement the bank's own efforts to encourage responsible corporate management.

All of these initiatives reinforce the bank's ethical stance and constantly remind staff of the need to uphold bank policy at all times.

Compliance with the bank's ethical policy in commercial lending activities is the responsibility of both the relationship managers and lending officers, but is principally monitored through the Advances Control Department. Since May 1992 relationship managers have been required to make specific comments regarding compliance when each business account is submitted for review. Lending officers are similarly obliged to endorse the file, confirming compliance, or alternatively to bring non-compliance to the attention of line management. Any new business applications must also contain comment on the business activities of the proposer in relation to the ethical policy, otherwise it will not be considered.

The bank's own Audit Department has also built into its standard audit procedures the requirement to check for compliance when undertaking its own investigations into the quality of the bank's lending portfolio and underwriting procedures.

The guiding principles are contained in comprehensive Policy and Procedures Manuals which are dispersed throughout the organisation. If further clarification or interpretation of policy is required, the case details may be referred to the Group Public Affairs Manager, who oversees and has line responsibility, through to the Chief Executive, for ethical policy compliance.

These procedures supplement the bank's training programmes and induction programmes for new recruits. Updating of the Policy and Procedures Manual is maintained in line with the bank's Total Quality Management systems, which are, in themselves, subject to audit.

11   Implementation of the Ethical Policy – A Vignette

[This vignette is based on an actual situation and follows the sequence of events faithfully. However, the names, financial information, account details and circumstances surrounding the case have all been changed to respect the confidential nature of banking relationships.]

David Williamson, the Relationship Manager for the North Eastern region, based in Newcastle, sat down to prepare the annual account review of Forest Products Limited, one of his better accounts, following an enjoyable visit to his client's premises in Jarrow. He had known the managing director, Andrew Campbell, for over ten years, and had retained full responsibility for the bank's relationship with this company, which he obtained from Midland Bank precisely eight years ago. He prided himself that there had not been one serious problem with the handling of this account and that he had been able to overcome Head Office reservations about the company, which stemmed from concerns about some of the entrepreneurial activities of Andrew Campbell.

It was with these reservations in mind that he commenced the write-up of the account review. He realised that this particular review would present the stiffest test of his ability to retain the account and would also test the bank's resolve to ensure compliance to its ethical policy, particularly bearing in mind the profitability of the connection.

Forest Products Limited's principal activity, until six months ago, was importation and wholesaling of timber, which it imported from Norway and Sweden. Reduced demand for natural pine had forced it to consider diversification and it instigated an ambitious plan to import mahogany (*Swietenia Macrophyllia*) from Brazil. Although many companies and local authorities no longer use tropical hardwoods because of public pressure, demand for mahogany in the North East of England for domestic use or re-exportation remains strong. There is little competition in the area and profit margins are much higher than in the pine trade. The decision to expand the product range was taken following a meeting with a wealthy American landowner, Dave Cromes, who had agreed to part-fund the venture through a £100,000 equity injection into Forest Products Limited.

David Williamson was obliged to draw attention to the company's involvement in mahogany in his submission to Advances Control. As a strong advocate of the bank's ethical policy, this requirement was readily accepted, but it was not clear how the bank would interpret the company's involvement in this activity, in terms of possible contravention of the policy not to invest monies in businesses which damage the environment. It was certainly not a clear-cut case in this instance.

Andrew Campbell had been quick to point out that while certain areas in Brazil, such as Randonia and Para, had experienced particularly high rates of deforestation (20% and 15% of these states were deforested by 1990), Forest

Products Limited had secured access to tropical hardwood from 'sustainable sources'. In Mato Grosso, where the company's operations are based, every effort is made to preserve the natural ecosystem of the forest and to limit the impact on tribal communities (the Yanonami) still resident in the area. The World Bank and European Community had funded similar projects in Amazonia and Andrew Campbell saw no reason why *The* Co-operative Bank should be concerned about his company's activities.

In an effort to support continuation of banking facilities, David Williamson obtained literature from Friends of the Earth and was disturbed to read some of the quotes in the briefing on sustainability and the trade in tropical rainforest timber:

> Management programmes . . . on sustained yield principles are not occurring anywhere in the humid tropical forest of the country. (Forestry Department, Food and Agricultural Organisation)

> in practical terms, no commercial logging of tropical forests has proven to be sustainable from the standpoint of the forest ecosystem, and any such logging must be recognised as mining, not sustaining the basic forest resource. (Lee Talbot, Advisor to the World Bank)

> sustainability is a smokescreen to cover destruction of irreplaceable forests for financial gain. (International Union for Conservation and Nature)

Friends of the Earth confirmed that *Swietenia Macrophyllia* was the most sought-after timber. The tree occurs singly or in small clusters. Clusters of more than four to eight trees are rarely found. Given that sawmills are prepared to travel longer distances to find this particular species, the level of rainforest destruction is correspondingly greater than it is with more common species. Recent studies had shown that, on average, twenty-six trees were damaged for every *Swietenia Macrophyllia* tree extracted. Annual deforestation in Brazil was running at a rate of thirty-five to forty thousand square kilometres per annum.

Despite assurances from Andrew Campbell that the Brazilian authorities had provided a statement to the British Government's Export Credit Guarantee Department stating that the company's activities were 'environmentally friendly', in order to help Forest Products Limited to obtain insurance cover for shipments of mahogany to the UK, David Williamson felt that Advances Control were more likely to be persuaded by the Friends of the Earth's views on this matter. Seeking guidance from them himself had placed him in a more difficult position.

It was a much easier task for him to provide evidence of the company's financial position, in the form of audited accounts for the year ended 31 December 1993.

The financial position of the company had been strengthened by the equity injection, but the gearing had increased substantially due to acquisition of special timber-cutting equipment costing approximately £250,000 on hire-purchase terms, repayable over seven years. Increased reliance on trade credit and bank funding was evident from the company's financial accounts and from the bank's own overdraft monitoring statistics. The limit of £60,000 had been breached three times over the past two months, albeit the excesses were cleared the following day.

Hardcore overdrawing of approximately £40,000 had developed over the past five months. Cashflow had been adversely affected by relaxation of credit terms to boost trade in the UK and delays in settlement on some European accounts.

The company had incurred a pre-tax loss of £(6,176) during 1993, compared to a profit of £22,476 the previous year, largely due to the higher interest charges, but Andrew Campbell was confident of a return to profitability in the full year to December 1994. The forecast was for a profit of £50,000 on turnover of £1,750,000, up nearly 70% from the year before.

The risk grade attached to this account by Advances Control was C. This grading reflected the fact that account conduct had been satisfactory, although the provision of financial information lagged behind that of other accounts allocated an A or B credit rating. Risk grade C was in keeping with the general profile of business accounts on *The* Co-operative Bank's books and David Williamson could see no reason why this rating should be changed on completion of the annual review.

The level of bank exposure to the company and security details to be forwarded with the review read as shown in Table 5.2.

TABLE 5.2   Forest Products Ltd

Facility	Limit £	Interest rate	Security	Security value* £
Overdraft	60,000	Base + 3.0% 1% renewal fee	First fixed charge Jarrow Warehouse and offices	70,000
Term loan (4 years remaining)	35,000	Base + 3.5%	First fixed and floating debenture over the assets and undertaking of the company	105,000
Duty deferment bond	40,000	2% of face) value		
Total	135,000			175,000

*Security values are shown at their written down values in line with Advances Control guidelines.

In addition the bank holds the personal guarantee of a director, supported by a first charge over otherwise unencumbered property valued at £125,000.

The profitability of the account to the bank was more than satisfactory. The latest business account review statistics from the finance department indicated a 135% recovery of costs, which exceeded the bank's minimum cost coverage requirement by 10%. In view of the increased level of turnover through the account in 1994 and the higher monthly commission charges agreed by Andrew Campbell, a further improvement in profitability to 150% recovery of costs was forecast for the coming year.

David Williamson was very keen to retain this particular account. Loss of the business and income from it would be hard to replace and he could ill afford to lose such a long-standing, fully secured and profitable business connection. He stressed these points in his final remarks in the account review. He was reasonably hopeful that the bank would feel able to renew facilities at the current level, subject to the assurances already received from the client that the company would continue to take all reasonable steps to minimise the ecological impact of its trade in Brazilian mahogany.

Attached to the review were the following Annual Report and Account details of Forest Products Limited, for the year ended 31 December 1993.

Forest Products Limited
Profit and Loss Account for the Year Ended 31 December 1993

	1993	1992
Turnover	1,043,641	453,896
Cost of sales	801,289	342,691
Gross profit	242,352	111,205
Administrative expenses	213,947	80,826
Operating profit (loss)	28,405	30,379
Interest payable	34,581	7,903
Profit (loss) on ordinary activities before taxation	(6,176)	22,476
Taxation	1,605	(7,866)
Profit retained	(4,571)	14,610
Balance brought forward	27,761	13,151
Balance carried forward	23,190	27,761

Forest Products Limited
Balance Sheet as at 31 December 1993

	31.12.93 £		31.12.92 £
Fixed Assets			
Tangible fixed assets	304,826		47,158
Current Assets			
Stocks	111,616		32,895
Debtors	257,336		99,185
Cash at bank	40,159		3,350
	409,111		135,430
Current Liabilities			
Bank overdraft (secured)	58,352		19,527
Bank loan	10,000		11,250
Hire purchase	21,250		–
Creditors	206,443		61,030
	296,045		91,807
Net Current Liabilities	113,066		43,623
Total Assets Less Current Liabilities	417,892		90,781
Creditors: Amounts Falling Due After More Than One Year			
Bank Loan	35,740		13,020
Hire purchase	208,962		–
Net Assets	173,190		77,761
Capital and Reserves			
Called up share capital	150,000		50,000
Profit and Loss (deficit)	23,190		27,761
	173,190		77,761

Internal Memorandum

To: Advances Control Manager

From: Group Public Affairs Manager

Date: 28 February 1994

Subject: Forest Products Limited

I refer to our recent telephone conversation.

I feel the time has come for us to make a decision about this customer, particularly in relation to its business activities which involve the importation of Brazilian mahogany.

The bank must be very concerned about the possibility of tropical rainforests being destroyed. Although the fresh 'Guidelines' for the sustainable production of rainforest timber issued by the International Tropical Timber Organisation may be being followed by the company in the Mato Grosso area, I do not feel that the bank can afford to associate itself with the trade in mahogany (Swietenia Macrophyllia), particularly bearing in mind our involvement in Global Forum 1994. The bank sought the views of Friends of the Earth when its ethical policy was formulated and their views on sustainable production of such timber must govern our actions.

Therefore, I feel that I have no option but to ask you to ensure that Mr Williamson be invited to seek another bank which might be prepared to provide banking services/ facilities to his company. If this means that we lose a customer and any associated profitable banking business, that is the price we will have to pay. Whatever the circumstances, we cannot compromise our policies in respect of business ethics and environmental requirements.

In line with legal advice, we are required to give customers a reasonable period of notice, thereby giving them the time to make alternative banking arrangements if they wish to continue a business activity we are not prepared to service. Accordingly, I shall be grateful if you will ask Newcastle Regional Office to inform our customer that we are no longer prepared to service any aspect of its trade in mahogany, adding that we will allow a minimum of three months in which to make alternative arrangements.

Please keep me advised of developments.

References and Bibliography

Burke, T. (1992) *The Co-operative Bank Survey of Business Ethics in the UK*, University of Westminster, London.

Clutterbuck, D., Dearlove, D., Snow, D. (1992) *Actions Speak Louder: A Management Guide to Corporate Social Responsibility*, Kogan Page, London.

Donaldson, J. (1992) *Business Ethics: A European Casebook*, Academic Press, London.

Donaldson, T. (1982) *Corporations and Morality*, Prentice-Hall, New Jersey.

Friends of the Earth (1991) 'Sustainability and the Trade in Tropical Rainforest Timber', Special Briefing, August.

Friends of the Earth (1991) 'Brazil – "Sustainability" and the Trade in Tropical Timbers', Briefing sheet, November.

Genfan, H. (1987) 'Formalizing Business Ethics', *Training and Development Journal*, November.

Murphy, P. (1988) 'Implementing Business Ethics', *Journal of Business Ethics*, vol. 7, pp. 907–15.

Ryan, L. (1994) 'Ethics Codes in British Companies', *Business Ethics*, vol. 3, no. 1, (January).

Thomas, T. (1993) 'The Banker as Ethical Businessman', *Banking World*, March.

Vallance, E. (1993) 'Good at Work: The Ethics of Modern Business', *Banking World*, March.

Webley, S. (1992) *Business Ethics and Company Codes*, Institute of Business Ethics, London.

CHAPTER 6

The *Co-operative Bank 2*

1 Introduction

The burgeoning growth of interest in business ethics has led to the search for examples of business organisations which combine principles with profits. This chapter examines the case of the British Co-operative Bank which is one of these organisations. However, our concern is not with the Bank's Ethical Policy (see Appendix 1) itself nor with its impact on the bottom-line. They help to provide the context for the research project which this chapter reports.

Policy statements on ethical issues abound. If all organisations which produce mission statements, codes of practice or ethical codes were therefore ethical in conduct and performance, business ethics would be non-problematic. However, the effectiveness of corporate codes of ethics is dependent, *inter alia*, on the day-to-day behaviour of managers.

Interest in the impact of ethical codes and mission statements on managerial behaviour has grown in recent years (Premeux and Mundy, 1993; Cohen *et al.*, 1993; Delaney and Sockell, 1992, Clutterbuck *et al.*, 1992; Stead *et al.*, 1990, Fritzsche and Becker, 1984). The assumption underlying this chapter is that one further way of enriching our understanding of the ethical behaviour of managers is to focus on actual behaviour in real organisations and to develop case-studies which test principles and concepts.

This chapter reports the findings of a research project aimed at discovering the extent to which *The* Co-operative Bank's Ethical Policy influences the behaviour of those managers at the bank who are responsible for achieving the bank's objectives in acquiring new business in the corporate market. We will seek to explore the impact of the bank's Ethical Policy on the day-to-day behaviour of a significant group of the bank's managers.

2 Successful Ethics

The Co-operative Bank is a commercially successful organisation with strong roots in cooperative values and history and with a high-profile stance on ethical issues. It operates in the competitive financial services market, the locus of several significant financial scandals, and it does so successfully, and at the same time promotes itself very clearly as an ethical organisation.

The bank's marketing strategy has been a classic niche marketing exercise with a strong emphasis on the cooperative values which created the bank and provide its dynamic in modern times. Its Ethical Policy provides a tangible outcome of a marketing strategy which has built upon the traditional values of the British cooperative movement and shaped the bank's current promotional stance.

Davis and Worthington (1993), writing about *The* Co-operative Bank within the context of traditional cooperative values, argue that the bank's commercial strategy and its market positioning have resulted in a confident re-statement of cooperative values within a highly receptive, if relatively small, sector of the financial services market.

The bank is convinced that its ethical stance has been good for business. Its 1992 Annual Report states (pp. 6–7): 'There is an increasing awareness of ethical issues in the UK and a broad spectrum of customers and potential customers would prefer to bank with a financial institution which has developed its customer service to this level of awareness.' It goes on to claim that 'The Ethical Stance is consistent with customer perception of *The* Co-operative Bank and represents a clear point of differentiation from its competitors.'

The success of the bank's strategy is reflected in the increase in operating profits (up by £11 million to £53 million in 1992) resulting from higher revenues from a depressed financial services market. Lynn (1993) asserts that the improved performance of the bank 'was the outcome of the bank's new ethical policy' (p. 44). Also, increased revenue is only one of the causes of higher profitability. The bank has also been bearing down on costs – particularly in relation to bad debts.

However, the enhanced profitability of the bank is a more complex phenomenon than simply a product of its ethical stance and reduction of bad debt. The bank has introduced new products, new methods of providing customer service based on considerable investments in new technology, a Total Quality Management programme and a process re- engineering programme which has resulted in some down-sizing and delayering of the bank's staffing structure.

3   The Organisational Context

The managers operate within an organisation which has an 'official' description which is reproduced in the organisation charts, job descriptions, remuneration systems and other organisational policies of the bank.

Figure 6.1 indicates the organisation structure of *The* Co-operative Bank as in October 1993. It is included here to indicate the place of the Retail Banking (Sales) Division within the corporate structure. Senior Commercial and Commercial Managers operate within this division. They are located at

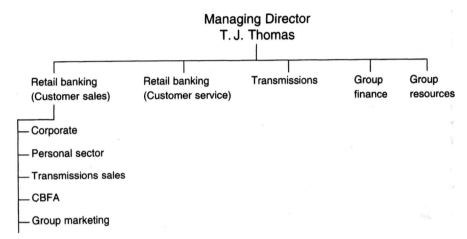

FIGURE 6.1   The Co-operative Bank plc: organisation structure and key functions

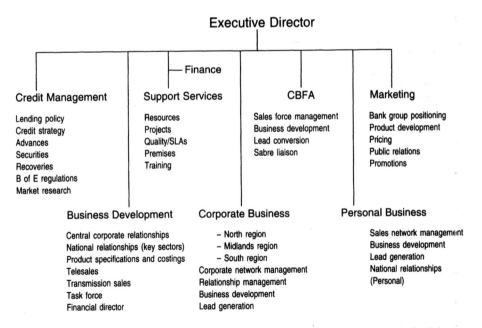

FIGURE 6.2   The Co-operative Bank plc: retail banking (sales) division

branches, known as Commercial Units, of the bank. Figure 6.2 indicates the structure of the Retail Banking (Sales) Division as in October 1993.

The Job Profiles of Senior Commercial Managers (SCM) require the SCMs to liaise with a wide range of other managers in the bank in order to ensure the provision of services to clients within a particular geographical area. They involve achieving targets for sales and services, generating new ideas for product and service enhancements, maintaining and developing client relationships, coordinating the work of subordinates, lending within their levels of discretion and preparing proposals for submission to credit assessors within the bank.

The Job Profiles also provide details of the knowledge base required by SCMs. The knowledge required is weighted (from 1 to 3, with 3 being the most important). Knowledge about the bank's ethical stance is weighted as '2'.

The Commercial Manager's Job Profile indicates his or her role in working with the SCM to ensure that business plans are devised and targets met, the importance of maintaining good client relationships, managing staff, lending within their discretionary limits and preparing proposals for submission to credit assessors. Knowledge of the ethical stance is also weighted at '2'.

Each Commercial Unit covers a given geographical area and the number of SCMs and CMs varies in accordance with the amount of the business being carried out in that area.

The remuneration of the managers is based on a structure with three elements. There is a basic pay element which is derived from the bank's grade and salary structure; there is a Christmas bonus paid to all staff; and, from 1993, an element derived from the bank's Performance Management Appraisal (PMA).

PMA is aimed at creating 'a performance oriented culture which will improve the Bank's position in the short, medium and long term' (PMA User Guide, p. 2). It has five performance principles:

- Maintain a competitive base salary (the job rate) for on-target performance.
- Pay people up to and at the job rate for on-target performance.
- Reward above target performance by means of additional payments.
- Recognise the importance of learning and development within a job by encouraging progression towards the job rate.
- Continue to employ on-target performers and take action to ensure that everyone meets these standards.

Rewards to staff can be developmental and monetary. 'How this works is that the Corporate Plan sets out the strategic direction of the Bank on a three-year rolling basis. The annual Group budget, Divisional Profit and Operating Plans translate this into targets for the current year. PMA turns targets into actions and actions into results. It pays for results and identifies any training and development that is needed to help people get even better results in future' (ibid, p. 2).

The bank's salary structure indicates the starting salaries for jobs at identified levels and a 'job rate' which is achieved through annual increments. To continue to be paid at the job rate requires the achievement of agreed performance targets. Performance above agreed targets will result in payment above the job rate.

The bank's recruitment policy has changed in recent years. The established practice, in common with other commercial banks, had been to 'grow' managers from internal sources. In recent years, the tendency has been to recruit more managers at a younger age from external sources. This is reflected in the findings below.

The job content of the SCM and CM has been radically affected by internal organisational change. These changes have aimed at developing centralised provision for customer services, incorporating, for example, the armchair banking service (telephone banking), the provision of centralised administrative support for non-personal accounts and the introduction of 'Financial Director' which is a real-time office finance system used in the Commercial Units (branches). The overarching aim of these developments has been to reduce the impact of day-to-day administrative demands on branches and to release branch-based SCMs and CMs from routine administrative chores to enable them to manage their client relationships more effectively.

4 The Research Findings

A total of 17 managers from 10 different branches were interviewed in their offices using a written schedule (see Appendix 2). Responses were recorded during the interviews. The ten centres were selected to represent the geographical spread of the bank's operations.

When examining the research findings, it is important to note that for many questions managers were not limited in the number of responses they could make, hence in several instances the recorded responses exceed the number interviewed.

From the total of 17 managers interviewed 10 were Commercial Managers and 7 were Senior Commercial Managers. Thirteen managers had been previously employed by a different bank. It should be noted that only two of these managers came from small banks. Most of them had experience of working for the larger clearing banks.

4.1 Job content

The purpose of this section is to identify the major components of the managers' jobs so that their responses to the request to identify which parts of their jobs are influenced by the bank's Mission Statement and Ethical Policy can be placed within the organisational context as experienced by the managers.

Managers were asked to identify the major components of their job. From the self-reported job content, the differences between Commercial and Senior Commercial Managers were not significant. This appears to reflect the heavy reliance on teamwork and trust at branch or centre level and the deeply shared assumptions about the purposes of the corporate and commercial work of the bank. Table 6.1 indicates the managers' self-reported job components and the frequency with which each component was reported. Clearly, the predominance of the first two elements, which are strongly interrelated, indicates a widely held view about the purposes of the job. This reflects the Bank's perception of the nature of the commercial management function as indicated in the job descriptions of Commercial and Senior Commercial Managers.

The focus for the managers is fundamentally based on target achievement within the context of competitive commercial banking.

TABLE 6.1   Managers' self-reported job components

Component	Frequency
Maintaining a portfolio of commercial accounts	15
New Business Development	14
Managing subordinates	7
Training and development	5
Meeting targets	3
Cross selling	3
Troublesome accounts	1
Team leader/motivator	1
Ensure things work	1

4.2   How the ethical policy influences job performance

Managers were asked to indicate which parts of their current jobs were influenced by the bank's Ethical Policy. Table 6.2 summarises their responses.

There was a clear view amongst the majority of managers that the Ethical Policy had proved to be very successful in attracting new business and had played a major role in the commercial and corporate sector of the bank's work. Three managers reported that existing businesses within their portfolio had been affected by the introduction of the Ethical Policy – some business had been released by the bank as a result of a search of existing customers to check their compliance with the policy.

TABLE 6.2   Ethical policy influence: summary of responses

Response	Frequency
All aspects	9
New business	11
Existing customers	3
Little impact	2
Partial effect	1

4.3   Incidents

The influence of the policy was further investigated by asking managers to identify incidents in which the bank's Ethical Policy had helped them in arriving at a decision about a particular client. Incidents which were reported included:

- A chemical waste company applied for loan facilities; the manager was concerned about the processes involved but further investigation reassured him that the processes were sound and environmentally acceptable.
- A group of hunt saboteurs were asked to withdraw their business when they failed to give reassurances about being non-violent in their approach.
- An incinerator business was investigated in more detail than would have been the case without the existence of the policy.
- the bank's policy not to speculate against sterling in the foreign exchange market enabled a manager to obtain additional business from charitable organisations.
- A manager used the policy to point out to a business that the attempts by that business to evade tax were against the bank's policy.
- A factory farming business was investigated in great detail and found to be operating within the spirit of the bank's policy.
- A waste disposal company was investigated and, after consultation with the bank's head office, approved.
- A political organisation was asked to produce a copy of its aims and rules and were asked to confirm that they would not be involved in illegal or violent action.
- A company wanted finance for a venture involving the processing of chicken manure to produce electricity. The manager was concerned about the links with factory farms from which the manure would need to be obtained. The business was approved.
- A charitable trust wished to deposit large credit balances at the bank. However, the Chairman of the trust was heavily involved in organising bird shoots and wanted to put the family accounts into the bank – his wife already had an account at the bank. The manager felt that the Ethical Policy raised the issue but did not provide an answer and he referred the matter to Head Office.

- During a 'sweep' of existing accounts following the introduction of the Ethical Policy, a manager became concerned about an account with an abortion clinic. He referred the case to Head Office.
- A manager reported a case, currently under investigation, of a company making lipsticks some of the raw materials for which were tested on animals. The company making the lipsticks did not itself do the testing on animals. The company was not doing very well and the manager was concerned that no other bank would be willing to take on the business if the bank decided to ask it to withdraw its account.
- One manager reported that from a 'sweep' of 5,000 accounts at his branch 12 or so had been 're-banked' (i.e. asked to withdraw their account).
- A manager who targeted business in the working mens' clubs sector was concerned that there were many smokers in these clubs, but as they were not involved in the manufacture of tobacco products their business was acceptable.
- A manager turned down a substantial new account because it breached the bank's code on the environmental impact of the business.
- A battery-hen operation was refused facilities by a manager because it breached the Ethical Policy. This manager indicated that his decision may have been different if later in the financial year he had not been hitting his targets for new business.
- A sports organisation approached the bank for accounting services. This organisation was partly sponsored by a tobacco manufacturer. The manager's view was that since they were not involved in the manufacture of tobacco and since the co-operative retail organisations also sold tobacco products, the business was acceptable.
- A public company put one of its businesses into receivership and wished to get it back as an attempt to evade tax. The manager declined to grant loan facilities.
- A manager was concerned that an approach from a part of the Territorial Army might have been in breach of the code; the business was approved.

From the 19 incidents reported, six managers checked with the Corporate Affairs Unit in the Manchester headquarters of the bank for advice and guidance, and eight felt compelled to carry out further detailed investigation into a proposition because of the existence of the Ethical Policy.

Seven managers reported no incidents at all. All of the above-cited examples came from the remaining ten managers. Two managers indicated that their decisions were affected by commercial realities – one was concerned that no other bank would take on a business which he felt he wanted to be rid of because it breached the policy and one admitted that a decision might have been different if he had been below his financial targets.

It is clear from the above that a significant number of managers have been influenced in their behaviour by the existence of the Ethical Policy. It is also interesting to note that even where a particular case does not directly breach the Ethical Policy as it is written, some managers feel that they need to apply the spirit of the policy as they see it. This applies in the cases of the hunt saboteurs and the political organisations mentioned above.

4.4 Someone to turn to?

Managers were asked whether there was someone at the bank for them to turn to if they had a problem of an ethical nature. This question did not refer specifically to the Ethical Policy but to ethical issues generally whether or not they were incorporated in the policy. Two managers stated that there was no-one to whom they felt they could turn for ethical advice or guidance. These were the exception. Twelve indicated that they would turn to the Corporate Affairs Unit at Head Office and eleven felt that they could discuss ethical problems with colleagues at their own branch.

4.5 Ensuring conformity

The methods used by managers to ensure that their investment or client related decisions conform to the Ethical Policy produced a variety of answers.

The bank's procedures require confirmation that the Ethical Code has been discussed with any new client and managers discretionary limits are set so that the larger advances are dealt with by head office staff. The bank also requires an annual review of each existing account. However, within this general framework managers appear to exercise their discretion in different ways.

One manager felt that this was not a real issue. Another stated that he discusses the policy with a new client and relied on the client to disclose relevant information. Other approaches included the view that the Ethical Policy was quite specific and conformity with it was unproblematic – it was clear when a client did or did not conform.

Nine managers stressed the importance of analysing the work of a company in some detail. Five indicated that they always met with new customers and the Ethical Policy was always discussed with them. However, two stated that small accounts were usually dealt with solely on documentation. One manager took the view that whether or not a client conformed to the policy was usually obvious from the nature of the client's business or operations.

The role of the annual review was mentioned as significant in this context by nine managers.

Since the exercise of discretion is always likely to lead to different approaches and outcomes, the variety of approaches indicated above is possibly remarkable in the sense that it does not demonstrate widely different approaches being taken. The major difference appears to be the extent to which managers rely on clients to disclose information. However, experienced commercial managers with successful track records are unlikely to be easily misled.

4.6 The managers' personal views

The managers were asked to identify which parts of the Ethical Policy were most important to themselves personally and which were least important. They were not limited in the number of items which they could identify in either category. One manager was not able to identify any section as most or least important to himself. Table 6.3 summarises the responses.

TABLE 6.3   Aspects of ethical policy: summary of responses

Ethical policy section	Most important	Least important
1. Oppressing human spirit	9	–
2. Oppressive regimes	3	–
3. Environmental impact	7	1
4. Ethical customers	1	–
5. Speculation against sterling	3	5
6. Money laundering Drug trafficking Tax evasion	2	1
7. Tobacco manufacturers	2	6
8. Customer charter	2	1
9. Animal experimentation	5	2
10. Factory farming	2	–
11. Animal fur	2	–
12. Blood sports	3	1

The very high level of identification of the first section of the Ethical Policy as personally important is worthy of note. When pressed to identify any regimes or organisations which fell into this category, respondents found some difficulty in doing so. It is also interesting that significant numbers of managers regard the bank's stance on tobacco manufacture and speculation against the pound as not significant parts of the policy.

Managers were clearly more able to identify elements which they personally regarded as very important than they were to identify the least important elements.

The overwhelming response to the question 'Does the bank's ethical stance accord with your own personal, ethical or moral views?' was positive. Eleven stated 'yes' without qualification. Two indicated 'yes' but felt that interpretations of aspects of the policy might differ between managers. Two indicated 'yes, generally speaking'. One claimed to have an open mind on this question and another was undecided but felt that some aspects of the policy went further than he personally might feel disposed to go.

The general support for the policy probably has two major sources. First, the bank, in developing the policy, consulted widely with customers and staff and found considerable consonance between the values of both groups and the cooperative values which formed the basis for the Ethical Policy. Second, managers were very clear that the policy was an important part of the bank's market positioning strategy and that it was instrumental in helping them to achieve the targets set (see the responses to the next question).

Sixteen managers responded positively to the question 'Does it help you to gain clients?'. The one not responding positively felt that the policy might have helped him, but not directly.

Managers predominantly felt that the ethical policy made no contribution to their ability to manage their staff. Eleven answered with a clear 'no' to the question 'Does it help you in your management of staff?'. However, five felt that it did help with the management of staff because it helped in the development of a shared set of values making leadership and control of staff less demanding for themselves. One of them was not sure.

To the question 'Does it help you in relating to your superiors?', thirteen answered 'no' and four answered 'yes'. Most managers reported that the Ethical Policy was less important in this context than organisational goals focused on targets and personal relationships with their superiors.

Claims made about the effectiveness of corporate codes and mission statements (see Campbell and Tawadey, 1992) emphasise their role within the corporation of creating the conditions for effective leadership and direction of staff by managers. It is not clear in this case whether the Ethical Policy does help significantly in this area of the managers' jobs.

The question 'Are there any aspects of the Code you would like to change?' produced a wide range of responses:

- 6 managers did not want to change anything in the code
- 1 did not wish to change anything but was personally more relaxed about some of the matters mentioned in the code
- 2 felt that the reference to tobacco manufacturing should be taken out.

There was a large number of individualised responses which produced the following statements:

- 'any extension of the ethical policy would require greater specificity or be more widespread in its coverage'
- 'the statement is rather long-winded and could be reduced to 5 paragraphs with a strong emphasis on the customer charter'
- 'the code has to be ever-changing; the detail is less important than the general statement'
- 'the code should be more down-to-earth and include categories such as cleaning up the streets'

- 'the bank should run diesel cars if it is genuine in its concern about the environment'
- 'endangered species should be added to the list'
- 'issues of race, ethnicity and creed should be included'
- 'alcohol should be included along with pharmaceutical products if tobacco is included'
- 'issues such as family instability and law-and-order issues should be included'
- 'there should be clarification of the tax evasion and tobacco manufacturing parts of the policy'

Most managers (11 out of the 17 interviewed) did wish to propose changes to the Ethical Policy. This does not imply a general dissatisfaction with the policy. It does, however, show that these managers felt that improvements in the policy could be made. There was a general perception amongst the managers interviewed that they would not be able to influence the content of the policy and that the processes involved in making changes were distant from their own working experience in the bank.

4.7   Hypothetical circumstances

Each manager was asked to indicate what he would do if:

    (a) 'one of the companies in which you invest goes bankrupt'
    (b) 'one of your clients was convicted of drunk driving'
    (c) 'a direct competitor of one of your existing clients approached you for a loan'

In relation to the first hypothetical circumstance, fifteen managers responded that they would instigate the bank's receivership procedures. 2 indicated that they would attempt to avoid this situation arising by being alert to developments and intervening to help the company before it got to the stage of receivership.

Four believed that *The* Co-operative Bank would be more sympathetic to the company than would other banks, but six stated that they felt that *The* Co-operative Bank's approach would be the same as any other commercial bank and this meant acting to protect the bank's interests. One manager, without prompting, stated that the bank's Ethical Policy was not relevant to this situation. No other manager mentioned the Ethical Policy in relation to this question.

Responses to the second hypothetical circumstance showed a similar degree of uniformity. Twelve managers indicated that their major concern was simply the impact of the drunk-driving case on the client's ability to run the business, and four indicated that they would do nothing.

Two felt that they should not make a moral judgement, but seven indicated that such an incident might affect their personal relationship with the client involved.

The third hypothetical circumstance produced a wider variety of responses than the earlier two. Although the predominant view was that commercial considerations would be the major factors in a decision, different reasons were given to support this view. Six managers felt that the new business should be taken because if they did not someone else would. Two argued that it is a competitive business world in which they operate and that this justified taking the new business on.

However, one manager asserted that he would definitely not take the new business because of the danger of having intimate knowledge of two competing clients. He felt that this ran counter to the underlying values of the Ethical Policy even if such matters were not explicitly included in the published statement. Two felt that if there was a conflict of interest they would turn the new business away. One manager would give the decision to another colleague not personally involved with either business, but went on to say that he would try to influence this colleague's decision. Another adopted the approach of turning down the new business but encouraging the existing one to repay the bank loan as soon as possible to protect the bank from any future decline in the fortunes of this business as a result of new competition.

Three managers introduced the bank's duty of confidentiality into the discussion. One of these stated that he felt that the question posed was not an ethical one because it was covered by the duty of confidentiality, which meant the new business could be taken on without alerting the existing client because the bank is bound by the duty of confidentiality not to tell clients about other client's business. The other two simply stated that the duty of confidentiality meant that they should examine the new proposition purely on commercial grounds.

The responses to the hypothetical circumstances indicate that managers would approach such cases on the basis of the established procedures of the bank, based on traditional banking practices as applied within *The Co-operative Bank*. The Ethical Policy does not provide clear guidelines to managers about what to do under the various circumstances. It is not intended to. There are rules, regulations and traditions which managers draw on in such circumstances.

5   Conclusions

Has the Ethical Policy made any difference to the way in which managers perform their duties?

At one level, it is possible to argue that the policy has had a significant influence on behaviour within the bank. Its procedures require managers to confirm that all clients, especially possible new ones, are aware of its Ethical Policy and job profiles indicate the need for managers to have knowledge of the policy. There was also a high degree of awareness of the existence of senior staff at head office in Manchester who could be consulted about particular problem cases. The bank appears to have been successful in integrating the policy into its processes.

However, within the complex and rapidly changing internal organisation of the bank, it is difficult to establish the precise influences which the policy has on managerial behaviour. Other factors, such as the process re-engineering, downsizing, vigorous marketing strategy and the new performance management system, are just as likely to have influenced managerial behaviour.

Further, the traditional cooperative values of the bank, which is an integral part of the cooperative movement, are felt by the managers to be significant in influencing the culture of the organisation and the behaviour of managers towards customers and colleagues. The bank could argue, with considerable justification, that its Ethical Policy is simply a market- oriented re-statement of these traditional values.

The managers do feel that the policy has had a major impact on their ability to attract new business amongst the target groups (educational establishments, professional bodies, charitable organisations) and has provided an entrée into discussions with these groups. However, they also take the view that the policy is effective in this regard only in so far as it is supported by efficient, helpful and effective services provided by the bank.

The Ethical Policy does not appear to have significant influence on behaviour in areas which the managers regard as covered by traditional banking practice. This is illustrated in their response to the hypothetical circumstances. In these circumstances, the more traditional banking virtues of confidentiality were seen as predominant in influencing their behaviour.

Chadwick (1993) argues that one danger of professional codes of conduct is that the behaviour of the person affected by the code loses autonomy. The code becomes a replacement for independent moral action. In the case of *The Co-operative Bank's* Ethical Policy, this does not appear to be happening. The policy is significant in marketing terms and is seen as helpful for managers in achieving targets. It does not dominate their thinking. Other values, beliefs and attitudes intervene in mediating the code. The more traditional banking values, particularly of confidentiality, are used by mangers in justifying their behaviour more frequently than reference to the Ethical Policy.

Finally, the Ethical Policy is the product of decisions to include certain features and, necessarily, to exclude others. The bank is committed to reviewing and changing its policy in the light of changing circumstances and the changes in the values of its customers. As indicated above, most of the interviewed managers wished to propose some changes to the policy although each manager's individual proposal would not result in major changes of emphasis. However, most of the managers were not aware of the procedures for review and change. Their sense of ownership of the policy as a marketing tool is considerable. Their use of it in other areas of work and their feeling of influence over its content are limited.

Bibliography

Annual Report and Accounts, 1992, The Co-operative Bank plc.

Campell, A. and Tawadey, K. (1992) *Mission and Business Philosophy*, Butterworth Heinemann, Oxford.

Chadwick, R. (1993) 'Codes and Ethics – An Unhappy Alliance?', Conference on Business and Professional Ethics, University of Central Lancashire (unpublished).

Clutterbuck, D., Dearlove, D. and Snow, D. (1992) *Actions Speak Louder – A Management Guide to Corporate Responsibility*, Kingfisher/Kogan Page, London.

Cohen, J., Pant, L. and Sharp, D. (1993) 'A Validation and Extension of a Multidimensional Ethics Scale', *Journal of Business Ethics*, vol. 1, pp. 13–26.

Davis, P. and Worthington, S. (1993) 'Cooperative Values: Change and Continuity in Capital Accumulation. The Case of the British Cooperative Bank', *Journal of Business Ethics*, vol. 12, pp. 849–59.

Delaney, J.T. and Sockell, D. (1992) 'Do Company Ethics Programmes Make a Difference? – An Empirical Analysis', *Journal of Business Ethics*, vol. 11, pp. 719–27.

Fritzsche, D.J. and Becker, H. (1984) 'Linking Management Behaviour to Ethical Philosophy – An Empirical Investigation', *Journal of Business Ethics*, vol. 27, 1, pp. 166–75.

Lynn, M. (1993) 'Terry Thomas', *Management Today*, (July), pp. 44–6.

Nash, L. (1991) 'American and European Corporate Ethics Practices', in J. Mahoney and E. Vallance (eds), *Business Ethics in a New Europe*, Kluwer, Dordrecht.

Performance Management Appraisal, 1993, The Co-operative Bank plc.

Premeux, S. and Mundy, R.W. (1993) 'Linking Managerial Behaviour to Ethical Philosophy', *Journal of Business Ethics*, vol. 5, pp. 349–57.

Stead, W.E., Worrel, D.L. and Stead, G.S. (1990) 'An Integrative Model for Understanding and Managing Ethical Behaviour in Organisations', *Journal of Business Ethics*, vol. 9, pp. 215–26.

Appendix 1   The Ethical Policy of *The* Co-operative Bank

1. **It will not invest** in or supply financial services to any regime or organisation which oppresses the human spirit, takes away the rights of individuals or manufactures any instrument of torture.
2. **It will not finance** or in any way facilitate the manufacture or sale of weapons to any country which has an oppressive regime.
3. **It will encourage** business customers to take a proactive stance of the environmental impact of their own activities.
4. **It will actively** seek out individuals, commercial enterprises and non-commercial organisations which have a complementary ethical stance.
5. **It will not speculate** against the pound using either its own money or that of its customers. It believes it is inappropriate for a British clearing bank to speculate against the British currency and the British economy using deposits provided by their British customers and at the expense of the British tax payer.
6. **It will try to ensure** its financial services are not exploited for the purpose of money laundering, drug trafficking or tax evasion by the continued application and development of its successful internal monitoring and control procedures.
7. **It will not provide** financial services to tobacco product manufacturers.

8. **It will continue** to extend and strengthen its Customer Charter, which has already established new standards of banking practice through adopting innovative procedures on status enquiries and customer confidentiality, ahead of any other British Bank.
9. **It will not invest** in any business involved in animal experimentation for cosmetic purposes.
10. **It will not support** any person or company using exploitative factory farming methods.
11. **It will not engage** in business with any farm or other organisation engaged in the production of animal fur.
12. **It will not support** any organisation involved in blood sports, which it defines as sports which involve the training of animals or birds to catch and destroy, or to fight and kill, other animals or birds.

Appendix 2   Questionnaire for Interviews with Managers

1. How long have you been in your present role in the bank?
2. What was your previous role?
3. When did you start your employment with the Bank?
4. What factors led to your being employed by the Bank?
5. Can you tell me your age and qualifications?
6. Please describe the major components of your current job (briefly).
7. Which parts of your current job would you say are influenced by the Bank's :
    (a)   Mission Statement
    (b)   Ethical Code
8. I would like you to describe up to three incidents in the last 2 or 3 years in which the Bank's ethical code assisted you in arriving at a decision.
9. If you have a problem at work of an ethical nature, is there someone at the Bank you can turn to for help?
10. How do you ensure that your investment or client-related decisions conform to the Bank's ethical code?
11. Which parts of the Bank's ethical code are most important to you personally?
12. Which parts are the least important to you personally?
13. What would you do if:
    (a)   one of your companies in which you invest goes bankrupt
    (b)   one of your clients was convicted of drunk driving
    (c)   a direct competitor of one of your existing clients approached you for a loan
14. In your opinion:
    Does the Bank's ethical stance accord with your own personal, ethical or moral views?
    Does it help you to gain clients?
    Does it help you in your management of staff?
    Does it help you in relating to your superiors?
15. Are there any aspects of the Code you would like to change?
16. In relation to day-to-day banking practice, does *The* Co-operative Bank differ from other banks?

CHAPTER 7

The Ethical Organisation

1 Individuals and Organisations

People, with very few exceptions,[1] are moral agents. In other words, their actions are governed by rules, explicit or implicit, which can be subjected to ethical appraisal. We may praise them for being courageous, charitable, just, sensitive, or magnanimous, or we may condemn their foolishness, envy or deviousness. We may neither praise nor blame, but wonder whether they were not fully responsible for what they did. Perhaps they were coerced or pressured or, perhaps, just did not know what they were doing. This language of moral evaluation does not only apply to adult human beings, but that is its primary and most typical use. Children may be selfish or act unfairly, but we accept that they only gradually acquire full moral responsibility for their actions. Animals, too, may be courageous or altruistic, but we may suspect a degree of anthropomorphism in extending moral language too far in their direction. The moral status of animals is a matter of debate, but no one thinks butterflies can have or lack charity or that jackdaws are dishonest. The rest of the world lies outside the moral realm altogether, except, perhaps, for our moral responsibilities towards it. Rocks and stones and trees do not have moral responsibilities.

At one end of the spectrum, then, there are adult, rational human beings with the full panoply of moral rights, duties, virtues and vices. At the other are inanimate physical objects to which moral language is entirely inappropriate. In the middle are small children and some animals to whom some moral categories may be applied. Where on this spectrum do organisations belong?

One answer is that organisations, which in this context means clubs, societies, incorporated bodies, companies and so on, belong with the rocks and stones and trees on the non-moral end. To that it is usually quickly added that, of course, such entities are made up of people and those people are moral agents, but the organisations as such are not. It would therefore be as absurd to require an organisation to act justly or to behave charitably as it would be to expect the sea to be responsible in deciding which bits of the coastline to erode or a tree in deciding which passers-by it dropped its dead branches on.

A second answer is that organisations may well be agents of a kind which it makes sense to praise or blame for their actions, even though they are not agents in exactly the same way as human beings are. Nonetheless it is not a good idea to lay social, moral or political obligations on organisations because they are not very effective or efficient (or, sometimes, that they are inappropriate) entities for carrying them out. A bank should operate according to financial principles, and not impose its political or social values on the community. Major concerns should not seek to remedy social problems through their hiring and firing policies because they are not very good at it. In any case, attempting to do so will detract from their main mission – making a profit – out of which some genuine social benefit might eventually accrue.

A third answer is that organisations have sufficient structural complexity to be agents whom it makes sense to call to account for their actions and the consequences of those actions. An organisation is, by definition, *organised*; it is not just a group or mass of people. This implies that it has *structure* which enables it to make collective decisions and act on those decisions. Such structures vary enormously. Some organisations have flat, relatively informal and open structures whilst others may be rigid, hierarchic and formal. This variation may be relevant to the questions of whether organisations take decisions readily or with extreme difficulty, whether they do so with the full consent of all involved or in the teeth of opposition and dissent, but it is not relevant to the question of whether they can take decisions at all. And if a body can take decisions and implement them, then it must be responsible for those decisions and their consequences. It may not be possible for such organisations to be responsible in the way that people can be, but they can be responsible in a way appropriate to organisations. Being profitable is a virtue of business organisations, but it is not the only virtue. We can expect organisations to be socially responsible because that is part of the contract out of which they were created, a condition of the permission that society granted that they exist in the first place.

We want to argue that the third answer seems to us to be the most plausible and defensible of the three, but first we need to explain what is wrong with the other two.

2   Organisations are not Agents

Margaret Thatcher once famously asserted that 'there is no such thing as "society", there are only individuals'. The argument that organisations cannot have moral or social responsibilities sometimes seems to take as its premise a similar assertion, that 'there are no such things as organisations, there are only individuals'. Such an assertion cannot be as simple as it seems, or else it would have to be taken as affirming what is obviously false: that Marks & Spencer, Crédit Lyonnais, the Catholic Church, the United Nations and Greenpeace and similar organisations all over the world do not, in fact, exist and the illusion that they do is one suffered by millions of people. Clearly any argument resting on such a foundation could be easily rejected.

Instead, we must read the premise as asserting something more sophisticated; namely that organisations are made up of people and that they have no real existence of their own apart from the people out of which they are constituted. This is like saying that rainbows do not (really) exist. It is not that if you think you have seen one you are mistaken, but that rainbows are made up out of the sunlight refracted through raindrops, and that were it not for the existence of raindrops and sunlight there would not be rainbows. And what *that* is saying is that rainbows are not material objects, though they are an effect caused by physical objects (raindrops) in certain circumstances.

There may be people now (as there certainly were in the past) who think that rainbows are material objects, at the bottom of which, could you get there, you would find a pot of gold. To such people the previous paragraph would be news. To the rest of us, the statement that rainbows are not real either tells us nothing we did not know before (read as telling us that rainbows are caused by raindrops) or else it is obviously false (read as telling us that rainbows are illusions).

Similarly, if the assertion that organisations are not real is saying no more than that the existence of organisations depends on people, then it is telling us nothing we did not already know. And, equally, if it is saying that organisations are illusions, then it is false. But perhaps we do need to be reminded that organisations are made up of people because we are inclined to attribute to organisations qualities which, properly, are properties of the people who make them up rather than of the organisations themselves. If we are inclined to think that a rainbow is a material object, then we may be puzzled as to why we cannot get closer to it in order to see it more clearly. If we are reminded that a rainbow is just the sun refracted through raindrops as seen from a particular position, then the puzzlement vanishes. For we can get closer to the raindrops, but once we do so, we are no longer seeing them from the right position for the rainbow to appear. It is not the rainbow which has a particular spatial location, but the raindrops.

Milton Friedman (1970) assumes that when we talk about the social responsibilities of business we are making just such a mistake. Businesses are not the kinds of things which can have responsibilities: 'Only people can have responsibilities'. Friedman does not attempt to defend this, except by saying that a corporation is an artificial person (and in this sense may have artificial responsibilities). By this he seems to imply that, just as artificial cream is not really cream, an artificial person is not really a person and artificial responsibilities are not real ones. But though artificial cream is not *real cream*, it is, in its own way, real enough. Incorporated organisations may not be real persons, only legal ones, but they are really organisations, and so the question of whether they can have duties, responsibilities, obligations, intentions, purposes, etc, has been left untouched. Indeed, on the face of it, the idea that organisations cannot have responsibilities seems obviously false once actual examples are considered. Even Friedman thinks that governments have responsibilities (the responsibility, amongst others, to leave businesses alone to make money and not to impose social obligations on them). And the fact that other institutions, such as law courts, professional bodies, pension funds, etc. also have responsibilities seems unarguable.

This last fact is what makes the argument advanced by Danley (1993) rather curious. It does not deny that organisations are real, but that like rocks and stones and trees they are entities that are not capable of assuming responsibilities because they cannot form intentions. He explains the fact mentioned above – that some organisations seem, on the face of it, to have genuine responsibilities – by agreeing with Friedman that to talk in this way is simply a shorthand way of saying that certain individuals within those organisations have responsibilities. His argument is a severely positivist one which assumes that we cannot make a sensible distinction between the way in which an organisation *ought* to function, and the way in which it actually does; between, that is, the decisions taken which are actually decisions of the corporation, and those which are decisions of its wayward members, acting outside the scope of their authority. The reason why this is a problem is that most organisations act in accordance with a corporate structure that is both much more complicated than and also quite different from the official organisational chart that hangs outside the MD's office or in the reception area (see, for example, Handy, 1978). Thus, argues Danley, we must accept either that most decisions are not decisions of the organisation as such at all (because they are not in accordance with the officially publicised decision-making procedure), or that *all* decisions made by *any* member of the organisation are decisions of the organisations (in which case we can no longer distinguish between decisions which are and those which are not decisions of the organisation).

As with many philosophically generated dilemmas, this one is quite bogus. Just because the officially produced organisational chart is both naive and over simple, it does not follow that there are no rules at all which determine what count as the proper procedures. Official grammars of English (or, indeed, any natural language) are also both naive and over-simple, but that does not mean that there are no implicit rules at all which people follow and that *anything* (and hence nothing) can count as a correctly formed English sentence. Without rules, however informal and imperfectly characterised, there could be no such thing as the English language. Equally, without procedures and protocols there could *be* no organisation as such, just an anarchic mass of people, even if such procedures and protocols are not what people would say they were, if asked to describe them.

This matters because it implies that organisations do have the complexity of internal structure that would permit us to say that they can take decisions and perform actions which are not either the decisions and actions of any one individual (even though in very small or very hierarchical organisations one person may actually take the decision), or an aggregate of the decisions and actions of all. This fact will be familiar to anyone who has served on committees (or boards of management, tribunals, juries, or anything of that kind), that decisions are taken and acted on which are not the decisions or actions that any individual member would have chosen or predicted. Whether this is something which counts for or against committees is another issue. Nor is it relevant that, of course, sometimes an individual member will succeed in securing the committee's agreement to his or her own personal wishes, or that it is seldom the case (though it can happen) that a body makes a decision that none of its members, individually, would agree to. The point is not that without its members acting and deciding there could be no body which could act and take decisions. A committee is not some kind of magical machine which can operate without people. And the people involved will, of course, be responsible for the decision arrived at. The point is, rather, that a procedure exists which, if followed correctly, will result in a decision which is corporate or collective rather than individual; the responsibility for it will be collective or corporate rather than individual too. And being responsible for an action means being morally responsible, where that action has moral implications.

3 Limited Liability

If we have established that the idea of collective responsibility makes sense and that organisations can have responsibilities just as people do, we have still to establish that organisations either can or should have ethical responsibilities. Friedman (1970 and 1980) argues (as does Hayek, 1982; and, arguably, as did Adam Smith, 1776)[2] that it is not prudent, even if it is possible, to require business organisations to take on responsibilities beyond those of making money and acting within the law.[3]

The argument for this view comes in a number of forms, but common to all of them is the idea that the collective good is an unspecifiable and unknowable value. Individuals have differing conceptions of the good, and it is better to allow each to attempt to realise their own version of the good in their own way than to enforce some preferred version on everyone. There are two reasons for this. One is that, because individuals are different, there will be genuine differences in what is good for each and the attempt to sum over those individual goods is fruitless and, probably, also harmful. The other is that there is no clear formula for establishing what the good is and, so, any attempt to do so is prone to error. If individuals are left to determine what is good for them by themselves, then the scope of any error is restricted to that individual who has, in any case, a considerably greater incentive to correct it, or, indeed, to get it right in the first place, than has any third party.

Organisations, then, should 'stick to the knitting'[4] and do what they do best. In the case of business organisations, this is to turn a profit by trading in the market place. They should not, still less should they be obliged to, attempt to impose their view of what is socially good on the rest of us. They are not especially well qualified to determine what that good is and, if they are wrong, we bear the consequences. And, because society is composed of individuals, that good is going to be so variable, so complicated and so diverse, that they are extremely unlikely to get it right.

The idea that business organisations are, because they are essentially money-making enterprises, best to stick to making money and, also, that they should not be obliged to strive to do anything else, is undoubtedly appealing in its simplicity. There is also an economic argument which allegedly proves that, in a market of perfect competition, they can do nothing else. (See Baumol, W. J. and Batey Blackman, S. A., 1991, ch. 1.) For any effort directed elsewhere than at profit must be a cost to the company. This cost can only be met by a decrease in profit or by a degradation in the quality of the company's product. In a perfectly competitive market a business which took this road would be forced out by competitors who chose not to bear this additional cost and could, therefore, increase their profits or sell a higher-quality product.

4 Society, Markets and Law

The idea of a perfectly competitive market is, however, an unrealisable ideal to which actual markets may only approximate. It requires that participants be small and anonymous and that entry to and exit from the market be rapid and costless. (Baumol and Batey Blackman, 1991, pp. 8–9.) The reason for this is that the larger and better-known a company is, and the greater its investment in the market, then the more the market is distorted towards monopoly. Advocates of free-market economics find this point troublesome, because it implies regulation of the market of a kind they would normally deplore, simply in order to retain the free-market whose benefits they are advocating. Friedman glosses over this point in a single sentence when he remarks that the responsibility of a corporate executive '. . .is to conduct the business in accordance with [the] desires [of his employers], which generally will be to make as much money as possible while conforming to the base rules of society, *both those embodied in law and those embodied in ethical custom*' (Friedman, 1970; our italics.) What, we believe, he has in mind here is that certain core legal and moral values are essential if business and trade within the market is to be possible. These would include promise-keeping, financial probity, honesty, integrity, and reliability. They would also require the avoidance of price-fixing, cartels and other monopolistic tendencies. This is because, unless a business paid its bills and met its orders it could not continue to trade and if it began to dominate the market then that market, to that extent, would no longer be a free one. But once this is spelled out it would seem that Friedman has conceded the case that corporations can and should be ethically responsible. The only way to avoid this conclusion is to draw a dubious distinction between positive and negative duties, between those things one should refrain from doing and those things one ought to do. An organisation can be required not to do harm. It ought not, in addition, be required to do good. This is partly because it is governments through the political process which are the appropriate organs for determining what social good is. It is also partly because doing good involves costs which it is not appropriate for a business organisation to have to bear if it is to remain in a competitive position within the market place.

Several highly questionable assumptions are involved in this argument. One is that positive duties have costs whereas negative duties are cost-free. But to refrain from exploiting or creating a monopoly market is certainly not cost-free, whereas anti-discriminatory hiring and promoting policies may well, after a certain initial investment, bear fruit in the form of a more highly qualified, better-motivated work force. A second assumption is that refraining from doing harm is readily distinguishable from doing good. But, clearly, to refrain from harming someone is to benefit them, whereas to fail to benefit someone when one is able to do so, just is to harm them. A third assumption is that to require organisations to act in a socially responsible way is to render them less competitive and, thereby, to injure the market which creates the wealth in the first place. But it is not clear that this is any different, in principle, from the requirement, which Friedman himself accepts, that businesses 'conform to the base rules of society'.

It is true that, in a perfectly competitive market, free-riders[5] can benefit from dishonesty and honest traders will be disadvantaged by it. (See Baumol and Batey Blackman, 1991.) This process can continue until the supply of honest traders runs out and the market is totally corrupted. (At which point it will, presumably, disintegrate, along with a substantial portion of the fabric of civil society.) Thus a perfectly competitive market must be maintained by legal and/or social regulation which imposes on all those obligations which honest traders impose on themselves. It is, therefore, in the interests of those who do not need to be regulated that they be regulated. That creates a level playing field in which free-riders are compelled to quit or else compete on equal terms. In other words, society creates a market it is prepared to live with, and there is no reason why it should be prepared to live with a market in which only minimal standards of honesty and decency prevail, rather than one which is able to take on a higher degree of responsibility towards the society which created it and the environment in which it operates and from which it benefits.

The question is not whether organisations can or should have ethical and social responsibilities. We believe that we have shown that they can and should. Indeed, it would seem that even Friedman has conceded this point, though he may well think that his position can avoid its implications. The question is, rather, since organisations do and must have such responsibilities then, whether and where a line can be drawn around what they can do and what we would wish them to do (or not do). What are the characteristics of a properly ethical organisation?

5   Characteristics of Ethical Organisations

If it is accepted, following on from the argument above, that there is a sense in which organisations can be said to have ethical responsibilities or, at least, to behave in ethical ways, then some organisations might be said to be more or less ethical than others.

How can it be known, either by organisational members or by external others, that a particular organisation is an ethical one? Or, as Nash (1992) asks, 'How to take the moral pulse of organisations whose workforce exceeds the population of small towns and whose operations are often spread over many geographic areas?' Bearing in mind the enormous size and complexity of some business organisations, to what extent does it make any kind of sense to ask the question?

As organisations grow, the likelihood of someone, somewhere, behaving in unethical ways is likely to increase. Does this mean that larger organisations are likely to be less ethical than smaller ones? Does unethical behaviour by a single employee mean that an organisation's claims to be ethical are thereby negated? If it can be shown that some aspect of the functioning of an organisation is questionable on ethical grounds, does this condemn the organisation?

It is probably unreasonable to answer 'yes' to any of the above questions. Most of us would accept that the occasional deviation from ethical conduct need not result in outright condemnation. We would tend to be even more confident in holding this view if we had evidence to show that an organisation had taken appropriate action following the revelation of shortcomings on its part.

How an organisation responds to unethical conduct by one or many of its employees may be taken as an indicator of the strength of its ethical pulse. One-off, episodic or uncoordinated responses to known transgressions may, however, be regarded as a weak vital sign. An organisation which has thought through its ethical stance and developed a fuller, better managed approach to ethical issues is more likely to be producing ethical behaviour on a regular basis than one which has only a reactive approach. Such organisations have a stronger claim to the view that they are ethical organisations. As interest in the study and practice of business ethics has increased, the search for the ethical organisation has intensified.

To identify the characteristics of ethical organisations, three different approaches can be used. These approaches are not mutually exclusive. Each of them offers useful insights. First, there is that approach which stems from a desire to build a model or theory of corporate moral excellence from a basis of first principles. Second, there is the approach which is based on stakeholder theory. Third, there is the approach which stems from a concern about issues of corporate governance.

6   Theories of Corporate Moral Excellence

The notion of corporate or organisational culture is well established in the field of organisation theory and behaviour. Although there are some significant divergences of view about the features and origins of corporate culture, there is widespread agreement amongst analysts that organisational culture significantly affects behaviour in organisations.

Fundamental to any corporate culture are the values which are embedded within the corporation. Deal and Kennedy (1982) express this view forcefully when they write 'Values are the bedrock of any corporate culture.' They assert that values produce a sense of direction for employees and help to guide and control their day-to-day behaviour.

One useful distinction between corporate values is that between espoused values and values in practice. Espoused values are those found in company mission statements, codes of ethics or credos. They state what the company stands for and describe the ethical perspective of those who are responsible for leading and directing the company. They are intended to indicate to employees, customers, competitors, suppliers and others the sort of behaviour and approach which is acceptable to the company.

These espoused values may be very different from 'values in practice'. For example, a company statement may contain a sentence which says 'We regard our employees as our most valued asset.' If this is the case in practice, then one might expect to see clearly thought-through and effective policies and procedures in relation to the appointment, induction, training and development, remuneration and other rewards of employees. If these do not exist, then the contrast between espoused values and values in practice may be apparent. If the company practices are seen as unfair and discriminatory or as repressive and outdated, then its employees will be conscious of the differences between espoused values and values in practice. No one would regard the publicly stated espoused values as, in themselves, an indication of an ethical company. There would be a reasonable expectation that espoused values are followed through in practice.

Michael Hoffman (1986) builds upon the concept of corporate culture in order to develop a powerful theory of corporate moral excellence. Hoffman holds the view that corporate culture has three main elements. First, there are the basic values, attitudes and beliefs of the organisation. Second, there are the organisational goals, policies, structures and strategies which are shaped by those basic values, attitudes and beliefs. Third, there is the organisational 'way of doing things'. These are the everyday, accepted, unchallenged processes and procedures. Almost hidden from view within these everyday forms of behaviour are the basic values, attitudes and beliefs of the organisation.

However, Hoffman asserts that within organisations it is individuals who are responsible for creating goals, criticising and evaluating the corporate culture and instigating and implementing change. He states that the morally excellent corporation is one that discovers the healthy reciprocity between its culture and the autonomy of its individuals. This reciprocity is a necessary but not a sufficient condition for corporate moral excellence. It is also necessary for the corporate culture to be a moral corporate culture.

This means that the espoused values and values in practice should be ethically acceptable. Although not directly concerned with issues of business ethics, the work of Peters and Waterman (1982) supports this view. They studied successful companies which had achieved excellence in their fields and concluded that, amongst other characteristics, excellent companies were clear on what they stood for and took the process of value shaping very seriously. They doubted whether it was possible to be an excellent company without clarity on values and without having the right sort of values.

Morally excellent organisations, therefore, according to Hoffman and Peters and Waterman have cultures based on ethical values.

How can an organisation ensure that its ethical values are reflected in its corporate culture? How can it ensure that its basic ethical beliefs are reflected and carried through in its goals, policies, structures and strategies and in its everyday ways of behaviour? Goodpaster (1983) offers an approach based on four steps. First, there is the need to look for ethical issues or situations which raise ethical questions. Second, rational principles are applied to produce ethical strategies and procedures. Third, there is a need to coordinate the ethical strategies and procedures with other demands, interests and constraints. Fourth, there is the implementation of the agreed ethical strategies and procedures. This produces action or 'good deeds' and involves integration within the everyday way of doing things in the organisation.

However, Goodpaster takes the view that such an approach could be dangerous to individual moral autonomy if it takes place within a corporate culture which is too strong or prescriptive. Excellent organisations are driven by a few key values and give space to individuals to use their initiative to support those values.

Morally excellent organisations, according to the approach exemplified by Hoffman and Goodpaster, are characterised by ethical values and clarity about those values. They also have good communications systems to aid the process of clarification and implementation, room for rational disagreement and protest, avenues of withdrawal for antipathetic individuals, and minimised bureaucracy and control.

However, according to Sinclair (1993) the prevailing approach to corporate ethical behaviour holds that creating a unitary cohesive culture around core moral values is the solution to enhancing ethical behaviour. Strong cultures are characterised by being shared by all employees, being deeply felt, being capable of determining behaviour and being consistent across the organisation. However, he argues that strong cultures present dangers. They can be simply a managerial ideology designed to serve the interests of those who exercise power within the organisation. They can run counter to the long-term performance needs of the organisation by blinding organisational members to the need for change. They can undermine ethical conduct by removing dissent and rational debate of issues.

Having identified the dangers of a powerful, uniform organisational culture, he goes on to identify the benefits of sub-cultural conflict within organisations. A sub-culture within an organisation can be defined as a sub-set of the organisation's members who identify themselves as a distinct group and who routinely act on the basis of collective understandings unique to that group. The prevailing approach described above sees sub-cultures as likely to undermine the dominant, unitary corporate culture. Sinclair argues that sub-cultural conflict can actually be beneficial to the organisation. It could enhance commitment to organisational goals if sub-cultural goals can be assimilated into the organisational purpose. It can help to prevent 'groupthink'. It can improve the overall performance of the organisation if its members have diverse norms and styles and it can help to prevent disasters by encouraging a critical approach to organisational management. Sub-cultural conflict can also stimulate ethical behaviour by preventing insulated or blinkered thinking on the part of the organisation's managers. However, sub-cultural conflict presents dangers to ethical behaviour. This is because it may develop into anarchy with no shared values across the organisation and a lack of perceived responsibility to the organisation as a whole.

These approaches to corporate moral excellence begin with models of ethical behaviour which offer rich insights into organisational life and often produce very practical approaches to the development of ethical behaviour within organisations. Having established, on the basis of principles or theory, the likely features of an ethical organisation, the next step is to consider ways in which such characteristics can be developed, embedded and encouraged within actual organisations.

There is considerable experience in the United States in the implementation of corporate ethics programmes and a great deal of guidance is given to managers about how to go about creating more ethical organisations. There are four major features of such advice and guidance, which rest upon a predetermined model of ethical organisations similar to those outlined above.

First is the need for an ethics audit – this is an exercise in self-assessment by the organisation, usually in response to a series of prepared questions dealing with major aspects of behaviour and operations within the organisation. Clutterbuck *et al.* (1992) identify three levels of audit: the policy level, the level of systems and standards, and the level of recording and analysing performance.

The second feature of advice and guidance is the need for publicly stated expectations about employee behaviour. There has been a proliferation of company codes of ethics in both European and US business over the last 20 years.

Third is the need for organisational structures to support ethical behaviour. For some organisations this has meant the creation of ethics committees with sometimes very wide-ranging powers. In others, it has meant the provision of confidential hotlines for whistleblowers.

Fourth is the need for ethical behaviour to be supported by the reward systems within organisations. Employees soon notice the difference between espoused values and values in practice. The ways in which an organisation responds to ethical or unethical behaviour are extremely potent influences on employees' perceptions and behaviour.

7   Ethics and Stakeholder Theory

A different approach to the problem of defining and developing ethical behaviour in organisations is provided by stakeholder theory. According to this approach, paying attention to the needs and rights of all the stakeholders of a business is a useful way of developing ethically responsible behaviour by managers. An ethical organisation is seen as one in which obligations to stakeholders figure prominently in the decision-making of managers within the organisation.

Stakeholder theory has a long tradition. John Donaldson (1992) writes that the term 'stakeholder' was created by Robert K. Merton in the 1950s and has enjoyed a vogue in recent years. Goodpaster (1983), on the other hand, states that the term appears to have been invented in the early 1960s as a deliberate play on the word 'stockholder', which is the American equivalent of the British 'shareholder'.

The Stanford Research Institute, in 1963, defined the stakeholder concept as including those groups without whose support an organisation would cease to exist. Its list of stakeholders originally included shareowners, employees, customers, suppliers, lenders and society. It was argued that unless business executives understood the needs and concerns of these stakeholder groups, they would be unable to secure the support necessary for the continued survival of the firm. Freeman (1984) widens the definition to 'any group or individual who can affect or is affected by the achievement of the organisation's objectives'.

Company law in Britain enshrines the view that the interests of shareholders of public companies take precedence over any other interests in the company. Companies are managed by those appointed by the board of directors who are themselves elected by shareholders to ensure that shareholders enjoy the largest possible return on their investment. The managers act as agents for the shareholders who are their principals. Of course, this bald assertion is not always the reality. James Burnham, writing in the 1940s, alerted others to the trend which he labelled 'the managerial revolution' (Burnham, 1945) and there have been many examples of boards of directors being taken to task by shareholders when they appear to have prioritised interests other than those of the shareholders – recent examples being those of Tiphook and Queens Moat House.

Stakeholder theory is an attempt to broaden the perception that there is one dominant interest – that of the shareholder – in public companies. It challenges the view that the primary or even sole purpose of a company is to maximise the return to shareholders. It does not directly challenge the Friedmanite view that businesses exist only to maximise profits. This is because a firm may aim to maximise its profits without necessarily maximising the return to shareholders. Conversely, a firm may maximise the return to shareholders without necessarily maximising its profits. Indeed, one of the concerns of theorists of the 'managerial revolution' tradition is that in many cases managers ensure maximum returns to themselves rather than to shareholders and that this is frequently done on the basis of business goals which are not focused on the maximisation of profits. Growth and market share are often the predominant objectives of managers. This may or may not lead to a maximisation of profits.

In challenging the predominant view, as enshrined in the legal codes of many societies, that the interests of shareholders have primacy, stakeholder theory introduces the notion that there are a variety of stakeholders in any business. The decisions of managers and boards of directors have an impact on many different groups, communities and individuals. Stakeholder theory asserts that companies have responsibilities and obligations beyond those to the shareholders.

But what kind of responsibility do organisations have to their stakeholders? Hosmer (1991) identifies five levels of managerial responsibilities: ethical, conceptual, technical, functional and operational. Ethical responsibilities include the distribution of benefits and the allocation of costs or harms created by the firm. Hosmer argues that if these functions are performed well the benefits and harms will be distributed in a way which stakeholders will see as right, proper and just. Ethical principles should be used to distribute benefits and allocate costs or harms because the decisions will be seen by stakeholders as ethical, and more acceptable, thus ensuring their continuing support.

However, there are significant differences within the tradition of stakeholder theory. The major differences revolve around the question 'How far do the responsibilities of companies extend?'

We have already looked at the Friedmanite view which holds that the role of business is to make profits and the only responsibility is to the shareholder. This view rejects the notion that there are any other stakeholders in business. A very different view is expressed by those who wish to argue that businesses do have wider social responsibilities. For example, in Britain, the work of New Consumer, a public interest research organisation, identifies a broad range of issues and stakeholders when describing the activities of many of Britain's major companies. Adams, Carruthers and Hamil (1991), writing on behalf of New Consumer, seek to evaluate company performance along dimensions such as disclosure of information, employment issues, pay, benefits and conditions, industrial democracy, equal opportunities, community involvement, environment, other countries, respect for life, political involvement, respect for people, oppressive regimes, military sales and marketing policy. There is an underlying assumption here that businesses have a very wide range of responsibilities and that many groups, including shareholders, have a stake in the business because they are affected by the actions of the business.

Between the Friedmannite and New Consumer approaches, there is a large gap. Raven (1994) draws a distinction between a narrow definition of stakeholders and a broader definition. The narrow definition would include the following groups as stakeholders: employees, shareholders, customers, suppliers, creditors and the local community. The wider definition would add the following: social activists, public interest groups, trade associations, local government, international organisations and society in general.

Some approaches include 'competitors' as stakeholders. This may seem rather strange at first sight but is worth exploring a little. There are many examples, particularly in the small business sector, of mutual interdependence between firms which are operating within the same industry. If a small garage, for instance, is presented with a repair job which requires specialist equipment it may be able to borrow the equipment from its 'competitor' around the corner. If it cannot cope with the repair it may recommend another of its 'competitors' to the customer. Collaboration with competitors is not unknown in big business. When several European companies combine their efforts to produce Airbus or the Channel Tunnel, it could be argued that they become stakeholders not only in that particular project but also in each other's future success. It is also the case that in entering into trade associations which are designed to protect and further the interests of businesses within a particular industry, competing businesses are acting on the assumption that their future success as individual businesses is intimately connected with the success of the industry, i.e. with the success of their competitors.

Stakeholder theory presents managers in business and other organisations with a significant challenge. Managing a business knowing that your primary responsibility is to the shareholders may not be easy, but at least it is likely to be a much less complex task than managing a business within the context of multiple claims from multiple stakeholders.

A significant challenge to the claim that stakeholder analysis is a way of introducing ethics into managerial decision-making comes from Goodpaster (1983). He argues that managers may carry out an analysis of stakeholder reactions to decisions for reasons which have little to do with ethics. They might be concerned that stakeholder reaction could impede the achievement of strategic objectives and that the effects of decisions on relatively powerless stakeholders might be ignored or discounted. Expanding the list of stakeholders who are taken into account may be a form of enlightened self-interest but Goodpaster doubts that it is really a way of introducing ethical values into business decision-making.

He also casts doubt on what he calls the 'multi-fiduciary view' of stakeholder analysis. This view argues that managers do not have only a single fiduciary duty to shareholders. They have multiple fiduciary duties to all stakeholders. If shareholders are the principals and managers act as their agents, which is a relationship that forms the basis of much of company law, then a major objection to the multi-fiduciary view is that the obligations of managers to shareholders takes precedence over all other obligations. The multi-fiduciary view imposes a neutrality on managers. They are required to be neutral regarding the competing interests of stakeholders and to produce decisions which effectively balance their competing claims. This neutrality undermines their moral responsibility, as agents, to act in the best interests of their principals, the shareholders.

The solution to this problem, for Goodpaster, lies in the argument that principals cannot expect of their agents behaviour that would be inconsistent with the reasonable ethical expectations of the community. The ethical challenges faced by managers are the same as those faced by other people. Goodpaster states: ' The foundation of ethics in management . . . lies in understanding that the conscience of the corporation is a logical and moral extension of the consciences of its principals. It is not an expansion of the list of principals.' Stakeholder analysis may assist managers in their strategic planning but it will not, of itself, introduce ethical considerations into their decision-making.

8 Ethics and Corporate Governance

Theories of corporate governance offer a further perspective on the characteristics of the ethical organisation. In his book *Management and Machiavelli* (1967), Anthony Jay draws a parallel between the large, modern public corporation and the independent or semi- independent states of the past. He feels that theories of government offer a way of fully understanding the behaviour of these large corporations. For Jay, management can only be properly studied as a branch of government.

Theories of government make use of concepts such as accountability, authority, power, consent, responsibility, policy-making and administration.

They are concerned to produce guidance about the best forms of government and the appropriateness of procedures of decision-making and execution. Classical theories of management (for example, Brech,1953) saw management as a process incorporating planning, control, organisation, delegation, responsibility and authority and accountability. They were concerned to improve the management of the modern large corporation and drew heavily on concepts developed in the study of government.

The connection between ethical behaviour and political or governmental processes are well established in the field of political philosophy. Aristotle, for example, saw a close link between his ethical theory and his political theory. He begins his discussion of ethics with the statement that every craft and every enquiry, and similarly every action and project, seems to aim at some good. He concludes that the good has been well defined as that at which everything aims. His discussion of ethics is followed by his treatment of politics. According to MacIntyre (1967), 'The *Ethics* shows us what forms and style of life are necessary to happiness, the *Politics* what particular form of constitution, what set of institutions, are necessary to make this form of life possible and to safeguard it.'

Theories of government applied to the large corporation can be expected, therefore, to be closely linked to a concern about ethical behaviour. Such theories tend to be labelled as theories of corporate governance. The use of the word 'governance' is partly based on fad or fashion but it emphasises the focus on the 'act, manner, function of government' (OED).

Before going on to examine some of the more significant aspects of corporate governance, it is important to note that for Aristotle and other major political theorists the formal mechanisms of government were produced and sustained by human action, and could therefore be changed by human action. There was nothing inevitable or necessary about particular forms of government. Also, the existence of a particular form of government was no guarantee of human happiness. People in positions of power and influence, within any system, needed to behave in ways which produced happiness, and this behaviour was shaped by their intentions which were in turn shaped by their values and beliefs.

The values and beliefs of those engaged in the processes of corporate governance are as significant in influencing their behaviour as are the formal procedures. Clearly, some procedures are more likely to produce ethical behaviour than others and discussions of problems in corporate governance do need to focus on issues of procedure, powers and responsibilities in a formal sense. However, the existence of formal procedures will not of themselves produce ethical behaviour.

Much of the literature on corporate governance is a response by businesses to problems of compliance with their obligations to their shareholders. Cannon (1992), for example, defines corporate governance as:

the sum of those activities which make up the internal regulation of the business in compliance with the obligations placed on the firm by legislation, ownership and control. It incorporates the trusteeship of assets, their management and their deployment.

This perspective on corporate governance sees senior managers as accountable to the owners of the business for the use of the firm's assets. The managers are stewards or trustees acting as agents on behalf of the owners of the assets. Cannon draws attention to the relationship between the poor performance of several large corporations and the increasing clamour during the late 1980s, and in the 1990s from shareholders who wished to be able to exert more control over those with responsibility for managing their companies.

This approach is based on the pursuit of the self-interest of the owners of the business. They are concerned to protect their investment and to enhance their income levels from share dividends. If their managers had performed well – in the sense of ensuring at least stable levels of income for shareholders – then concerns about corporate governance issues would be less likely to be raised.

This does not seem to be a very promising basis for the development of an ethical organisation. The argument is that changing the style and methods of corporate governance is justifiable because it will result in enhanced income for shareholders and that, therefore, one ought to be concerned about corporate governance and try to produce models of corporate governance reflecting this justification. Such an approach might produce ethical behaviour, or at least encourage it, but not intentionally. The intention is to produce enhanced income for shareholders through enhanced corporate performance.

A second perspective on corporate governance derives from a concern with the excessive pay increases which directors have received in the 1990s, the perks and conditions of senior executives and the golden handshakes received by executives leaving their organisations. The relationship between company performance and executive pay is perceived as having broken down. Despite relatively poor market performance, the pay of senior executives has outstripped that of middle and junior managers and of other employees. Many scandals have been reported in the media.

This concern has developed within the private sector and is particularly powerful in the newly privatised areas. It has also spread to the public sector. For example, the decision in 1994 of the Council of the University of Huddersfield, England, to offer a package amounting to over £500,000 to its retiring vice-chancellor was a subject of parliamentary investigation and, as a result, changes to the instruments and articles of government of the 'new' universities have been proposed. In this case, the vice-chancellor was retiring early following a bitter dispute over the representation of staff, students and the local community on the university's governing council. This dispute resulted in an overwhelming vote of no confidence in the governing council by the staff of the university.

In Britain, concern about corporate governance in the private sector led to the production of what became known as the Cadbury report. In 1991,the Financial Reporting Council, the London Stock Exchange and the accountancy professional bodies established a committee, chaired by Sir Adrian Cadbury, to examine the financial aspects of corporate governance.

The particular reasons for the establishment of the committee were based upon a concern about the lack of confidence in financial reporting and in the value of audits, which was heightened by several failures of major public companies, whose financial statements gave no forewarning of their true state of affairs. Interest in the work of the committee extended beyond what might have been expected from such a technical and fairly narrow brief and the work of the committee became a focus for a wide debate about issues of corporate governance in general.

The committee's report, published in 1992, presented a voluntary Code of Best Practice which is aimed at the boards of listed companies based in the UK. It argued for adequate disclosure of financial information and for checks and balances within the governance structure of companies. Their view was that disclosure of financial information was necessary to ensure that all those with a legitimate interest in a company have the financial information they need in order to exercise their rights and responsibilities towards it. They argued that openness by companies is the basis of public confidence in the corporate system.

The proposals in relation to checks and balances within the structure of a company were based on the view that they assist the directors in fulfilling their duty to act always in the interests of the company and guard against undue concentrations of power. These proposals included a recommendation that there should be a clear division of responsibilities at the head of a company between the chairman of the board of directors and the chief executive of the company. These roles should not be combined in one person. Recommendations to strengthen the role of the non-executive directors were made. These included having a formal process for their selection, that they should be independent of the management of the company, and that they should not have business interests which conflict with those of the company.

The report also proposed that the non-executive directors should form a Remuneration Committee to decide on the remuneration package of executives and that full details of remuneration packages should be disclosed in the annual reports of companies. The establishment of an Audit Committee was also proposed. This should have at least three non-executive directors. This was designed to bring greater objectivity into the auditing process and ensure greater public confidence in the published, and audited, accounts of public companies.

In June 1993 the London Stock Exchange introduced an obligation on listed companies to state in their annual reports whether they comply with the Code of Best Practice and to give reasons for any area of non-compliance. This Stock Exchange requirement does not mean that companies must comply with the Cadbury Report's recommendations. It requires only that companies make a statement about compliance. The committee took the view that it was in the best interests of companies to comply with the code as this would enhance their market standing. They also argued that non-compliance might lead to greater statutory control in the future. If companies could not be seen to comply with a voluntary code, the threat was that the government would feel obliged to introduce legislation to enforce compliance.

Theories of corporate governance focus attention on the policy and decision-making structures of large companies. They stem from a concern with the rights of shareholders and place responsibilities on directors and senior executives. They emphasise the need for openness in decision-making and for a clear demonstration that the company is being governed in accordance with perceived business virtues.

Judgements about undesirable business practices are usually based on a notion of business virtues. Clearly, perceptions of virtuous behaviour differ over time and place. Equally clearly, perceptions that some forms of business behaviour are unacceptable are based on a model or theory which indicates what is acceptable. These views arise from and exert great influence within the relevant community. Actions and behaviour can be labelled excessive or unacceptable only if the labellers have a standard by which to judge. The concerns about excessive secrecy in annual company reports, about a lack of suitable checks and balances within company decision-making structures, about the excessive power of the one person who combines the roles of chief executive and chairman of the board of directors, are all based on some commonly held standards which apply at the time the judgments are being made. These standards are based on what are seen as business virtues.

If an organisation adheres to the requirements of a code of best practice in relation to corporate governance, is it likely to be an ethical organisation? A board of a UK company may decide to implement fully the Cadbury Committee's recommendations but it does not mean that the company is an ethical organisation. It may still produce shoddy or dangerous goods, pollute the environment, impose adverse condition on its workforce or tell lies in its advertising. However, the following of a code such as that found in the Cadbury report is more likely than not to lead to a corporate governance regime with greater openness of information, less likelihood of domination by one or a few people and fewer excesses in the remuneration packages of senior executives.

Notes

1. The exceptions are those who cannot be agents because they lack, have lost or have still to acquire the relevant capabilities. This group might include infants, those in coma or with severe dementia or extreme learning difficulties.
2. 'Arguably', because the interpretation of Smith as a champion of untrammelled free enterprise is contested. See Smith (1976). Sen (1987) arhues that Smith's doctrine of the 'invisible hand' has, and was meant to have, a much more limited application than twentieth-century economic liberalism has supposed.
3. For a discussion of this point from an economist's point of view, see Chapter 9, below.
4. A phrase from T. Peters and R. Waterman (1982).
5. Those who profit from a situation without incurring the costs of maintaining it, (those who ride for free on a transport system maintained by those who buy tickets); in this case those who dishonestly exploit an honest market. (They could not, of course, continue to exploit the market once it became dishonest anymore than a transport system could continue if everyone managed to avoid buying a ticket.)

References

Adams, R., Carruthers, J. and Hamil, S. (1991) *Changing Corporate Values*, Kogan Page, London.
Baumol, W.J. and Batey Blackman, S.A. (1991) *Perfect Markets and Easy Virtue*, Blackwell, Oxford, ch. 1.
Burnham, J. (1945) *The Managerial Revolution*, Penguin, Harmondsworth.
Brech, E.F.L. (1953) *The Principles and Practice of Management*, Longman, London.
Chryssides, G.D. and Kaler, J.H. (1993) *An Introduction to Business Ethics*, Chapman & Hall, London.
Cadbury, A. (1992) *The Financial Aspects of Corporate Governance*, Stock Exchange, London.
Cannon, T. (1992) *Corporate Responsibility*, Pitmans, London.
Chadwick, R. (1993) 'Codes and Ethics – An Unhappy Alliance?', Conference on Professional and Business Ethics, University of Central Lancashire (unpublished).
Clutterbuck, D., Dearlove, D. and Snow, D. (1992) *Actions Speak Louder*, Kogan Page/ Kingfisher, London.
Danley, G. (1993) 'Corporate Moral Agency: The Case for Anthropological Bigotry', in Chryssides and Kaler (1993), pp. 279–86.
Deal, T. and Kennedy, A. (1982) *Corporate Cultures*, Addison-Wesley, New York.
Donaldson, J. (1992) *Business Ethics – A European Casebook*, Academic Press, London.
Freeman, R.E. (1984) *Strategic Management – A Stakeholder Approach*, Pitman, London.
Friedman, M. (1970) 'The Social Responsibility of Business is to Increase Its Profits', *The New York Times Magazine*, 13 September, 1970. Reprinted in Chryssides and Kaler (1993) pp. 249–54.
Friedman, M. and Friedman, R. (1980), *Free To Choose*, Avon Books, New York.
Goodpaster, K.E. (1983) 'The Concept of Corporate Responsibility', *Journal of Business Ethics*, vol. 2, pp. 1–22.
Handy, C. (1978) *Understanding Organisations*, Penguin, Harmondsworth.

Hayek, F. (1982) *Law, Legislation and Liberty, Vol. 2, The Mirage of Social Justice*, Routledge & Kegan Paul, London (first published 1976).

Hoffman, W. M. (1986) 'What is Necessary for Corporate Moral Excellence', *Journal of Business Ethics*, vol. 5, pp. 232–42.

Hosmer, L. T. (1991) 'Managerial Responsibilities on the Micro Level', *Business Horizons*, July/August, pp. 49–55.

Jay, A. (1967) *Management and Machiavelli*, Penguin, Harmondsworth.

MacIntyre, A. (1993) *A Short History of Ethics*, Routledge & Kegan Paul, London.

Nash, L. (1992) 'American and European Corporate Ethics Practices' J. Mahoney and E. Vallance (eds), in *Business Ethics in a New Europe*, Kluwer, Dordrecht.

Peters, T. J. and Waterman, R. H. (1982) *In Search of Excellence*, Harper & Row, New York.

Raven, W. (1994) *Considering Stakeholders' Interests*, Corporate Social Responsibility Consultants.

Sen, A. (1987) *On Ethics and Economics*, Blackwell, Oxford.

Sinclair, A. (1993) 'Approaches to Organisational Culture and Ethics', *Journal of Business Education*, vol. 12, pp. 63–73.

Smith, A. (1976) *An Inquiry into the Nature and Causes of the Wealth of Nations*, Oxford University Press, Oxford (first published 1776).

CHAPTER 8

Corporate Codes and Ethics

1 Introduction

According to Nigel Harris (1989) professional codes have increased in number nearly ten-fold in the last thirty years. At the same time, but especially since the mid 1980s, there has been a similar increase in the numbers of codes designed for the use of employees of a single company. Webley (1988 and 1992) surveyed 300 companies in the UK in 1988, and from 100 usable responses 55 had a company code. In 1992, he surveyed 400 of the largest companies in Britain, and from 159 usable responses he noted that 113 had codes. Langlois and Schlegelmilch (1990) surveyed 1,481 UK companies and, on a response rate of 25%, reported that 50.5% had codes of ethics, 22.8% had a policy statement on ethics and 42.6% had guidelines for the proper conduct of business.

In the USA, the numbers and percentage of companies with codes of ethics is higher than in the UK. Weaver (1993) reports two surveys which took place in 1992. In the first, 83% of the surveyed US companies had codes and only 50% of the surveyed European companies did. The second survey, focused on Fortune 1000 companies, reported that 93% had codes. Nash (1992), in a comparative survey of European and US companies, reported that, in the USA, corporate ethics activity was, in comparison to five years previously, more widespread, more sophisticated and moving deeper into the organisation. Many European firms, on the other hand, were still not attracted to formalised ethics statements and codes. In Europe, codes and ethics programmes appeared to be less frequent, newer, more dominated by large companies and more widely disseminated than in the USA: 83% of the US respondents and 50% of the European respondents had some kind of ethics document.

One reason for adopting a code of conduct may be a wish to be seen as self-regulatory in order to avoid regulation by government. This is a strategy adopted by the press, the stock market and the tobacco industry in regard to advertising. A second reason, connected to this, is a wish by a profession or a company to improve its image with the general public, or with its peers in the industry. Such reasons are clearly *prudential* in the sense that they are aimed at benefiting (or avoiding harm to) the company or profession in question. Some would argue (for example, see Chadwick 1993) that acting out of prudential motives is not to act morally[1]. However, some reasons for drawing up codes of behaviour are clearly moral in character. Professional bodies or companies may feel that there are special problems or particular temptations involved in the field in which they operate which ordinary moral judgement cannot cope with. Special advice and guidance may be needed in order to protect their members or employees from moral risk. And, in the end, they may feel the need for disciplinary sanctions against a minority for the sake both of the general public and their own members or employees. A code can also play a training role in inculcating and promoting the particular values and standards which characterise a profession or a company and which members or employees need to internalise in order to play a full role.[2]

So far what we have said applies indifferently both to professions and to companies. There are, however, obvious differences between professional and company codes in at least some respects. The first is that a company may employ members of many different professions as well as members of no professions at all. There is therefore a problem about *applicability*, i.e. to whom does the company code apply? Does it, on one level, apply to the chartered accountant currently a financial manager and director, who is also subject to the professional code of the Institute of Chartered Accountants? And, if it does, which is to take precedence should their requirements come into conflict with each other? On another level, does a company code, given that it is a code for corporate action, apply only to those empowered to act for and on behalf of the company, or to all those employed by the company in whatever capacity? Does it apply to consultants retained on a long-term basis, to sub-contractors or to satellite suppliers with no other outlets? Does it regulate only behaviour expected of its employees by the company, or does it also cover the behaviour of the company towards its employees? Company codes must recognise these problems and allow for some method of resolving them if they are not to be unworkable.

Company codes may be called codes of practice, codes of conduct, codes of ethics, mission statements or value statements. What difference there is between these may be characterised by increasing generality, in that codes of practice tend to be the most specific whereas value statements are the most general. Codes of practice and codes of conduct also tend to be the most prescriptive in tone (see Harris, 1989). But for the most part, the differences between them are less significant than the fact that they exist at all. What are they for, and why are they felt to be necessary? Isn't it true, as some might argue, that good people will not need the guidance of such a code and that the malicious, selfish or stupid will ignore it? In neither case, of course, will the existence of a code make any difference.

Such a position depends on the assumption that good people always know what to do, and that those who do the wrong thing always do so for reprehensible reasons. (It also, though this is more transparently false, depends on the assumption that we can divide people neatly into the good and the bad.) It is not always obvious what the right thing to do is, for ethics is more than a simple set of injunctions that any fool could grasp, and well-meaning people can often go astray for lack of experience or a momentary weakness which in other circumstances might have done no harm at all. We all need to know, or to work out, how general principles are to be made to apply to concrete particular cases. Different people may, in good faith and quite justifiably, come to different conclusions about the rightness of a particular act in particular circumstances, and in private life this may not matter. But in the public domain there is also a requirement of consistency which may force us to replace the workings of the individual conscience with a written code or an impersonal process. This may be needed not just to ensure (as far as it can) consistency of outcome, but also to protect those who must make judgements. In employment, for example, a judgement to promote a particular person may be totally defensible, but it has to be seen in the light of a company's record on promoting, say, women, or members of ethnic minorities. Those promoted, or not, have a right to be treated not just reasonably but equitably. And those who operate the procedures, so long as they operate them properly, must not be seen as personally responsible for the outcome.

One way, therefore, of seeing codes is by analogy with the law. Just as case law and rules of process are needed in order to make it possible for statute and common law to be implemented, so a code of practice mediates between general principles and particular cases. This is, at any rate, how they should operate. It is not, of course, how they always do. Sorell and Hendry (1994, pp. 14–15) point out some of the problems which can be caused by codes or mission statements which are so vague, general and uncontentious that, on the one hand, no one could possibly disagree with them, or, on the other, hope to get any real guidance from them as to what to do in a particular case. Chadwick (1993, p. 3) quotes the Johnson and Johnson organisation's 'We must provide competent management and their actions must be just and ethical' as an example of this. As inspirational rhetoric it may have a function, but as a basis for a code of ethics it is virtually useless without a detailed commentary.

2   The Development of Codes of Ethics

Many of those political and economic thinkers and practioners who claim an intellectual lineage back to Adam Smith may be surprised to learn that Smith himself was concerned to demonstrate the need for ethical values as an essential part of a market economy. He saw the role of moral values as one of exercising reasonable constraint on the single-minded pursuit of profit. It is interesting to note the widespread use of *The Wealth of Nations* as a traditional justification of rampant free-market policies and the almost total disregard for Smith's equally important, but much less influential, *A Theory of Moral Sentiments*.

In recent years, the concerns expressed by Smith have been echoed in the literature on company codes which has expanded considerably (see, for example, Webley, 1988; Donaldson, 1989; Campbell and Tawadey, 1992; Manley, 1992). Three major traditions can be detected in the literature:

- a concern for how businesses may make effective use of company codes with practical guidance on how to draw one up (see, for example, Clutterbuck *et al.*, 1992)
- a concern for the impact of company codes on business practice from a variety of perspectives (for example, Peters and Waterman, 1982; Hoffman, 1986: Drucker, 1981; Adams *et al.*, 1992)
- a concern to analyse company codes using theories of ethics (for example, Shaw and Barry, 1989).

All of these traditions have something to offer.

The philosophical basis for company codes appears to be eclectic in nature. Individual codes draw upon a variety of philosophical traditions combining utilitarian and deontological statements with those drawing on the Golden Rule and prudential approaches. The content of the codes often lacks philosophical consistency. This lack of consistency can, at least in part, be explained as a product of the circumstances in which the code is drafted and the positions of those responsible for drafting it.

Many codes are developed from a defensive posture by senior managers in the company and they tend to have a prudential tone with some basis in utilitarian theory. The example of Fiat is a case in point. After considerable damage to the international reputation of the company resulting from the revelations concerning the connections between the Mafia, big business and government in Italy, Fiat produced a code for its employees which lays down clear and enforceable rules concerning relations with government officials at all levels. The code ignores many other aspects of employee behaviour which have ethical implications. It was fashioned in particular circumstances for particular reasons.

Unilever provides a clear statement of a prudential approach in its company code, developed in circumstances very different from those of Fiat.

> The success or failure of a company – and Unilever is no exception – largely depends on its people, particularly its managers. Its reputation depends on the way its managers behave. (Unilever company code, 1981, p. 6)

Unilever's code reflects the company's position as a major multinational corporation. It contains statements about its support for the guidelines for international businesses produced by the OECD and ILO as well as those of the United Nations Commission on Transnational Corporations.

The Royal Dutch Shell Group of Companies provides a similar 'Statement of general business principles' (see Clutterbuck *et al.*, 1992, pp. 304–6). It recognises responsibilities to shareholders, employees, customers and society, asserts the importance of profitability and the benefits of a market economy, supports the OECD and ILO codes, requires honesty and integrity from its employees (any form of bribery is unacceptable), and declares itself as an abstainer from party politics. Running through the statement is a concern to be seen as a responsible citizen in all the countries in which it operates. This is a prime example of a code drawing upon a variety of different philosophical bases – Kantian duties for the workforce, prudential considerations for different Group companies in different parts of the world and a utilitarian approach to the market economy.

The Body Shop's code is in part based upon the Golden Rule:

We declare that:

1. The Body Shops goals and values are as important as our products and our profits.
2. Our policies and our products are geared to meet the needs of real people both inside and outside the company.
3. Honesty, integrity and caring form the foundations of the company and should flow through everything we do.
4. We care about each other as individuals: we will continue to endeavour to bring meaning and pleasure to the workplace.
5. We care about our customers, and will continue to bring humanity into the market place.
6. We care about humanising the business community: we will continue to show that success and profits can go hand-in-hand with ideals and values.

(Clutterbuck *et al.*, 1992, p. 303)

The Charter fits neatly with Body Shop's position as a leading supplier of 'ethical cosmetics' and clearly plays a significant role in its business strategy. It originates in the aims and views of the company's founder.

On the other hand, the code of British Gas plc reflects an overwhelming concern with vulnerability to allegations of impropriety (Clutterbuck *et al.*, 1992, pp. 306–8). It covers conflicts of interest, dealing in British Gas shares and those of other companies, purchasing and supplies, declarations of interest, gifts, and confidentiality of information. It warns employees that breaches of the code may result in disciplinary action and that they should seek the advice of their superiors if in doubt about any matter concerning conduct.

3   Company Codes and Managerial Control

Hosmer (1987) distinguishes between codes of ethics and rules of ethics. He sees ethical codes as 'statements of the norms and beliefs of an organisation' and as 'the ways in which the senior people in the organisation want others to think. This is not censorship. Instead the intention is to encourage ways of thinking and patterns of attitudes that will lead towards the wanted behaviour' (p. 153). He sees ethical rules as consisting of requirements to act in particular ways, as more than mere expectations or suggestions.

For many employees this distinction may appear to be a fine one, and company codes, in practice, tend to slip easily from being codes of ethics into becoming rules for behaviour. As defined by Hosmer, codes of ethics are produced by senior managers as a deliberate attempt to influence the ways in which others think. They are products of the managerial urge to control the behaviour of their subordinates. This applies with greater force to rules for behaviour.

Business codes, then, tend to have a strong imperatival nature in the sense that they expound the duties of the company and, especially, its employees. There is a clearly identifiable strand within the literature on business ethics which sees the use of a code of conduct as an important contributor to managerial control of employee behaviour. Shaw and Barry (1989) state the case for a corporate code of ethics very clearly: 'If those inside the corporation are to behave ethically, they need clearly stated and communicated ethical standards that are equitable and enforced' (p. 196).

Snoeyenbos and Jewell (1989) suggest that there are three elements in a successful strategy to institutionalise ethical behaviour. These are, first, the adoption of a corporate ethical code; second, the establishment of an ethics committee; and third, a management training programme which includes ethics training. All three elements are essential if the behaviour of company employees is to reflect well on the company itself.

Campbell and Tawadey (1992) perceive the benefits of a company having a sense of mission as follows:

> People are more motivated and work more intelligently if they believe in what they are doing and trust the organisation they are working with. . . If an organisation can provide meaning for an employee on top of pay and conditions, it will inspire the greater commitment and loyalty that we have labelled a sense of mission. (p. 6)

Other significant benefits include clarity of strategy, better decision making, clearer communication, and greater ease in delegation with lower costs of supervision.

Manley's (1992) comprehensive analysis of company codes identifies eighteen benefits of written codes. They are:

- providing guidance to and inculcating the company's values and cultural substance and style in managers and employees;
- sharpening and defining the company's policies and unifying the workforce;
- providing overall strategic direction;
- helping managers to deal with outside pressure groups;
- signalling expectations of proper conduct to suppliers and customers;
- delineating the rights and duties of the company, managers and employees;
- effectively responding to government pressures and rules;
- enhancing the company's public image and confidence;
- preempting legal proceedings;
- improving bottom-line results;
- enhancing the self-images of employees and improving the quality of new recruits;
- promoting excellence;
- realising company objectives;
- responding to stockholders' concerns;
- strengthening the British free enterprise system;
- encouraging open communication;
- integrating the cultures of acquired or merged companies;
- deterring improper requests of employees by supervisors and vice versa.

The underlying approach here appears to be one in which those who prepare, pronounce and protect the company code are in an active mode whereas those employees (usually below the level of senior management) who are faced with operational problems are passive recipients of the wisdom of their betters.

Although some of the companies which responded to his questionnaire indicated that employees were consulted and their views taken into account, Webley (1988) confirms the perception that a 'top-down' approach is the one most frequently found in the development of codes of ethics by British companies.

It seems likely to be the case that the recipients of the code and all the apparatus which goes with it will themselves have at least some beliefs on ethical issues or, at the very least, some general moral attitudes, which will affect their behaviour as much as the official code. Kitson (1994) reports that the managers within *The* Co-operative Bank appeared to interpret and apply the Bank's Ethical Policy in ways which reveal the mediating effect of their own values. Forsyth (1992) identifies four different moral philosophies amongst managers. They are differentiated along two dimensions – relativism and idealism. Forsyth produces the taxonomy shown in Table 8.1.

Managers with different moral philosophies will, Forsyth argues, react in complex but different ways from each other to the same objectively defined problem. The company ethical code, indeed any ethical code, will be more

TABLE 8.1   A taxonomy of personal moral values

Ideology	Dimensions	Approach to moral judgement
Situationists	High relativism High idealism	Reject moral rules; ask if the action yielded the best possible outcome in the given situation
Subjectivists	High relativism Low idealism	Reject moral rules; base moral judgements on personal feelings about the action and the setting
Absolutists	Low relativism High idealism	Feel actions are moral provided they yield positive consequences through conformity to moral rules
Exceptionists	Low relativism Low idealism	Feel conformity to moral rules is desirable but exceptions to these rules often permissible

Source: Forsyth (1992).

important for some than for others. It will be more important for those whose personal moral philosophy has some congruence with the values expressed in the company code.

This problem (of active and passive roles) can be looked at from a different perspective. It is possible to argue that any codification of ethics removes, at least in part, the personal autonomy which philosophers in the Kantian tradition argue is essential for any moral actor. One practical consequence is the 'loophole seeking' mentality. This is the antithesis of the behaviour normally stated as the expected outcome of company codes.

4   Who is being Protected by the Code?

Many companies state that their codes have been produced to help those employees who may be faced with a difficult ethical problem at work. Customers also frequently appear in company codes as the recipients of the intended ethical action. Sometimes the focus is on shareholders and on other occasions the target is society or the environment.

However, often unstated, the long-term interests of the company seem to represent the paramount cause for the production of the code and the audience appears to be influential sections of the public – mainly political and media groups and organisations.

Clutterbuck *et al.* (1992) identify the interests of the company as the prime reason for developing a code of ethics. Damage to the company's reputation is not, however, the only thing at risk. There is also the problem of the motivation of people in the company. Unethical behaviour may focus managers' attention on to short-term, pragmatic goals and lead to the exclusion of long-term objectives. Furthermore, a company engaging in unethical conduct towards customers, shareholders, suppliers or employees may encourage unethical behaviour towards itself. The case is stated with some force:

> The dilemma for top management is that it is expected to maintain an ethical climate, yet has only limited control over the hearts and minds of the people who work in the organisation. . . There are at least two major issues here:
>
> - how do executives keep themselves out of trouble?
> - how do they control the activities of perhaps thousands of individual employees, any one of whom may be mis-guided or mis-motivated into behaving in ways that may damage the corporate reputation? (Clutterbuck *et al.*, 1992, p. 269)

Senior executives are being encouraged to see the development of a code of ethics as a device for controlling their possibly unruly employees, as a way of keeping out of trouble and preserving the long-term future of their business.

Within the context of increasing political and public concern about (possibly) unethical behaviour (Guinness, Polly Peck, British Airways) and what appears to be a swing of the pendulum of public opinion away from the rampant free-market economic policy of the Thatcher years, not only do executives need to keep themselves out of trouble, they also need to be aware of a changing public mood in relation to unethical behaviour in business. Developing a code of ethics as a defensive measure in such a context seems to be a rational response. Whether such codes will bear the test of time remains to be seen.

5 Implementing Company Codes

There is a growing body of experience in the processes of implementing company codes and this practical experience is increasingly reflected in the literature on business ethics.

Ferrell and Fraedrich (1994) suggest that the implementation of strategies to encourage employees to make more ethical decisions is not very different from implementing other types of business strategies. They propose an approach to implementation based on four aspects: organisation, coordination, motivation and communication.

They assert that the structure of the organisation is a crucial influence on the implementation of an ethical policy and that authority should be delegated in such a way as to ensure appropriate levels of ethical performance. This may require, depending upon the particular circumstances of the company, greater centralisation or decentralisation.

Coordination involves 'arranging and synchronising the activities of all employees so that the company achieves its objectives efficiently, effectively and ethically' (p. 177). Coordination is needed to ensure that different parts of the organisation are not pursuing different ethical goals.

Motivating people to behave ethically involves applying the same principles of motivation that managers apply to other areas of employee performance. These include recognising that different people are motivated in different ways, and that modern employees are motivated by the quality of their work environment, their opportunities for personal growth, and the ethical performance of their companies. Job enrichment programmes are seen as providing motivation for such employees to improve their ethical decision-making.

Finally, communication by senior managers is essential to maintaining the ethical climate of a company and as an underpinning to effective coordination and motivation.

This approach to implementation seeks to incorporate ethical issues into the traditional management functions. It is heavily influenced by classical management theory. Classical management theorists (see, for example, Brech, 1953) identified a range of managerial functions and gave detailed guidance and advice on how these functions should be carried out. Ferrell and Fraedrich (1994) take the view that it is within these traditionally accepted managerial functions that ethical policies should be implemented.

MacDonald and Zepp (1989) adopt a more sophisticated approach to the problem of implementation. They propose an approach based on three perspectives – the individual dimension, group/peer influence and organisational strategies.

The individual dimension emphasises the need for individuals within the organisation to develop appropriate ethical values and sensitivity. MacDonald and Zepp assert that although individuals will possess different ethical values it is possible to enhance ethical behaviour through training programmes. They advocate a 'basic awareness programme' and specific ethical training programmes, based mainly on seminars focused on ethical dilemmas and encouraging the examination of the actual dilemmas faced by the managers participating in the programme. They refer to the work of Lickona (1987) who has provided specific strategies for corporate training programmes. Lickona advocates:

- the use of socratic questioning in order to isolate views and confront reasoning,

- creating open, integrative discussions,
- eliciting a full range of ethical views,
- utilising an experiential approach drawing upon the participants' own personal cases showing value conflict and ethical dilemmas,
- taking care not to present cases which continually show the most difficult choices and high levels of cognitive strain.

MacDonald and Zepp also argue that if a business is concerned about the ethical behaviour of their employees, it is easier to hire individuals with appropriate ethical standards than to try to change those of current employees.

The strong effect of peer influence on individual behaviour coupled with the frequent perception of peers as having lower ethical standards than themselves, may, according to MacDonald and Zepp, encourage individuals to behave unethically. They argue that greater understanding of the ethical values of one's peers, rather than unfounded perceptions, could help to make an individual feel more secure in his or her own value system. They advocate small group discussions on ethical issues but warn against the dangers of 'groupthink' which sometimes occurs with strongly cohesive groups. Mentor schemes are also seen as useful. Mentors can provide a private and confidential avenue for discussion and guidance.

Organisational strategies include the development of codes of ethics and ethical policy statements. However, they argue that it is ethical leadership rather than ethical policies or statements which is most effective in encouraging ethical behaviour throughout the organisation. The use of an ethical ombudsperson, with an investigative, counselling and advisory role is still unusual, but increasing, in large organisations. MacDonald and Zepp warn that such a person must be seen as independent and as having appropriate experience. More widespread, particularly in the United States, is establishment of Ethics Committees. These deal with policy formulation and sometimes with specific violations of the organisation's ethical code or complaints from employees and others. Reward and payment systems, which are often based on performance and output, may encourage unethical behaviour in the pursuit of a target. Reviewing reward systems may faciltitate a recognition of the need, on occasion, not to achieve a particular target if doing so would mean having to behave unethically.

Clutterbuck *et al.* (1992) offer very clear guidance in relation to the maintenance of an ethical climate. They suggest that senior managers should set an example through their behaviour, rather than by sending memos. Ethical issues should be on the board agenda and included in the annual report. Opportunities to demonstrate ethical commitments should be taken, the company should be active in charities and it should deliver the same messages internally and externally.

If a company does produce a code of ethics, it should ensure that its drafting is participatory, and all employees should receive a copy and be able to discuss its meaning and implementation. Performance against the code should be monitored. Monitoring takes several forms – requiring all managers to confirm that they have not deviated from the code and following this up with sample audits, asking non-executive directors to monitor compliance, establishing an ethics committee, giving the responsibility for monitoring to a senior manager.

Further proposals from Clutterbuck *et al.* include using the reward and punishment mechanisms to reinforce correct behaviour, recruiting ethical people, training, creating a framework for registering concern, and building openness into the workplace.

Manley (1992), based upon a detailed study of 125 British companies, argues that the following factors are crucial to the successful implementation of a code of conduct or similar policy document:

- management involvement and oversight;
- constant consciousness of those written, codified values and standards in recruiting and hiring;
- stressing code values and standards in educating and training employ-ees;
- recognition and tangible rewards for conduct which exemplifies desired values and standards;
- ombudsmen or other designated persons assigned to field employees' questions and reporting;
- thorough concentration on high-risk jobs and areas in terms of violating code values and standards;
- periodic certification and auditing to assure compliance with those code values and standards;
- well defined and fair enforcement procedures, including sanctions.

There is, then, a significant body of experience and guidance in relation to the implementation of codes of ethics developed by organisations. The process of implementation or ensuring compliance with the code is not the last thing to think about in the process of developing the code. The style and approach taken to implementation are often implicit in the process of development. The implementation of a code which is produced as a quick reaction to a controversy (for example, the British Airways case) will be very different from one which is produced following a lengthy and exhaustive process of consultation both within and outside the organisation (as with *The Co-operative Bank*). Those responsible for the coordination and leadership of the processes leading to the production of the code need to be aware of the problems of implementation from the very beginning of the process. Producing a code which cannot be effectively implemented is an act of cynicism.

The process of production should replicate the values which are being codified and lay the basis for implementation. Process and product are inextricably intertwined.

The crucial issue here is that of ownership. Some managers seem to define teams as 'lots of people doing what I want them to do'. Organisations with codes of ethics may define ethical behaviour as that which is in accordance with their code. If, however, the code has not been developed through prolonged and extensive discussion it is unlikely to reflect the ethical views of the people affected by it. The process of discussion and debate can help to produce a code which is understood by more people and owned by more of them than is likely to be the case if a code appears overnight as a management bulletin. The process of development of the code is an opportunity for people in the business to collectively come to some sort of agreement (total agreement may be undesirable as well as unlikely) about the basic values of the business and how to resolve at least some of the ethical issues faced in business.

Of course, such discussion may be seen by senior managers as something of a luxury when, for rational purposes, they need to develop a code very quickly. However, once a code, any code, has been published there is then an opportunity to initiate widespread and effective discussions, provided there is a genuine willingness to adapt it, which could lead eventually to a more open and rational discussion of ethical problems and a greater degree of ownership of the code (suitably amended). It seems that the choice facing companies with a code is either to allow it to ossify, in which case it will fall into disrepute sooner rather than later, or to see the code as merely a starting point in a long-term development – indeed as a significant part of strategic planning.

6   Conclusion

There is a real risk that codes may exist only on paper and not in practice. Where this is true then there will be justice in the cynic's claim that codes are for impressing outsiders and not meant to affect the behaviour of the company or its employees. For codes must not only be explicit and sufficiently detailed, they must also be internalised by those to whom and by whom they will be applied. In the end, a code which is to be worthy of the name must be embodied in the behaviour and the practices of the relevant group of people. This means that actually producing the written part of the code is only one part. The other part is implementing it, and this is something which cannot be done just once. It must be a continuous process. To succeed, a code must be the result of satisfying (at least) the following three conditions:

1. it must be the result of an extensive period of research, consultation and discussion by, on behalf of and between all affected parties;

2. it must be owned by all who are affected by it and not merely imposed by executive fiat;
3. it must be backed by a programme of staff development and training which is on-going and which opens the code up to amendment in the light of experience.

Notes

1. Though this is a distinction more easily made than defended.
2. A good example of this is the, somewhat inspirational, Charter of the Bodyshop and the role it plays in staff development.

References

Adams, R., Carruthers, J. and Hamill, S. (1992) *Changing Corporate Values*, Kogan Page, London.

Brech, E. F. L. (1953) *The Principles and Practice of Management*, Longmans, Green & Co., London.

Campbell, A. and Tawadey, K. (1992) *Mission and Business Philosophy*, Butterworth Heinemann, Oxford.

Chadwick, R. (1993) 'Codes and Ethics – An Unhappy Alliance?', unpublished paper, conference on Professional and Business Ethics, University of Central Lancashire.

Clutterbuck, D. *et al.* (1992) *Actions Speak Louder*, Kingfisher/Kogan Page, London.

Donaldson, J. (1989) *Key Issues in Business Ethics*, Academic Press, London.

Drucker, P. F. (1981) 'What is Business Ethics?', *The Public Interest*, Spring.

Ferrell, O. C. and Fraedrich, J. (1994) *Business Ethics*, Houghton Mifflin, Boston.

Forsyth, D. R. (1992) 'Judging the Morality of Business Practice: The Influence of Personal Moral Philosophies', *Journal of Business Ethics*, vol. 11.

Harris, N. (1989) *Professional Codes of Conduct in the U.K.: A Directory*, Mansell, London.

Hoffman, W. M. (1986) 'What is Necessary for Corporate Moral Excellence', *Journal of Business Ethics*, vol. 5, pp. 233–42.

Hosmer, L. T. (1987) *The Ethics of Management*, Irwin, New York.

Kitson, A. (1994) 'Managing Ethics: The Case of *The* Cooperative Bank', *European Case Clearing House*, no. 494–009–1.

Langlois, C. C. and Schlegelmilch, B. B. (1990) 'Do Corporate Codes of Ethics Reflect National Characteristics? Evidence from Europe and the United States', *Journal of International Business Studies*, pp. 519–39.

Lickona, T. (1987) 'What Does Moral Psychology Have to Say to the Teacher of Ethics?', in D. Callahan and S. Bok (eds), *Ethics Teaching in Higher Education*, Plenum Press, New York.

MacDonald, G. M. and Zepp, R. A. (1989) 'Business Ethics – Practical Proposals', *Journal of Management Development*, vol. 8, no. 1, pp. 55–66.

Manley, W. W. (1992) *The Handbook of Good Business Practice*, Routledge, London.

Nash, L. (1992) 'American and European Corporate Ethics Practices: A 1991 Survey', in J. Mahoney and E. Vallance (eds), *Business Ethics in a New Europe*, Kluwer, Dordrecht.

Peters, T. J. and Waterman, R. H. (1982) *In Search of Excellence*, Harper & Row, New York.

Shaw, W. and Barry, V. (1989) *Moral Issues in Business*, Wadsworth, Belmont.

Snoeyenbos, M. and Jewell, D. (1989) 'Morals, Management and Codes', in Snoeyenbos *et al.* (eds), *Business Ethics*, Prometheus Books, New York.

Sorell, T. and Hendry, J. (1994) *Business Ethics*, Butterworth Heinemann, Oxford.

Weaver, G. R. (1993) 'Corporate Codes of Ethics: Purpose, Process and Content Issues', *Business and Society*, vol. 33, no. 1, p. 46.

Webley, S. (1988) *Company Philosophies and Codes of Business Ethics: A Guide to Their Drafting and Use*, Institute of Business Ethics, London.

Webley, S. (1992) *Business Ethics and Company Codes*, Institute of Business Ethics, London.

CHAPTER 9

Markets and Morality

1 Introduction

Is there any link between markets and morality? Is it really possible or even sensible to talk of any link between them? Isn't the role of markets to bring about economic efficiency? And isn't efficiency the only 'legitimate' criterion to be applied to markets' own working? To discuss morality in relation to markets is surely to confuse issues and misunderstand markets' intrinsic nature and significance, and hence is not only inappropriate but also potentially harmful to their proper functioning?

It is clear, runs this general argument, that to burden markets with any consideration other than the pursuit of economic efficiency – considerations such as equity, income distribution, justice, fairness, trust, honesty – is only likely, if not bound, to distort their operation, interfering with and damaging to efficiency. For there is an obvious trade-off between economic efficiency and any other value-criterion. Similarly, and as Milton Friedman (1962) argues, to impose on business any duty other than that of making money 'shows a fundamental misconception of the character and nature of a free economy', in which 'there is one and only one social responsibility of business – to use its resources and engage in activities designed to increase its profits so long as it stays within the rules of the game, which is to say, engages in open and free competition, without deception or fraud.' In other words, it is not merely that firms, as an empirical matter, *will* aim simply to maximise their profits due to their natural and strong impulse to gain or make money – i.e. in accordance with the 'profit motive'. Rather, as Friedman and mainstream neoclassical economists maintain, firms *ought* to maximise profits as their own and only social obligation or moral duty, with the only (moral) constraint of *playing by the rules of the game.*

An extreme view of what the rules of the game are is that of Albert Carr in his renowned article 'Is Business Bluffing Ethical?' (1968). Carr argues that 'business, as practised by individuals as well as by corporations, has the impersonal character of a game – a game that demands both special strategy and an understanding of its special ethics'. And 'the ethics of business is game ethics, different from the ethics of religion', and indeed with its own norms and rules different from the rest of society. To better illustrate this point, he uses the poker analogy. The game of poker

> calls for distrust of the other fellow. It ignores the claim of friendship. Cunning deception and concealment of one's strength and intentions, not kindness and open-heartedness, are vital in poker. No one thinks any the worse of poker on that account. And no one should think any the worse of the game of business because its standards of right and wrong differ from the prevailing traditions of morality in our society.

Thus, in the business game, as in poker, it is right and proper to bluff in order to win, provided the bluffs are 'ethically justified', with the justification resting on the very nature and rules of the game. And 'an occasional bluff may well be justified in terms of the game's ethics and warranted in terms of economic necessity'. Indeed, 'A man who intends to be a winner in the business game must have a game-player's attitude.' And, according to Carr, although sound business strategy does not necessarily run counter to ethical ideas and they may even frequently coincide, 'the major tests of every move in business, as in all games of strategy, are legality and profit', not ethics.

The assumption of profit maximisation is the assumption underpinning the neoclassical economic theory of the firm; likewise the assumption of utility maximisation underpins consumer theory. Thus according to the theory, the rational pursuit of maximum profits and maximum utility, by firms and consumers respectively, is the only (and hence proper) perspective for them to adopt in their own decision-making and economic interaction, i.e. the only relevant goal to be pursued. And it is, moreover, socially desirable, since it is only in this way that the fundamental and primary goal of economic efficiency can be achieved, and economic well-being can be maximised.

In conclusion, according to this line of argument, morality has no place in the market. Economics and ethics have nothing much to do with one another: economics may be relevant to policy but its relevance is purely technical, with ethics determining the ends and economics the means. (Hausman and McPherson, 1993, offer a lucid exposition of this view, as well as an excellent critical discussion of it.) Indeed, as neoclassical economists, supporters of the free-market *laissez-faire* economy, claim, the market is a morally neutral and beneficent institution, 'colour-blind' and 'accent-deaf' and so a neutral arbiter (neither just nor unjust) in the active resolution of conflicts of interest. Moreover, as David Miliband (1993) notes, the market is assumed to be a natural institution – with its existence claimed to be antecedent to society – and thus governed by unchanging rules.

Contrary to this position, many economists and others insist that economic markets, far from being ethically neutral (amoral and apolitical) and natural, are in fact historico-socio-political and culural institutions, which reflect and are influenced by the morality of individuals and society as a whole. In other words, according to this alternative view, the morality of economic agents (consumers, firms, policy-makers) does influence their behaviour and economic choices – as it may influence both their preferences and constraints – and does hence influence economic outcomes. Therefore, markets and morality cannot be divorced.

2 Neoclassical Economic Theory: Economic Man, Efficiency and Markets

The neoclassical paradigm is a utilitarian (hedonistic and self-centred), rationalist and individualist ethical theory. The individual agent at the centre of the theory, *homo economicus*, is a selfish, rational, utility-maximiser, who acts independently and non-cooperatively, and whose behaviour is strictly motivated by narrow self-interest. Economic man is a totally unemotional and coolly calculating human being, supposedly amoral and asocial – albeit he often appears to be rather immoral/unethical and markedly anti-social – and his view of other individuals is a mirror image of his own.

In a more extreme version, which seems to dominate modern economics, the troublesome activities of *homo economicus* include, in Oliver Williamson's (1985) words, 'the full set of *ex ante* and *ex post* efforts to lie, cheat, steal, mislead, disguise, obfuscate, feign, distort and confuse'. Thus, the new economic man appears to be living in Hobbes' 'state of nature', i.e. in a permanent state of war, where *homo homini lupus* and where life is 'solitary, poor, nasty, brutish, and short' (1651).

Beside this characterization of *homo economicus*, neoclassical economic theory makes several other crucial assumptions. Individual subjective preferences are given, i.e. fixed, exogenously determined, set or stable. The individual derives utility or satisfaction from consumption of goods and services and from leisure. Hence work is a 'disutility', a pain necessary to earn the pleasures of income and leisure. The individual (consumer or producer) is the decision-making unit, each individual atomistically pursuing his/her own self-interest. Society is simply and only the sum of individuals. Economic acts are not to be morally judged. According to the accepted 'means–end' scheme, acts/means are rationally selected to realise goals/ends, and their selection is based on positive (rational, logical/empirical) ground, and not on normative (ethical/prescriptive, value-judgemental) ground. (This latter point is strictly linked to the emphatic distinction that is generally made between positive and normative analysis, hence dismissing the fact that the two are often intermingled, and at the same time insisting that economics is, as a science, a positive discipline.)

This theoretical framework gives rise to several highly controversial explanations and predictions of economic phenomena, behaviours and outcomes. First, cheating and betrayal on the part of economic agents are to be expected, since greed and mistrust are individuals' inherent traits, and hence widespread phenomena of non-cooperation and coordination failure will result. Therefore, individuals will tend to be locked into 'Prisoner's Dilemma' game situations (see Chapter 1, section 2) and will invariably choose the mutually costly defection strategy, rather that the mutually beneficial cooperation strategy; This will result in an inefficient, sub-optimal, equilibrium outcome. Also, individuals will tend naturally to 'free-ride' whenever the opportunity arises, and hence, unless forced to do so they will never voluntarily contribute to the public good; here, the result will be private inefficient under-provision of public goods. In other words, altruism and cooperation cannot be expected from economic men.

Second, efficiency (allocation of resources) is the main, if not the only, criterion of economic valuation, and hence equity (distribution of resources) is mostly ignored. That is, the income distribution problem as well as fairness and social justice considerations are to be left to politicians. Third, an idealised view emerges of competitive, unregulated, free markets as capable of achieving – with the (providential) help of Adam Smith's *Invisible Hand* – an efficient, Pareto-optimal and hence socially desirable economic outcome. Also, the over-emphasis on the virtues and merit of competition and markets implies, as the other face of the coin, a negatively biased view of state or government intervention, not only as not required (for free markets, if not interfered with, eventually lead to an optimum competitive equilibrium solution), but also as likely to be harmful – i.e. the 'more harm than good' philosophy in relation to any government intervention in the economy.

Neoclassical economics can, however, be challenged both on theoretical and empirical grounds, and in economic, social and moral terms. Theoretically, each of its basic assumptions can be legitimately questioned, from the presumed nature of human beings as essentially selfish, rational, utility-maximising economic agents (rather than more complex and morally responsible creatures); to their allegedly unexplicable subjective tastes or preferences (rather than being affected by moral values and social factors); to their presumed conception of work as a pain to be endured in exchange for the pleasure of income (rather than as a major source itself of individual satisfaction); to their presupposed standing in isolation and fierce competition with each other, and having no sense of community or society; to their presumed-to-be purely instrumental rational acts, not to be subjected to moral appraisal. Moreover, individuals' proclaimed self-interested and non-cooperative behaviour need not be accepted or justified, or indeed legitimised and fostered by the alleged neutrality of the theory.

Similarly, the nearly exclusive emphasis on efficiency as the criterion for economic assessment may well be challenged, for efficiency is as much a normative notion as equity is, i.e. is a value itself; and, as Joseph Stiglitz (1993) stresses, issues of efficiency and equity cannot be separated, for the distribution of income matters for economic efficiency, and greater income equality may well increase economic efficiency, and 'the neat dichotomy between distribution and efficiency that characterised neoclassical economics is not, in general, valid', nor is, in general, valid the claim of a conflict or trade-off between efficiency and equity. As Hausman and McPherson (1993) note, citing Fred Hirsch (1977) and others, 'economic efficiency and economic policy depend crucially upon ethical values which may be undermined by the development of market economies'.

Also, the utopian view of the competitive unfettered market economy, as the most efficient, productive and hence morally preferable economic system, can be disputed at a theoretical and practical level. One may ask whether the overall picture of the *laissez-faire* economy is an internally coherent and realistic one, or whether it is not in fact intrinsically flawed, given that some among the numerous conditions required for its working seem to contradict others, or at least undermine the feasibility of some other, even from a purely 'allocative efficiency' perspective. Arguably, the most crucial and questionable tenet of the theory concerns the 'labour market'. The presumed self-regulating tendencies of a totally free and flexible labour market, with the wage naturally finding its 'market-clearing' level and hence eliminating unemployment, rests on a highly disputable view of labour as a 'commodity', no different from any other. That is, the alleged efficiency of a flexible, deregulated labour market – not hindered by 'rigidities' – is based on a conception of it as a purely economic institution, rather than also, or even more, a social and moral one. For workers are not commodities but human beings and so their interaction with employers cannot be interpreted as the usual interaction of supply and demand in a typical 'good' market. Moreover, even if one were to abstract from the highly unrealistic and questionable content of the theory's assumptions, and concentrate on its value in terms of its predictive power – as Friedman (1962) would insist -, one might still be disappointed by the theory's limited capacity to generate valid predictions and by its more frequent tendency to generate incorrect ones.

Furthermore, one may ask whether the *laissez-faire* capitalist system does indeed promote competition – a crucial feature of its very existence – or whether in effect it also calls for protective measures. Does it breed oligopolies and monopolies by naturally leading to a concentration of property and hence resources and power, as famously argued by Karl Marx? In fact, an analysis of mature capitalist economies seems to call into question their effective level of competition, by pointing instead to strong monopolistic tendencies.

Finally, one may ask whether the urge and need for profitability and the tendency toward a concentration of power in competitive markets lead to an exploitation and alienation of workers, i.e. of the 'proletariat' by the capitalists, or 'bourgeoisie', as well as leading to the exploitation of consumers and society by producers and the corporate sector in particular. This latter effect could be said to be created by the consumerist, materialistic society, or by what Hirsch (1977) has called a 'commodity bias': 'a commodity fetishism in the fundamental sense of excessive creation and absorption of commodities and not merely an undue conceptual preoccupation with them in the original sense of Marx – a masking of social relationships under capitalism by their mediation through commodity exchange.' This is linked, Hirsch argues, to a 'commercialisation effect', i.e. the increasing commercialisation of life with the growing substitution of commercial market exchange for social convention, and which 'feeds on itself in a way that may retard rather than advance social welfare'. A similar argument is that of the 'materialisation of society' as a result of business self-interestedly propagating a certain view of humanity and the good life, as argued for example by Paul Camenisch (1981).

Thus, rather than supporting the assumption of 'consumer sovereignity', or, better, of the sovereignity of consumer purchasing power, this argument holds that the 'logic of the market', in an advanced capitalist economy, is more likely to lead to overt 'consumer exploitation', with a crucial role played by advertising and marketing. The result is over-consumption, since business's (selfish) goal is to maximise profits and hence consumption, which is, though, opportunistically alleged to maximise human well-being. For in the logic of the market, and according to neoclassical economic theory, individual welfare is identified with consumption and in turn with subjective wants, rather than with objective needs.

3   Social Responsibilities of Business

In an influential article, 'Social Responsibility and Economic Efficiency', Kenneth Arrow (1973) discussed the limits of the social desirability of profit maximisation and the need for the social responsibility of firms. Thus, 'Under the proper assumptions profit maximisation is indeed efficient' in the Pareto-optimality sense, with the first and foremost assumption being that of 'perfect competition'. But the forces of competition may be weak and so competition may be highly imperfect, in which case, and in particular in the case of monopolies, there is no social justification for profit maximisation. Also, a competitive unrestrained maximising economy may well be efficient, but it also leads to a very unequal income distribution, with a socially undesirable and/or unacceptable gap between rich and poor. Moreover, altruistic motives are not sustained, and may in fact be discouraged, by profit-maximising, self-centred economic behaviour. But, as Arrow argues, 'a great deal of economic life depends for its viability on a certain limited degree of ethical commitment. Purely selfish behaviour of individuals is really incompatible with any kind of settled economic life.' In other words, the narrow pursuit of individual self-interest may indeed result in a less efficient economy, for in almost every economic exchange transaction some element of trust and confidence is required.

Setting aside these problems, there are two additional situations which, as Arrow notes, greatly undermine the economic efficiency and social desirability of profit maximisation. The first and well-known case is that of *externalities,* such as pollution or congestion, where society's economic welfare and social justice require that firms 'internalise' the negative (unintended) side-effects or by-products of their economic activities, which are spilling over to third parties. Yet, a pure profit-maximising behaviour on the part of firms can only lead to their natural tendency to overlook the social costs imposed on others. Hence, in the presence of externalities, a competitive free-market economy will result in an inefficient allocation of resources, since externalities do not have a market or a price. The second, also well-known and common situation is that of *imperfect* or *asymmetric information* between firms and consumers about the quality or safety of products. A critical assumption for economic efficiency is perfect or full information among the parties to the transaction, but this assumption is clearly violated in many instances where the seller has considerably more knowledge about his product than the buyer. The most famous example is that of the 'second-hand car market', also known as the 'market for lemons', which exhibits an asymmetry of information with the buyer at a clear disadvantage. (Conversely, in insurance markets the information asymmetry works against the seller of insurance policies: it is insurance companies which face 'adverse selection' and 'moral hazard' problems, for insured individuals may well know more about their risk situation, with people with the highest risk being the most likely ones to buy insurance, and also with individuals once insured possibly changing their behaviour so increasing the likelihood of the insured event to occur at their financial advantage.)

The two situations considered are important cases of *market failure* – when free unrestrained markets fail to achieve allocative efficiency. More generally, market failure arises in relation to imperfect competition and monopoly, externalities and public goods, imperfect (asymmetric) and costly information, and all types of 'missing markets' associated with time, risk and uncertainty, and informational problems. In addition, two socially undesirable effects of a competitive, profit-maximising, free-market economy have also been underlined: high levels of income inequality and a decline in altruism, trust and confidence, effects which can both lead in the long run to economic inefficiency.

The above discussion thus points to the need, as well as providing a rationale, for government intervention in the economy, to correct for market distortions and improve economic performance. In other words, the analysis supports the view that the 'visible hand of government' is required alongside the 'invisible hand' of markets, due to the limits of the 'invisible hand' in promoting the general good. This view is also defended by those, like Kenneth Galbraith, who maintain that firms' social role is purely economic and should not be seen as moral, and that, as economic institutions, firms are hence quite properly profit motivated. But, as Shaw and Barry (1989) note, by recognising that 'what is profitable is not necessarily socially useful or desirable; and what is socially useful and desirable is not always profitable', such arguments call for the strong hand of government, via regulations, to control firms'natural and insatiable appetite for profit', so as to reconcile society's conflicting interests and to guard and promote society's moral values and ideals.

State/government intervention can clearly take many forms, ranging from direct provision of goods and services, to the use of taxes and subsidies, laws and regulations and various economic incentives. The type and extent of government intervention in the economy is a highly controversial issue. Also controversial is whether any type of intervention is, in theory and/or in practice, desirable and likely to improve upon free-markets' economic outcome. However, and as Arrow (1973) argues, in situations in which profit maximisation is socially inefficient and undesirable, it is also clearly desirable for firms 'to have some idea of social responsibility, that is, to experience an obligation, whether ethical, moral, or legal'. But to be meaningful, any such social responsibility or behavioural role of firms should, according to Arrow, be institutionalised through the establishment of stable ethical codes.

In discussing business's social responsibilities, one may ask what exactly these social responsibilities are. However, it is evident that there is no general consensus, but indeed an intense controversy, over the issue. And a main reason for the lack of consensus seems to be a disagreement about the nature of the business firm itself. In fact, alternative views on the type and extent of a firm's social responsibilities reflect differing underlying views on what a company is and which individuals or groups have claims on it. In general terms, it seems possible to distinguish two main positions on the social responsibilities of business: a narrow view and a broader view. The latter can, in turn, be subdivided into two versions: a narrowly broad view and a very broad view.

The _narrow view_ – which is strongly advocated by Milton Friedman (1962) and Theodore Levitt (1958) – contends that the sole social responsibility of business is 'profit maximisation'. Thus, firms ought to maximise profits, for it is their moral duty to do so, and in pursuing their own interests they will moreover maximise society's overall economic welfare, as if led by the 'invisible hand'. The only restraint on firms' pursuit of profits is to play by the rules of the game, that is, as Friedman says, without deception and fraud and in general obeying the law. Underpinning this narrow view is a conception of the firm that Ronald Dore (1993) has called *the property view* – which is 'the dominant one among business practitioners in the Anglo-Saxon world', and which sees the firm as a legal entity. In Dore's words, 'A company is an entity set up by its members to further their own material interest; the managers are their agents with a duty to give priority to that shareholder interest.' There is hence a 'promissory' relationship between managers and shareholders according to which managers' only obligation is to the firm's 'owners' (to make profits) and which is inconsistent with any other social responsibility.

The _broader view_ insists, in contrast, that firms have other social responsibilities in addition to profit maximisation. In particular, according to the *narrowly broad view*, firms have social responsibilities to various groups that are directly financially connected to them: consumers, employees, shareholders, and suppliers, including possibly also businesses' competitors. The concept of the firm underlying this view can be said to be what Ronald Dore calls *the arena view* – which is the 'one favoured among academic analysts. . . The firm is seen as an arena in which individuals or groups of individuals (. . .usually referred to as stakeholders) make, often implicit, contracts of various kinds.' Consequently, firms have a variety of obligations grounded in their various relationships. Finally, according to the *very broad view*, business's social responsibility is not only to all relevant stakeholders and concerned connected groups, but also to the community or society in general, as well as to the environment. Thus, firms should refrain from socially undesirable behaviour and contribute actively and directly to the public good. In other words, business's obligation is, as Ferrell and Fraedrich (1994) put it, 'to maximise its positive impact on society and to minimize its negative impact.' The reason for extending firms' social responsibilities to include all possible effects on society is, according to this view, that firms, and especially big corporations, have very great economic and social power. Thus, in return for granting companies their legal status as separate entities, society is entitled to expect from them a significant net positive contribution to the general good. Firms are seen as certainly playing a vital role in society, but also as being major players with correspondingly major obligations to discharge.

The distinction between the narrow view and broader view of firms' social responsibilities somewhat overlaps with the other distinction of narrow versus broad business ethics – concerning the rules, standards and moral principles that guide behaviour in the world of business. In fact, the two concepts of business ethics and social responsibility are closely linked: 'narrow business ethics' encompasses both the narrow view and narrowly broad view of social responsibility, while 'broad business ethics' broadly coincides with the very broad view of business's social responsibility.

A more precise conceptualisation of business's social responsibility includes, following Ferrell and Fraedrich (1994), four types of responsibilities: *economic* and *legal*, both of which society requires of business; *ethical*, which society expects from business; and *voluntary/philanthropic*, which society desires from business. The four types of responsibilities are moreover listed according to their standing in Archie Carroll's (1991) pyramid of social responsibility, with the economic ones as the building block of the pyramid, the foundation for all business activities upon which all other levels of responsibility rest. Specifically, the economic responsibilities are to produce goods and services that society needs and wants and to be profitable. The legal ones require business to obey the established laws and regulations that reflect society's codification of what is right and wrong, i.e. to play by the rules of the game. The ethical ones relate to business's obligation to do what is right, just and fair, and avoid harm, i.e. to behaviours or activities that are expected of business, albeit not codified in law. The voluntary/philanthropic ones refer to business's contributions of financial and human resources to the community and society to improve the quality of life and the welfare of society, such as charitable givings or support to community projects.

Clearly, the narrow view of firms' social responsibilities includes only the economic and legal dimension of social responsibility, with the other two dimensions seen as falling outside the proper sphere of business activity. Indeed, the latter dimensions should, according to the narrow view, be actively opposed as potentially seriously damaging to business's proper function and hence to society's economic efficiency.

Two additional questions could be raised in relation to firms' social responsibilities. The first is whether business's social responsibility is in the business's interest. More precisely, is ethical business good business? Is it in the firm's self-interest, and is it in fact 'enlightened self-interest'? The second is whether the business activity itself should not constitute the primary concern of a business ethics or social responsibility perspective.

As to the first question, according to Friedman (1962) and Levitt (1958), it is obvious that corporate social responsibility is not in the firm's interest and is indeed bad for business. Thus, despite any temptation to describe or rationalise some business activities as an exercise of social responsibility, any such activities can only be intended to promote the firm's long-run interest and are hence entirely justified in the firm's own self-interest. Only profit maximisation can and should motivate business actions. For, in line with the neoclassical utilitarian framework, rational economic agents' behaviour is strictly driven by self-interest; or, in the terms of game theory, businessmen must have a game-player's attitude, as Carr (1968) argues. Indeed Carr's position is similar, if only more radical: 'The illusion that business can afford to be guided by ethics as conceived in private life is often fostered by. . .such phrases as, "It pays to be ethical", or, "Sound ethics is good business". Actually this is not an ethical position at all; it is a self-serving calculation in disguise.' Thus, although it may well be true that 'in the long run a company can make more money if it does not antagonise competitors, suppliers, employees and customers by squeezing them too hard', this 'has nothing to do with ethics', and is simply in business's strategic interest. In fact, 'as long as a company does not transgress the rules of the game set by law, it has the legal right to shape its strategy without reference to anything else but its profits'. For business decisions 'are, in the final test, decisions of strategy, not of ethics'. And indeed 'The ethics of business are not those of society, but rather those of the poker game.' In conclusion, any actions of social responsibility that are not in the firm's interest are to be resisted, as ultimately detrimental to business and, in turn, to society.

This argument is clearly opposed by those who take a broader view of business's social responsibilities, and strongly reject Carr's poker analogy. For business activity is not a game, but the economic basis of society, and with very significant effects on it. It may well have its own distinctive rules, but these should still be morally evaluated; likewise business goals should not be exempt from moral assessment. Certainly, when business discharges some social responsibilities that are beneficial to society but also in the business's interest, then the moral worth of such activities can legitimately be questioned. Thus, taking a strictly Kantian perspective, such desirable but instrumental (self-interested) actions would be granted some value but not a moral one. By contrast, from a utilitarian viewpoint the same activities may well be said to have a moral worth, and certainly so according to ethical egoism. But as Sorell and Hendry (1994) argue, 'it is hard to find a convincing moral theory that both allows self-interested acts to have moral value and does not demand acts that go *beyond* self-interest.' Indeed 'the demands of morality may introduce forms of corporate social responsibility that are very far from being justified by self-interest'. Thus, justice requirements would clearly demand that firms correct any negative externality that they have caused, even if doing so is not in the firm's interest. Moreover, firms may be required to intervene in situations of emergencies or crises, even if this can involve a serious economic loss, as for instance when banks are urged and expected to outrightly forgive or at least partially write off Third World debts.

Turning to the second question, which relates directly to the *nature* of business, a very common position here seems to be that of abstaining from any moral judgements about the business activity itself, provided only that the activity is not illegal. In contrast to this view, Camenisch (1981) argues that the 'heart' of business ethics consists indeed in an assessment of business's primary function, that is the *provision of goods and services*. Certainly, the other essential element of business, *profit-making* – which is a necessary means by which business enables itself to survive – can also raise moral concerns. But it is business's central activity, its goal of producing goods and services, which raises the most important moral/ethical issues. Thus the business activity itself must be scrutinised according to how it affects 'human flourishing directly through the kind of products or services it provides, and through the responsible or irresponsible use of limited and often non-renewable resources'. In other words, business's social and/or moral responsibility does not certainly lie only on its profit-making function, as Friedman argues, but rather, Camenisch claims, on its very contribution to sustaining and enhancing human life through its essential and primary function.

Undoubtedly, the choice of criteria by which to assess business activity in terms of its contribution to 'human flourishing', that is in terms of the true human value of the goods and services it produces, is, as Camenisch acknowledges, a difficult and controversial task. Nevertheless, his emphasis on the fundamental nature of business *as business* points not only to the market system's bias in favour of expanding output and hence consumption – ie to Hirsch's (1977) 'commodity/commercialisation bias' – with its inherent overriding stress, as Camenisch notes, on 'dollar-value, profitability, marketability, efficiency, contribution to the gross national product, etc.', at the clear expense of other values, such as equity, justice and fairness. It also directs attention to the markets' seemingly unstoppable move, in mature capitalist economies in general and in the Anglo-Saxon ones in particular, from the traditional manufacturing sector to the service sector, and moreover from production to finance. The increasing stock market/foreign exchange market financial domination of the economy seems thus the result of a fundamental shift in the moral evaluation of different kinds of human activity.

The 'productivist' ethic, which values production rather (or more) than finance – for, as Dore (1993) puts it, 'producing goods and services which enhance the lives of others is good. Spending one's life in the speculative purchase and sale of financial claims is bad' – appears in fact to be increasingly receding under the attack of neoclassical free-market theory, which holds that the market is driven by individual self-interest and the pursuit of short-run profits. Thus *laissez-faire* insists on the importance of 'free' markets, and in particular of a flexible and deregulated labour market (since labour 'rigidities' impede the proper functioning of the market); with the maximum mobility of resources – so that they can be allocated to the uses that guarantee the highest return – as the fundamental necessary precondition for economic efficiency and hence for economic growth. A main effect of the systemic shift away from the productivist ethic, and the shift in the balance of power between finance and industry in favour of finance, is not only a growing lack of interest in production *per se* (for 'manufacturing does not matter' after all) and the consequent proliferation of, and speculation in, secondary markets; but also a related growing preoccupation with short- term business performance and short-term profit, that is a spreading endemic short-termism, induced by the increasingly market-based financial system, at the expense of long-term strategies and long-term investment.

4   Regulation and Self-regulation

The neoclassical *laissez-faire* economic doctrine points to the ability of a free, flexible, unregulated market economy – populated by selfish, rational, utility-maximising agents – to achieve the most efficient, Pareto-optimal and hence socially desirable economic outcome. Thus, the superiority of such a perfectly competitive market system, benignly helped by the 'invisible hand', is, at least theoretically, established. The market mechanism is, above all, a self-regulating natural order, and hence any government interference in economic affairs, no matter how well-meaning, is bound to have harmful effects on the economy and should thus be limited as much as possible. Laws and regulations that are supposed to improve the economy are actually more likely to obstruct the proper working of the market: the market can by itself solve all the economic problems and so economic decisions should be left to the marketplace.

This is, no doubt, a very idyllic view of a free, perfectly competitive economy. However, and as already discussed, the reality is quite far from it. The free-market system suffers from several instances of market failure and produces an arbitrary, very unequal and socially unacceptable distribution of income and wealth. In addition, big firms and especially corporations have significant power – economic, social and political – over consumers and employees in particular, and the community, society and the environment in general. Therefore, to correct the market flaws and protect individuals or groups from exploitation or abuse, the 'visible hand of government' is called upon, in the form of government intervention in the economy, through public spending and taxation, as well as by means of laws, regulations and controls.

Legislation governing economic and social affairs is clearly dynamic and also continuously changing in response to society's demands; and it certainly varies from country to country. However, the range of such legislation has everywhere become very wide. Following Ferrell and Fraedrich (1994), most of the laws and regulations governing business activities can be said to cover essentially four areas. The first is *regulation of competition*, 'to prevent the establishment of monopolies, inequitable pricing practices, and other practices that reduce or restrict competition among businesses', including chiefly antitrust and fair trading legislation. The second is *consumer protection*, requiring businesses 'to provide accurate information about products and services and to follow safety standards', as well as health standards. The third is *environmental protection*, to protect individuals and the environment from pollution or toxic waste (industrial and nuclear) in the air and water, depletion of scarce natural resources, as well as noise pollution and environmental degradation in general. The fourth is *promotion of equity and safety* in the workplace, 'to protect the rights of older persons, minorities, women and persons with disabilities', and the rights and safety of all workers, thus including equal opportunity and equal pay legislation and protection of trade-union rights; as well as investor and borrower protection legislation.

Such an extensive range of legislation over economic and social affairs clearly reflects a large consensus in society that regulation is needed in many areas of economic activity, and for several diverse reasons. Employees, consumers, borrowers, and even shareholders and firms themselves, all require some degree of legal protection, as does the environment in which business operates. Some regulation can clearly be justified on paternalistic grounds, while some other can also be defended on non-paternalistic grounds. And when paternalism is the motive, it is evident that individual freedom and autonomy have to be balanced against the public interest or society's welfare. Indeed, the criticism of (and opposition to) paternalistic intervention, on the grounds that it limits and interferes with individual freedom, by above all curtailing the range of individual choice, thus on grounds of liberty, is frequently used as a major argument against government's economic and social regulation and in favour of self-regulation. Moreover, self-regulation is also strongly advocated by those, including many businesspersons, who endorse the *laissez-faire* doctrine and so regard self-regulation as a more efficient method for market control. And these, it may be added, are also likely to be the ones who appeal to the libertarian argument and against paternalism.

Self-regulation can take the form of individual firms' voluntary codes of ethics, or else of industry-wide self-regulatory rules, of professional or business associations' codes of conduct. Ethical guidelines, codes and rules can be implicit or explicit, can be narrower or broader in their coverage of potential problems and moral issues, and their actual enforcement and implementation can greatly vary across businesses or professions. Self-governance can certainly contribute to promoting 'good' economic behaviour, discharging business's social obligations and avoiding conflicts of interest among different economic parts. However, as Shaw and Barry (1989) argue, 'self-regulation can easily become the instrument of subordinating consumer interest to profit making when the two goals clash. Under the guise of self-regulation, businesses can end up ignoring or minimising responsibility to consumers.' And self-regulation or deregulation may not be 'compatible with consumer safety or the economic interests of society'. Clearly, the same argument for not relying solely on business's self-regulation, and hence for not endorsing total deregulation, goes also for protecting the interests of individuals other than consumers, such as employees, borrowers and also small shareholders. But government regulations also have limitations, for they can be silently evaded, or simply the risk of being fined can be accepted, especially if the threat of punishment (the value of the fine) is not regarded as high compared to the actual cost of complying with regulations. Moreover, the public policing of business compliance with regulations can be difficult, besides being very costly.

In summary, government regulation over economic and social affairs is needed to protect and promote the health and safety of consumers and workers; to control and restrain firms' monopoly and market power, preventing in particular monopoly pricing abuses, and to promote competition; as well as to protect the environment. But although often necessary, legal regulations may not be sufficient, and hence other mechanisms, such as economic market incentives including fiscal measures, can be used by government to this end; and businesses' and markets' self-regulation can also help to improve economic efficiency, if not equity.

Finally, it should be noticed that *laissez-faire* supporters, who favour the minimal role of government in (socio)economic activity, strongly oppose government regulations and typically advocate economic deregulation, not only by using the libertarian anti-paternalistic argument, and pointing to the virtues of competitive unfettered free-markets as self- correcting mechanisms. They also argue that the regulatory process does actually (or is likely to) benefit the regulated industry or business at the expense of consumers, thus creating monopoly power rather than curbing it, and preventing competition. However, the experience of the deregulation of financial and labour markets and of the self-regulation of several business activities does cast serious doubts on the effective ability of competitive unregulated free-markets to restrain their vested greedy interests and contribute to the public good; and indeed it raises serious concern about the unrestrained markets' potential destabilising effects on the economy and society in general, which might thus lead to clearly undesirable economic social and political instability.

More important, as the 'second-best' economic theory explains, unless all the conditions of the perfect competition model are simultaneously met, the benefits of the competitive free market are not available; and when even only one condition cannot be fulfilled, trying to satisfy the others, even if possible, is no longer desirable. Consequently, when some of the assumptions of the perfect competition model are clearly missing, then, as Amitai Etzioni (1988) stresses, 'when an economy moves toward perfect competition, say as the result of the deregulation of one industry, one cannot assume that such a step will yield some of the benefits of perfect competition. Competition is either perfect or it is not;. . . it cannot be had in degrees.' Thus, as David Miliband (1993) points out, the effective models of the economy (the 'mixed-economy' or 'second-best' solutions, departures from the 'first-best' perfect competition model) 'are not simply diluted versions of the perfect system: they have their own logic and equilibrium'. Indeed 'each mixed economy, and each part of each mixed economy, has its own logic, institutions and character based on a complex interdependence of state, market and citizen'. And, as Miliband also argues, while the debate about the relationship between the market and the state has almost exclusively focused on the question of the desirable degree of perfect competition and of state intervention, that is on the issue of the 'boundary' of (and balance between) market and state, 'the real question is what sort of markets we want to create and what sort of state we want to develop, not how much we have of each'. For 'markets and the state not only co- exist, but stand interdependent' and hence 'The important issue is not the opposition of market and state but the nature of the interdependence between them; on it depends the logic and rationality of different markets and different economies.'

To conclude, businesses and markets are socio-polical and moral institutions as much as economic institutions. Their powers, interests and values may well conflict with those of individuals, communities or society. Thus, government intervention and regulation is fundamental not only in establishing or changing the 'rules of the game', but also in mediating and resolving any conflict in the general interest of society. That is, the ultimate social responsibility for social harmony and well-being lies with the government.

5 Business and Government

As discussed in a previous section, from the perspective of the very broad view of business's social responsibilities and of broad business ethics, business has several obligations which society requires of, or expects and desires from it. However, if firms' economic resposibilities (to provide goods and services and maximise profits) and legal responsibilities (to obey the law) are always accepted as natural dimensions of business activity, the other two dimensions – the ethical and voluntary/philanthropic ones – raise, as also discussed, some controversial issues. Thus, the issue arises (also already discussed) of whether business's broader social responsibility is in the business's interest, or whether in fact it does interfere with and hence impede business's primary economic function. Yet another important issue is, as Sorell and Hendry (1994) put it, 'whether certain ventures in corporate social responsibility saddle business with projects that the state ought to (morally ought to) initiate and maintain'. Here, as they argue, 'What is at issue is the morality of dividing up the social responsibilities of state and business in one way rather than another.' In fact, 'By taking on obligations that are properly those of government, it could be argued, businesses discourage government from discharging its obligations itself. If businesses then have to withdraw through financial circumstances, those who might reasonably expect support are deprived of it.' And it is thus morally wrong for a business to go beyond certain limits.

This very point could also be put in terms of 'the moral boundaries of the market', following Russell Keat (1993), who addresses the broad question of 'how, and upon what basis, the boundaries should be drawn around the domain of activities to be governed by the market.' Thus the question about the precise scope and boundaries of the market domain concerns not only the issue of potentially morally inappropriate or undesirable involvement of business in certain areas on a voluntary/philanthropic basis – such as, notably, charitable donations to, or sponsorships of hospitals, schools, universities, etc. – but also, and arguably more important, the issue of business's direct engagement in activities such as health care and education, and more generally the extension of market forces and the introduction of commercial forms of organisations to 'social practices or institutions of a broadly cultural character: broacasting and journalism, museums and the arts, education, sports, academic research and many others'. The question is whether the 'colonisation' by the market of these areas – thus turning these activities that have traditionally or more commonly been run on a non-market basis into commercial, for-profit, activities – is acceptable, and indeed socially desirable, for supposedly improving economic efficiency; or whether the 'dominance' of the logic of the market and of free-market values (i.e. profit making) is not in fact likely or even bound to 'contaminate' the very character and nature of these practices.

A reason for opposing the subordination of these activities to the market logic of profitability is, as Sorell and Hendry (1994) say, that although 'profit does not necessarily pollute', 'there is a risk of profit polluting' and moreover 'profit doesn't necessarily purify'. In particular, 'the idea that the market-oriented, profit-motivated approach is morally improving because of its tendency to promote choice and responsibility' seems to be highly questionable. For, as they argue, it rests on an interpretation of the concepts of choice and responsibility in a purely commercial sense – of consumer choice and market responsibility – that has no moral significance, as opposed to the morally valued concepts of autonomy and conscientiousness.

As to the issue of privatising public enterprises, it seems doubtful, as Sorell and Hendry also argue, 'Whether there can be good general arguments for or against the privatisation of just *any* state-owned industrial enterprise in just *any* circumstances.' In other words, the boundaries between state and market, or public sector and private sector, should be drawn on a case-by-case pragmatic basis, since there seem to be no firm theoretical grounds for defining those boundaries, that is no general economic case or rationale for preferring public or private ownership of specific firms or industries.

The neoclassical *laissez-faire* doctrine clearly favours the 'minimal state' and a virtually wholly privately-owned economy, with government's economic involvement limited to basic functions (defence and justice) and elementary regulation. However, the implied case against nationalisation and for widespread privatisation of public enterprises rests on a number of controversial or even fallacious tenets. Firstly, it seems to put undue emphasis on the importance of ownership, as the central determinant of how property is used and organised, hence overlooking the crucial issue of control and of tensions between ownership and control. The same 'fallacy of ownership' is certainly also true of the case of public ownership, where the problems of control are arguably even more severe, as sustained by Geoff Mulgan (1993). Secondly, the privatisation case, as Sorell and Hendry (1994) underline, is based on the presumption or defended on the ground that the widening of share-ownership is morally a good thing, whilst it may well be argued that 'neither share owning nor ownership in general is necessarily morally desirable'. Moreover, as they also note, 'Although the transfer of businesses to the private sector is supposed to increase competition', privatisation may actually usher in predatory behaviour that reduces competition (as the evidence from the British Airways case seems to show). Finally, in a wholly privatised economy, serious problems arise in relation to private monopolies, and the underprovision of public goods and of quasi-public goods (those with significant externality effects).

6 International Business and Morality

Domestic economies have become increasingly internationally interdependent and part of a 'global economy'. Issues of *international trade* (economic protectionism versus free trade, international competitiveness and exchange rate systems), of *international finance* (global financial markets, perfect capital/ asset mobility, role of major financial institutions and commercial banks operating on an international level, and of international economic institutions such as the International Monetary Fund and the World Bank), and of *international cooperation* among countries in economic and social policies (international trade agreements, international monetary arrangements and macroeconomic coordination); they have all become more important as a result of the growing interdependence of national economies.

In the new 'global market', more and more companies have extended their activities from the domestic economy to other countries and multinational corporations operate on a global scale. The internationalisation of business activities and transactions raises additional ethical issues, over and above those that firms operating only in their domestic economies face. Major ethical issues in international business may arise when companies operate in foreign countries with different cultures, values and ethical standards, and/or under different socio-economic circumstances. Firms doing business in different cultural and/or economic environments have in fact to decide which standards to adopt in their decision-making. Is it the host-country or home-country norms and laws that should take precedence, especially when from the firm's perspective the former appear to be substandard or socially or morally unacceptable?

International ethical issues can in particular arise in relation to:

employment practices – including the issues of wage levels (fair wage or minimum wage standards or laws), number of working hours, child labour, health and safety conditions, as well as the issues of non-discrimination and equal opportunity treatment;
use of bribery and corruption in general in business practices – concerning both the size of bribes (small or large) and the types of bribes ('facilitating payments', i.e. small and often standardised tips or gifts to petty officials; or 'middlemen commissions', i.e. large disbursements to agents and consultants often to secure aircraft and arms/military contracts; or 'political contributions', i.e. large kickbacks to politicians, government officials or political parties);
environmental/green standards – where controls and standards can greatly vary across countries;
product marketing practices – including the issues of exporting harmful or potentially harmful products that may have been banned in the home country while still being legal in other countries; of aggressive promotion

techniques; and of selling advanced sensitive technology that may be employed for military use;

international pricing practices – including the issues of unethical or even illegal price discrimination (applying price differentials as a result of artificial market segmentation not justified by costs), and of gouging or dumping (i.e. selling products abroad at an unjustifiably higher or lower price, respectively, than that charged at home, for various commercial unethical reasons).

Moreover, as Ferrell and Fraedrich (1994) point out, the activities of multinational corporations can raise particular ethical issues. In fact, because of their size and financial power, multinationals can have a serious impact on the countries in which they operate and especially on less-developed/Third World countries, where they can exercise an enormous, potentially destabilising, economic and political influence and control. And this may create ethical issues related to exploitation of natural and human resources and unfair competition.

In resolving international ethical issues, businesses may take one of two extreme positions – that of ethnocentricism (or moral absolutism) or that of cultural (moral) relativism – both of which are, however, open to serious criticism. Thus, on the one hand, an ethnocentric view – which means adopting home-country norms – presupposes equating, as Sorell and Hendry (1994) say, 'home-country standards with some absolute standards of morality. . . However, the assumption that our moral standards. . . are in some sense absolute, or even just exemplary, is rather difficult to defend.' For what may seem to be 'moral absolutes' in a society, at a particular moment, are in fact values that are partly shaped by the specific social and economic circumstances of that moment, as well as being the result of historical circumstances and religious and cultural traditions. And what are regarded as, if not absolute, at least 'exemplary moral values', compared to those of underdeveloped or less- developed countries – where, mainly because of poor economic conditions, the permissible local standards and practices are normally far worse or looser than those of economically more developed, richer, countries – may simply reflect the greater economic development, with no particular moral claim attached to them. As Sorell and Hendry argue, 'rich' is not necessarily 'right'. Moreover, and as they add, 'even among the economically most advanced nations, such as Japan, the USA, Germany and Sweden, there are strong cultural differences', and also quite different economic and social practices. Therefore, the simplistic view that richer countries have intrinsically better moral values and standards than poorer countries seems weak and untenable. And claiming the moral superiority of any one system or culture over any other seems more an act of ethnocentric arrogance than anything else. After all, so-called 'most developed' countries not only have different laws and public opinions on many issues involving social and moral value judgements – such as the use of tobacco, alcohol or drugs, sex and decency, abortion and birth control, punishment, torture or death penalty; they also show different degrees of 'tolerance' for diversity within their own national boundaries.

On the other hand, the position of ethical relativism – which means accepting the host – country standards – may suggest consideration, respect and understanding for other cultures' values and norms. However, even if the 'When in Rome, do as the Romans do' proverb seems appealing, both in logical and pragmatic terms, it can be (and often is) used, as Thomas Donaldson (1985) argues, 'to justify practices abroad which, although enhancing corporate profits, would be questionable in the multinational's home country'. In other words, it can be a rather convenient licence to adopt significantly looser host-country standards, and indeed 'mask immoral practices in the rhetoric of "tolerance" and "cultural relativity"'. Moreover, as Sorell and Hendry (1994) note, 'to accept the relativist position is in some sense to deny any objective grounds for morality at all, and so to reject the very concept of morality as commonly understood', and moral values would hence 'lose completely their imperative force'. Thus they argue 'that it is morally irresponsible for businesses to act on the basis of "anything goes"', but also 'that in many areas of business practice there is an element of cultural relativism, and that for a business to assume that its own values are necessarily the only or best ones is also irresponsible'.

Consequently, in solving international business ethics problems, the two extremes of ethnocentricity and moral relativism should both be avoided, in favour of an appropriate and reasonable compromise. This is clearly not an easy task, although an awareness and understanding of cross-cultural differences seems to be at least a starting point. Various criteria or approaches have been suggested, typically dependent on the particular type of situation that gives rise to the ethical problem. The least morally demanding approach is a *pragmatic economic calculation*, by the firm's local managers in the host country, mainly based on a cost–benefit analysis that however takes also into consideration the home-country opinion on the issue. A more stringent approach is the *criterion of openess* suggested by Sir Adrian Cadbury (and reported by Sorell and Hendry, 1994), which concerns specifically the issue of bribery and corruption. Since in many countries bribes and kickbacks seem to be a necessary or accepted business practice, then depending on whether the practice requires secrecy, or whether it could be made public without embarrassment for the recipient, one may well infer how ethically defensible or acceptable the practice is. Thus the criterion helps in judging the specific situation and so partly counteracts the dangers of cultural relativism. A more complex approach is Thomas Donaldson's (1985) two-stage *ethical algorithm*. In the first stage, a situation is identified as a type 1 or type 2 conflict, depending on whether or not the moral/cultural differences are dependent on the relative level of economic development. In the second stage, depending on the type of conflict, a special test is applied to determine the permissibility of a business practice. Specifically, in a type 1 conflict, a practice is permissible if and only if home-country members would, under economic conditions relevantly similar to those of the host country, regard the practice as permissible. The criterion therefore rightly requires putting oneself in the host-country position and then applying to it one's knowledge and experience, hence avoiding cultural relativism. By contrast, in a type 2 conflict, a practice is permissible if and only if it is impossible to conduct business successfully in the host country without undertaking the practice *and* the practice is not a clear violation of a basic human right. Here, however, both the word 'successfully' and the phrase 'basic human right' seem to be rather controversial, as being open to several interpretations, and this criterion may thus be regarded as not very satisfactory for being potentially too permissive. Yet another useful approach, suggested by Sorell and Hendry (1994), is 'to transpose the situation from one in which ours is the home-country culture to one in which ours becomes the host-country culture', and which thus 'can help to protect us from the. . . danger of ethnocentrism'.

Finally, multinational businesses face serious international ethical problems also in relation to the very fact of operating in countries ruled by oppressive regimes, such as, notably, the former one of South Africa. Here the issue in not that of deciding which standards to adopt, but indeed that of deciding, as Sorell and Hendry (1994) put it, 'whether it is morally acceptable to operate in a country at all'. In fact, if a country's government policies are politically and ethically unacceptable, such as was *apartheid*, then by doing business in that country a company can, arguably, be said to be endorsing that immoral regime. Moreover, serious international business ethics problems arise in connection with the operation of global financial markets. Apart from the issue of insider-dealing, another and possibly more important issue relates to the conduct of major commercial banks and financial institutions toward Third World countries' borrowing and debt crisis. For, arguably, banks and financial markets in general can affect the welfare and economic development of poorer nations even more than big international companies and multi-national corporations.

Clearly, in all international ethical issues, as for national issues, public opinion and pressure groups can help improve businesses' ethical conduct. However, in relation to the international context – even more than for the domestic context – the role played by governments and international institutions may be not only important, but indeed fundamental. It can in fact be argued that only by an active international policy coordination may the partly conflicting issues of economic development and of the environment find a politically and ethically acceptable solution.

7 Concluding Remarks

Economic markets perform a fundamental function for society, ensuring the provision of goods and services that society wants and needs, whilst aiming at the most efficient use of resources. Markets, however, are not ethically neutral, apolitical and inherently beneficent institutions; nor are they 'natural' institutions. Indeed, markets are historico-socio-politico-cultural and moral institutions, as much as economic. Markets reflect and are influenced by the morality of individuals and society as a whole, but markets' morality can in turn affect economic agents' choices and behaviour.

Instances of market failures are rather pervasive, leading to inefficient and socially undesirable economic outcomes. Conflicts of interest among economic agents are common phenomena, but are not always satisfactorily resolved by the allegedly neutral arbitration of the market. In particular, the market produces an arbitrary, very unequal and hence unacceptable distribution of income and wealth. Moreover, the market, if simply driven by individual self-interest and the profit motive, is not able to nourish and sustain, and may well discourage or undermine, important social values. Trust, truth-telling, honesty, goodwill, cooperation, altruism, restraint, non-aggression, obligation, and in general non- self-interested moral commitment – these are all values relevant, or even crucial, to the functioning of markets and to economic efficiency, as emphasised by several economists and others. But in the individualistic, contractual market economy, as Bowles and Gintis (1993) argue, 'The anonymous nature of [market] exchange appears hostile to the evolution of these values', and indeed 'fosters norms hostile to the efficient solution of coordination problems.'

Competition among firms is certainly fundamental for efficiency and innovation. But cooperation between firms – provided it does not amount to collusion or cartels at the expense of other firms and consumers – can also be beneficial to the economy and society. Thus, the pooling of resources and technical expertise, and especially collaboration in R&D, may well increase productivity and efficiency, with obvious gains for the cooperating firms and society as a whole.

The pursuit of profit is, clearly, a necessary condition for firms' economic survival and success. Profit maximisation is hence a social responsibility of business. Managers have a moral obligation to the firm's shareholders to make money, and, moreover, by doing so they also promote society's welfare, as well explained by the 'invisible hand' doctrine. However, a business firm has also social responsibilities to its other stakeholders, its employees, consumers, suppliers, as well as to its competitors, and more generally to the community, the society at large and the environment. These other obligations, in addition to maximising profits, can be said to be justified by firms' economic, social and political power. Firms play indeed a vital role in society, but they are major players and have hence major obligations to discharge.

In recognising a broader social and moral dimension to business activity, society expects not only that firms refrain from unethical behaviour and internalise any negative externality, but also that they positively contribute to the general good. Certainly, businesses' ethical codes and markets' self-regulation can help in sustaining 'good' economic behaviour, and enhance economic efficiency. Nevertheless, the ultimate social responsibility for economic and social harmony and society's well-being can only rest with the government. There can be no presumption that businesses' and markets' interests, norms and values coincide rather than conflict with those of individuals and society in general. Markets alone cannot (and should not) be relied upon always to deliver efficient and socially and morally desirable economic outcomes. Government intervention in the economy and regulation of business activities, far from being an unnecessary interference and also likely to be harmful, is indeed required if the collective interest is to be upheld.

References

Arrow, K. J. (1973) 'Social Responsibility and Economic Efficiency', *Public Policy*, vol. 21.

Bowles, S. and Gintis, H. (1993) 'The Revenge of Homo Economicus: Contested Exchange and the Revival of Political Economy', *Journal of Economic Perspectives*, vol. 7, pp. 83–102.

Camenisch, P. F. (1981) 'Business Ethics: On Getting to the Hearth of the Matter', *Business and Professional Ethics Journal*, vol. 1, pp. 59–69.

Carr, A. Z. (1968) 'Is Business Bluffing Ethical?', in John Drummond and Bill Bain (eds) *Managing Business Ethics*, Butterworth-Heinemann, Oxford, 1994, pp. 28–38. Reprinted from *Harvard Business Review*, vol. 46, 1968, pp. 162–9.

Carroll, A. B. (1991) 'The Pyramid of Corporate Social Responsibility: Toward the Moral Management of Organizational Stakeholders', *Business Horizons*.

Donaldson, T. (1985) 'Multinational Decision-Making: Reconciling International Norms', in John Drummond and Bill Bain (eds), *Managing Business Ethics*, Butterworth-Heinemann, Oxford, 1994, pp. 136–48. Reprinted from *Journal of Business Ethics*, vol. 4, 1985, pp. 357–66.

Dore, R. (1993) 'What Makes the Japanese Different?', in Colin Crouch and David Marquand (eds), *Ethics and Markets. Co-operation and Competition within Capitalist Economies*, Blackwell, Oxford, 1993, pp. 66–79.

Etzioni, A. (1988) *The Moral Dimension. Toward a New Economics*, The Free Press, New York.

Ferrell, O. C. and Fraedrich, J. (1994) *Business Ethics. Ethical Decision Making and Cases*, Houghton Mifflin, Boston, Mass.

Friedman, M. (1962) *Capitalism and Freedom*, University of Chicago Press, Chicago.

Hausman, D. M. and McPherson, M. S. (1993) 'Taking Ethics Seriously: Economics and Contemporary Moral Philosophy', *Journal of Economic Literature*, vol. 31, pp. 671–731.

Hirsch, F. (1977) *Social Limits to Growth*, Routledge & Kegan Paul, London.

Hobbes, T. (1962) *Leviathan, or The Matter, Form and Power of a Commonwealth Ecclesiasical and Civil*, Collier Books, New York [1651].

Keat, R. (1993) 'The Moral Boundaries of the Market', in Colin Crouch and David Marquand (eds), *Ethics and Markets. Co-operation and Competition within Capitalist Economies*, Blackwell, Oxford, pp. 6–20.

Levitt, T. (1958) 'The Dangers of Social Responsibility', *Harvard Business Review*, vol. 3, no. 6, 1958.

Miliband, D. (1993) 'The New Politics of Economics', in Colin Crouch and David Marquand (eds), *Ethics and Markets. Co-operation and Competition within Capitalist Economies*, Blackwell, Oxford, pp. 21–30.

Mulgan, G. (1993) 'Reticulated Organisations: The Birth and Death of the Mixed Economy', in Colin Crouch and David Marquand (eds), *Ethics and Markets. Co-operation and Competition within Capitalist Economies*, Oxford, pp. 31–47.

Shaw, W. and Barry, V. (1989) *Moral Issues in Business*, Wadsworth, Belmont, Calif.

Sorell, T. and Hendry, J. (1994) *Business Ethics*, Butterworth-Heinemann, Oxford.

Stiglitz, J. (1993) 'Post Walrasian and Post Marxian Economics', *Journal of Economic Perspective*, vol. 7, pp. 109–14.

Williamson, O. (1985) *The Economic Institutions of Capitalism*, The Free Press, New York.

PART II

MANAGEMENT AND ETHICS

Introduction to Part II

This part of the book is intended to provide insights into and analysis of the major ethical issues presented within the contexts of different managerial functions or roles.

We believe that a context which is grounded in business practice is essential to develop an understanding and appreciation of the severely practical and philosophically challenging field of business ethics. Ethical issues, problems and dilemmas are everyday problems. This is in the sense that they occur every day, in every organisation and for almost every member of those organisations. Managers' ability to deal with ethical issues rests partly on their ability to recognise such issues and partly upon their understanding of how particular issues relate to or exemplify general principles. In the chapters which follow, each of the authors will explore the range of ethical issues within a specific function or role and will ground their discussion of ethical issues within that context.

It begins with Peter Davis's examination of ethical issues in strategic management. The centrality of values within the strategic planning process is becoming increasingly recognised (see Campbell and Tawadey, 1992). Indeed, the many failures of traditional approaches to strategic management can frequently be seen as the result of a lack of thinking about the core values of the business and the absence of attempts to shape strategy as an outcome or development from those values.

The study of ethical issues in marketing is quite well developed and Greta Richards and Collette Blanchfield have developed a helpful review of the major ethical issues in marketing, based in part on their own previous work and pulling together several strands of enquiry. Whereas the ethics of marketing is a well-developed field of study, the study of purchasing has lagged behind. Purchasing as field of management practice has long been recognised as an area rich in the presentation of ethical dilemmas. It is strange, therefore, that it has not been a fruitful area for academic investigation. Graham Wood has begun to redress the balance with his work. His chapter provides a comprehensive review of the field and the ethical dilemmas presented by it.

Brian Elliot offers a systematic and concise review of ethical issues within the field of operations management, referring to both the manufacturing and the service sector. Basing his analysis on different models of operations managers, he offers alternative methodologies for the analysis of typical dilemmas faced by these managers.

Unlike the study of marketing, the literature on human resource management in Britain does not reveal a significant preoccupation with ethical issues. Wes Haydock argues that nearly all decisions relating to human resource management present ethical problems. He discusses this paradox and, by focusing his analysis on specific aspects of human resource management, he identifies and evaluates significant ethical issues in the field.

Margaret Leigh and Richard Scholefield review the various roles of members of the accounting profession and identify the major ethical issues involved in this area. They analyse the limitations of current accounting theory and practice from an ethical perspective, both from the point of view both of accountants in professional practices and of those working in businesses. They offer an illuminating analysis of the effects of the nineteenth century origins of much of modern accounting practice.

None of the authors of the chapters in Part II sit on the fence. There is a common assumption that ethical behaviour is the only acceptable basis for conduct in business. Their work, however, is not based on mere opinion. In all cases, it is based on experience as practitioners and on an informed knowledge of the field of study. Their work reflects a conviction of the centrality of ethical concerns and issues in their various fields of expertise.

Reference

Campbell, A. and Tawadey, K. (1992) *Mission and Business Philosophy*, Butterworth Heinemann, Oxford.

CHAPTER 10

Ethical Issues in Strategic Management

1 Introduction

Strategic management is the locus for the most far-reaching decisions (in scope and time) that any organisation makes, hence one could argue that it is in this sphere that ethics also has its most decisive role to play. Since strategic decisions have a major integrative and directive role for the other functions, then ethics at this level will also inform the ethics of other functions. Moreover, it is at the strategic level (articulated in mission statements, aims and objectives) that the most fundamental questions about the ends and means of a business organisation are tackled:

Ends: What is the real purpose of this organisation? (What is its scope to be? Where do we want it to be in 5, or 10 years' time?)

Means: How are we going to get there? (What ethics and values will guide the process of change? What limits will be put on the means justifying the ends?)

The relevance of the ethical nature of the answers to such questions can be seen in the enduring difference of many companies founded on a purposely different ethic, such as Quaker companies in the last century (Bradley, 1987). Other notable examples include the Co-op bank and Scott-Bader, and also smaller companies such as Traidcraft.[1] What this points to is the power of those at the top of any business organisation (particularly its founders) to shape its strategy (for good or ill) and also to set the ethical tone of the organisation in terms of acceptable behaviour. Certainly newspaper headlines of corporate misdemeanours have highlighted the involvement of very senior managers, not just because they make crucial strategic decisions, nor just because their high profile strongly links them with the organisation's reputation, but because the public now expects them to give ethical leadership as well.[2] Strategic management involves top-down decisions with concrete outcomes such as closing certain plants, operating in different countries, management buyouts, mergers and acquisitions, major organisational restructuring, and so on. But strategic management also depends equally on those lower down the organisation who have to make these changes work; otherwise even the most brilliantly conceived strategy will fail. A consideration of strategy and ethics therefore cuts across all levels of an organisation.

2 Significant Ethical Issues in Strategic Management

Ethical issues of particular concern in strategic management need to be discussed with reference to the current debate about stakeholders. How stakeholder interests are balanced depends partly on the legal structure of business organisations, so to some extent ethical issues in strategic management must be worked out within what is 'given'; but this is not always adequate. MacIntyre (1977) argues that we live in an imperfect (and imperfectly structured) society, but that to live in such a society is something that can of itself be done well, or badly. If you want to ensure you do it badly, then either you say that the problems and injustices are not yours (and take a Friedmanite view of business and society), or, you can say they are a legitimate concern, but you cannot do anything about them. MacIntyre deems neither approach as morally adequate. From the point of view of far-reaching strategic decisions, business has an obligation to both work within the given structures, and go beyond them.[3] The following then emerge as the most significant ethical issues in strategic management.

2.1 Setting the vision, aims and objectives

Although the linear approach to strategic management is coming increasingly under fire (Mintzberg, 1994; Stacey, 1993), there seems little doubt about the importance that a strategic vision plays in strategy and ethics (Whittington, 1993). This is usually articulated in the form of a mission statement. It seems it does not matter whether you write it down or not, so long as the company has thought long and hard about what the company is to be, and the rules and values it is to live by (Campbell and Yeung, 1994). The ethical issue is: to what extent do other stakeholders have a right (or even duty) to be involved in developing and articulating the strategic vision which will greatly affect their lives? Success stories suggest that a charismatic CEO has this vision and does it all him/herself. 'Failure' stories point out the weakness of this approach; employees and other stakeholders are reluctant to make work a vision they had no part in developing. Employees in particular will have to live with the resultant organisational culture. Remembering that there is no such thing as a purely rational decision based on pure data, and all decisions have a significant value element (Andrews, 1989), it seems legitimate that more than just the CEO and senior managers should be involved both on ethical grounds and on grounds of good strategic management.

2.2   Leadership and senior managers' remuneration

David (1991, pp. 21) suggests that the very high salaries of those at the top of a business organisation are justified on the grounds that those people not only make the long-term success-or-failure strategic decisions, but also carry the 'moral risks' of the firm. Directors can be said to have a number of 'contracts' with other stakeholders (Cannon, 1994, p. 88). For example, the 'knowledge contract' is to use their competence and skill for the benefit of the enterprise as a whole; their 'efficiency contract' is to minimise waste, and sustain effort-reward standards. They also have a 'psychological contract' to motivate and give recognition to stakeholders, and offer some security. Obviously these contracts are severely at risk when senior executives award themselves protectionist remuneration packages (golden parachutes, etc.), especially in the face of major company redundancies. We are back to stakeholders and the question of 'whose company is it anyway?' and, 'for whose benefit is it to be run?'

Moreover, in terms of ethical leadership 'managerial capitalism' sends certain signals cascading down through the organisation, sanctioning opportunist behaviour. There is no doubt that actions at the top of an organisation carry a heavy symbolic and concrete element which both contribute to the culture of an organisation and strongly influence what people understand as ethically acceptable behaviour in that organisation. If David's (1991) argument is right, what if moral leadership is not forthcoming? Remuneration committees are one outcome to give a sense of justice being seen to be done, but the continuing existence of a strong 'corporate veil' begs their validity (Chryssides and Kaler, 1993, pp. 241–7). When such huge personal financial implications are tied up with strategic decisions, there must be an unreasonable temptation to compromise fiduciary duties, prejudicing the management of the company *as a whole*, with certain stakeholders unjustly losing out. This raises ethical issues of loyalty and the 'psychological contract'.

2.3   Implementing strategic change

Strategic management often entails large-scale changes in the nature of our work, the people we have to work with, our work space, and lifestyles. The nature of change has altered in several ways in the twentieth century, not least in its speed and scope (Toffler, 1970; Lynch and Kordis, 1990). But regarding strategic management, there is another aspect of change that requires attention. Before the Industrial Revolution when 80% of the population worked on the land, people were used to change but in a different manner. The seasons changed regularly and reasonably predictably; there were occasional one-off changes such as earthquakes, floods, and unexplained crop failures. The 'imposed' nature of such changes were accepted with resignation because they were 'acts of God'. Nowadays, though, many major changes (particularly in the nature of our working lives) are imposed upon us clearly by the acts of other humans, and as such people are less ready to accept them as legitimate.

The ethical question in strategic change again draws in the notion of stakeholders who can legitimately ask to what extent the change is really necessary. Could not a different strategic solution be found which had fewer negative impacts? Does the factory have to close? Do I *have* to move 300 miles to a new location? The way these questions have been resolved in the past is simply by the exercise of raw stakeholder power. The option is that if one does not like the changes, one is free to leave. Is this really ethically adequate?

2.4 Changes in organisation ownership

In the 1980s a favourite strategy was growth through mergers and acquisitions; this in turn also generated an increasing number of Management Buyouts (MBOs) as unwanted parts of acquired businesses were sold off.[4] More such activity is currently taking place in the early 1990s as companies re-appraise their strategies in the light of the recession and get back to their core businesses and competencies. The strategic rationale behind such moves has always been to either diversify, or gain a more dominant position within a particular industry. The latter are subject to the Monopolies and Mergers Commission (MMC), but the former have mainly gone ahead without much scrutiny.

What has been left out of the debate is the ethical issues in such activities (Cooke and Young, 1990, pp. 254–69). Historically, takeovers involved a healthy company rescuing a failing one, but now even the most healthy company may be subject to a takeover bid. Although many acquisitions are friendly and mutually beneficial, hostile takeovers have increased. Does the maxim: 'the strong do what they will, the weak do what they must' always have to apply? Another ethical issue is that of 'Corporate Raiders' who use the threat of a takeover to force the target company to buy back shares at a premium – a technique known as 'greenmail'.[5] Not surprisingly such activities have provoked defensive strategies such as 'poison pills' whereby various tactics ensure that the potential buyer will have to put up a disproportionate amount of capital in order to gain a controlling interest. An ethical issue here is: what is the cost in time, energy and money of all this, and wouldn't stakeholders be better served without the attitudes that drive such behaviour? Who really are the stakeholder winners and losers in all this activity?

Moreover, will the merger genuinely enhance the company mission? Synergy gains are not automatic, let alone resolutions to merging two company cultures and management styles.[6] Above all, how does the concept of company loyalty (to and by employees) fit with all this?

2.5 Global strategic operations

The growing size and geographical scope of business organisations has been perhaps *the* key feature in post-war economic development. A number of Multi-National Companies (MNCs) wield more financial muscle than the GNP of some countries (Goyder, 1993, p. 4). Legally, MNCs can be everywhere and nowhere as they transcend national legal frameworks and tax authorities. They can invest rapidly, having a major effect on the local communities of the host countries; and they can pull out almost as fast – as comparative and competitive advantage are sought on a global playing field. Indeed, some developing host countries deliberately lower their employment standards in order to attract companies, and their less-developed consumer regulations invite the dumping of unsafe or inappropriate products.

The key ethical question in global strategic management is simply: when in Rome should one do like the Romans? (Bowie, 1990). The issues go beyond mere cultural sensitivity (for example, should Europeans be obliged to go without alcohol in an Arab country?) They go beyond whether a westerner should offer bribes in order to get a sales contract. They concern the level of employment rights and safety standards when operating a plant in another country; one might be easily achieving the host country's standards, but be quite far below the standards of one's own country. Should a chemical banned in one country be sold in another that legally allows it? Which standards should be adopted (or some standard in between), and why? The answer to such questions is discussed under the ethical theory of (cultural) relativism.

3 Illustration: Strategic Visioning and Mission Statements

Traidcraft's 'Statement of Objectives' (1986) was developed over a six-month period by ordinary employees of the company; the executive directors attended very few meetings, believing that the staff should decide what the business was all about. Their mission states:

> Traidcraft aims to expand and establish more just trading systems, which will express the principles of love and justice fundamental to Christian faith.
>
> Practical service and a partnership for change will characterise the organisation which puts people before profits.

Its objectives are listed under five main headings:

1. Just Trade – Fairer Systems
2. Just Trade – Developing People's Potential
3. Just Trade – More and Better Jobs
4. Just Trade – Fairer Relationships within Traidcraft
5. Just Trade – Efficient and Practical Structures

(Evans, 1991, p. 875)

Compare this with IBM's Mission Statement given by the CEO Louis Gerstner:[7]

> IBM's mission is to be the world's most successful and important I.T company, helping customers apply technology to solve their problems. IBM's success will be based on being the basic resource for much of what is invented in this industry.
>   IBM's strategic imperatives (objectives) are based on:
>
> - Exploiting technology much better
> - Increasing market share
> - Re-engineering the way value is delivered to customers
> - Rapid expansion in key emerging geographic markets
> - Using their size to achieve cost and market advantages.

It is clear that the process of arriving at, and the content of, these two sets of mission statements and objectives will send different ethical messages down through their respective organisations. Although the examples compare a David with a Goliath, the principles remain valid. The IBM example sets a tone of self-aggrandisement, the use of corporate muscle, and an implicit assumption of profits before people.

Compare these with the middle road, a medium size organisation like BAA. After wide consultation, they arrived at the following mission statement:[8]

> BAA's mission is to be the most successful airport company in the world. This will be achieved by always focusing on customer needs and safety, and by seeking continuous improvements in the quality and costs of service. The company culture will enable BAA employees to give of their best.

BAA's chairman Sir John Egan stated that their mission statement made it absolutely clear what BAA wanted to do. Their mission statement evolves continually.

It is clear that strategic management starts with articulating and communicating a vision of what a business organisation is to be all about. The mission aims and objectives and their interpretation are all influenced by people's values and ethics (in turn influenced by existing organisational forces). Strategic management is also about real change, which requires changes in beliefs, values and assumptions – a change in ethical orientation. In short, ethics dictate strategy formulation. There appears to be no reason why any be excluded from having some sort of say in what the ⁀n is to be, nor in how the changes are achieved.

nderlying an Ethical Approach to Strategic

4.1 Stakeholder theory, strategy and ethics

Stakeholder theory stems from the suggestion that business should be regarded as an activity of society, and hence business has responsibilities to a much wider range of stakeholders than merely its shareholders, directors and creditors. It therefore concerns who should have what level of say in strategic issues within a company. Hence it challenges the traditional belief in a manager's right to manage, and raises questions about responsibility and accountability. Stakeholder theory is also an attempt to avoid a 'bolt-on' ethics mentality. This stems from the very persistent basic picture of self-understanding that the business community has about itself, which is the organisation doing its best to 'survive' in a 'hostile environment' (Davies, 1992, pp. 1–40). The danger with a wide acceptance of this approach is that it promotes the habit of seeing strategy merely as a reaction to internal and external threats (which where they have an ethical dimension need likewise responding to – in ethical terms). Ethical strategy then becomes some kind of bolt-on veneer forced upon businesses by various stakeholders. Good ethics are therefore only acceptable when they contribute to good business sense in the prevailing climate; if this requires being 'ethical', then so be it.

An alternative way of looking at ethics, strategy and stakeholders is to view business as having a pro-active role in creating an ethical society (Goyder, 1993). The argument is that business activity is such a pervasive and powerful force in contemporary life, shaping lifestyles and expectations, that (even if it is an unwanted responsibility acquired merely by historical default) it can no longer legitimately understand itself as essentially a narrow universe of accounting goals separate from society.

4.2 Loyalty and the psychological contract

Strategic change often breaches what is known as the 'psychological contract'. This is implicit in the relationship between every employer and employee, and is often couched in terms of loyalty. There are philosophical problems with the notion of loyalty to 'an organisation' (Ladd, 1982; Baron, 1991) but it is still a key perceived element of the psychological contract. An employee will have built up certain expectations about how they will be treated (based on personal relationships with organisational members). They are then prepared to make sacrifices for 'the organisation' in return. All changes require sacrifice of time and energy; but changes in ownership often additionally shatter the relationships with key people on which someone's psychological contract is based. A new owner buys the assets and liabilities of a company, but what expectations of loyalty to, and from, does it also 'buy' in that same transaction? Overnight many years' worth of 'loyal' sacrifices for 'the company' may count for nothing: a whole level of management may be removed *en masse* regardless of the actual contributions and competence of the individuals concerned; a whole factory may be closed by the new owner just because it is now considered strategically to be in the 'wrong' geographical location. Whilst shareholders may gain, a lifetime employee may lose their job. There is a question of justice here: why should the latter suffer more than the former? If such actions become commonplace, why should an employee have any loyalty for the new employer? But successful strategies require strategic change, and this in turn requires the commitment, energy and creativity of the organisational members – in other words their loyalty, undergirded by perceptions of their psychological contract. The ethical issue therefore lies in persuading people that the changes are legitimate. If their own perceptions of the psychological contract must remain unbroken, then a sense of loyalty to the company will continue.

4.3   Cultural relativism

One solution to the problem of how to react to differing cultural standards has been to accept what is known as 'cultural relativism', which means one should adopt the norms of the country one is in. In other words, you cannot take moral beliefs across national borders (Bowie, 1990; Donaldson, 1989). If bribes are part of normal business practice, then that fact must be accepted.[9] At first cultural relativism seems plausible enough. But to be a genuine cultural relativist one must accept *any* practices within national cultures, across time, and even hypothetical situations however extreme. Jailing a thief is no better (or worse) than chopping off their hand; the old Samurai practice of testing a new sword by cutting an innocent traveller in half is acceptable; one would even have to accept the sacrificing of first-born children to 'the gods', were it a national cultural practice. If an unequivocal endorsement cannot be given to all these situations, then one is not a cultural relativist. The moment this admission is made, (that some practices are *universally* wrong no matter what the supporting cultural belief system) then we have to look elsewhere for some international framework to guide the strategic actions of MNCs when operating in other countries (Donaldson, 1989).

Being a global player is an increasingly important strategy for continued long-term survival, and so the difficult ethical issues surrounding cultural relativism and the regulation of MNCs are likely to increase. But ten or more years' worth of negotiations have so far failed to produce any UN Code of Conduct for Transnational Corporations (Donaldson, 1989). Some better way of coping with cultural diversity is still needed. As a possible starting point, MNCs, and most other business, have in the last decade begun to seriously accept the arguments of environmental rights; so why not human rights?[10]

5   Conclusion

As pointed out in the introduction, strategic management first and foremost addresses fundamental questions about a business organisation's purposes, its ends and means. But the strategic question 'what is to be the purpose of this organisation?' is informed by assumptions and beliefs about a deeper question: 'what should the purpose of business organisations be anyway?'

The answer to this question has for many years been strongly influenced by the legal status of companies which has in essence remained unchanged for well over 100 years (Goyder, 1993). The Companies Act of 1862 recognises only shareholders, creditors and directors; this remains the same today. It was made long before the world of MNCs, the welfare state, trades unions, giant privatised monopolies and of social expectations of certain democratic rights. Company law does not recognise shop-floor workers, technicians, managers and wider stakeholders; it is now wholly out of line with social reality and expectations.

To this extent, debates about the moral status of corporation (can companies be held criminally negligent?), and corporate governance (the Cadbury Report), are unable to get to the heart of the matter because both company law, and beliefs about the general purpose of business organisations, have not been radically re-examined and updated. The growth in the stakeholder concept is an attempt at second best, given the above. As such it falls into the category of bolt-on ethics, rather than being recognised within company law.

Although ultimately ethics drives strategy, business still suffers from a low status, being viewed only as a quasi-profession. With the traditional professions the driving ethic is easy to identify. For law, it is justice; for medicine, it is health (and the Hippocratic oath); for the priesthood, it is spirituality. What is it for business? No one single ethical concept springs easily to mind. Suggestions such as sustainable development will remain side-tracked until there are legal changes, such as in the annual reporting of results. If wages were on the profit side (contribution to the economy), and businesses' free use of 'the commons' was properly costed in, then the ethics that drive business strategy would be taken more seriously.

Notes

1. The Co-op bank has now been in existence for over 120 years. Scott-Bader (a 'common-ownership' company) with a turnover of about £50m has been in its present form since 1951 (Bader, 1988). Traidcraft (an 'alternative trading

company') has a turnover of about £5m and has been in existence since 1979 (Evans, 1991).

2. Lord Laing, Chairman of United Biscuits in the forward to the company's 'Ethics and Operating Principles' states: 'United Biscuits' business ethics are not negotiable – a well-founded reputation for scrupulous dealing is itself a priceless company asset and the most important single factor in our success is faithful adherence to our beliefs. . . To meet the challenges of a changing world, we are prepared to change everything about ourselves except our values.'

3. Scott-Bader did just this and got the first certificate of the new legally recognised 'common ownership' companies after the passing of the *Industrial Common Ownership Act* in 1976; the owners had in fact transferred ownership to the 'Commonwealth' in 1951 (Bader, 1988).

4. The UK use of the term 'Management Buyout' (MBO) differs from the American. MBOs in the UK sense refer to the purchase of *part* of a business by its managers – the equivalent American term is 'Leveraged Buyout'. MBOs in the American sense refer to the purchase of a *whole* company from the shareholders by its management (Williams, 1993, p. i).

5. 'Greenmail' is an analogy to 'blackmail'.

6. For example, the benefits of the 1969 merger between Cadburys and Schweppes remain mainly elusive even 25 years later (see case study by Tony Eccles and Martin Stoll, originally published in J. Hendry and T. Eccles (eds), *European Cases in Strategic Management: A Resource Pack*, Chapman & Hall, London, 1993. See also newspaper article by William Gleeson, 'Accountants Add Up Cultural Differences', *The Independent on Sunday*, Business Section, 17 July 1994, p. 4.

7. These details taken from an article by Jack Schofield entitled 'Mission Impossible', *The Guardian*, Thursday, 14 April 1994, p. 19, © *The Guardian*.

8. These details taken from an article by Jane Simms entitled 'When a Corporate Resolution Becomes Mission Impossible', *The Independent on Sunday*, Business Section, 6 February 1994, p. 15.

9. Under German law companies can get the tax back on bribe payments to foreign companies.

10. This was proposed at the Amnesty International British Section Business Group inaugural meeting held at London Business School on 28 April 1994.

Further Reading

Allinson, R. E. (1993) *Global Disasters: Inquiries into Management Ethics*, Prentice-Hall, New York. (Deals with how ethics are built into the strategic management decision-making processes; explores this via four major management disasters – Challenger, Kings Cross, Herald of Free Enterprise, Mount Erebus.)

Miles, G. (1993) 'In Search of Ethical Profits: Insights from Strategic Management', *Journal of Business Ethics*, vol. 12, no. 3, pp. 219–25. (Evaluates three standard strategy paradigms by historical criteria of ethical profits; gives grounds for including ethics in strategic management, even if ethics does not pay.)

Rowe, A. J. *et al.* (1994) *Strategic Management: A Methodological Approach*, 4th edn, Addison-Wesley, New York. (See ch. 3, 'Strategic Visioning, Goals, Ethics and Social Responsibility'.)

Special edition (25th Anniversary) of the *Journal of Management Development*, (1992), vol. 11, no. 4. (Special theme issue on (organisational) ethics and strategic management.)

170   *Management and Ethics*

References

Andrews, K. (1989) 'Ethics in Practice', *Harvard Business Review*, vol. 67, no. 5, pp. 99–104.
Bader, G. E. S. (1988) 'New Frontiers in Planning – Strategic Issues for the 1990's', *Long Range Planning*, vol. 19, no. 6, pp. 66–74.
Baron, M. (1991) 'The Moral Status of Loyalty', in Johnson (ed.), pp. 225–40.
Bowie, N. (1990) 'Business Ethics and Cultural Relativism', in Madsen and Shafritz (eds), pp. 366–82.
Bradley, I.C. (1987) *Enlightened Entrepreneurs*, Weidenfeld & Nicolson, London.
Campbell, A. and Yeung, S. (1994) 'Creating a Sense of Mission', in Dewit and Meyer (eds), pp. 147–56.
Cannon, T. (1994) *Corporate Responsibility: A Textbook on Business Ethics, Governance, Environment: Roles and Responsibilities*, Pitman, London.
Chryssides, G. D. and Kaler, J. H. (1993) *An Introduction to Business Ethics*, Chapman & Hall, London.
Cooke, R. A. and Young, E. (1990) 'The Ethical Side of Takeovers and Mergers', in Madsen and Shafritz (eds), pp. 254–69.
David, F. R. (1991) *Strategic Management*, 3rd edn, Macmillan, Basingstoke.
Davies, P. W. F. (1992) 'The Contribution of the Philosophy of Technology to the Management of Technology', Ph.D. thesis, Brunel University with Henley Management College.
Dewit, B. and Meyer, R. (eds) (1994) *Strategy: Process, Content, Context (An International Perspective)*, West Publishing Company, St Paul, Minnesota.
Donaldson, T. (1989) *The Ethics of International Business*, OUP, New York.
Evans, R. (1991) 'Business Ethics and Changes in Society', *Journal of Business Ethics*, vol. 10, no. 11, pp. 871–6.
Goyder, G. (1993) *The Just Enterprise*, Adamantine Press, London (first published in 1987 by Andre Deutsch).
Johnson, D. G. (ed.) (1991) *Ethical Issues in Engineering*, Prentice-Hall, Englewood-Cliffs, N.J.
Ladd, J. (1982) 'Collective and Individual Moral Responsibility in Engineering: Some Questions', *IEEE Technology & Society Magazine*, vol. 1, no. 2 (June) pp. 3–10.
Lynch, D. and Kordis, P. L. (1990) *Strategy of the Dolphin: (Winning Elegantly by Coping Powerfully in a World of Turbulent Change)*, Arrow, London (first published by Hutchinson in 1989).
MacIntyre, A. (1977) 'Why are the Problems of Business Ethics Insoluble?', Conference proceedings from Bentley College, Mass, pp. 99–107.
Madsen, P. and Shafritz, J. M. (eds) (1990) *Essentials of Business Ethics*, Meridian, New York.
Mintzberg, H. (1994) *The Rise and Fall of Strategic Planning*, Prentice-Hall International (UK) Ltd, Hemel Hempstead.
Singer, A. E. (1994) 'Strategy as Moral Philosophy', *Strategic Management Journal*, vol. 15, pp. 191–213.
Stacey, R. D. (1993) *Strategic Management and Organisational Dynamics*, Pitman, London.
Toffler, A. (1970) *Future Shock*, Bodley Head, London.
Whittington, R. (1993) *What is Strategy – And Does it Matter?*, Routledge, London.
Williams, J. G. (1993) 'Management Buyouts: Technical Problems or Ethical Dilemmas', Conference on Professional and Business Ethics, October 1993, University of Central Lancashire (unpublished).

CHAPTER 11

Ethical Issues in Marketing

1 Introduction

Whilst most people may be able to agree that an ethical code in marketing practice is desirable, reaching agreement on a systematic application of even the most rudimentary moral principles becomes more problematic as one moves from considering broad generalisations to particular examples (Laczniak, 1983). This is not confined to marketing but applies to business conduct generally. As consumers, most people believe that stealing from employers is wrong, but as employees, this sense of probity seemed to diminish as the value of the item fell. A Gallup poll in the US cited by Ricklefs (1983) indicated that 74% of a sample of business executives had supplied their children with materials for their homework and 78% had used company telephones for long-distance calls. A decade later a similar mismatch of public expectation and private behaviour was noted in the UK. Blanchfield, Lea and Richards found, unsurprisingly, that the consumers surveyed believed financial institutions should observe strict standards of honesty and accountability, and yet a survey carried out by Leicester University showed a high proportion of their sample of consumers filing dishonest insurance claims, without apparent moral qualms (see Blanchfield, Lea and Richards, 1994).

2 Marketers and Ethics

Ferrell and Gresham (1985) take the view that there is 'no clear concensus about ethical conduct'; that ethical standards are neither absolute nor constant and that attempts to determine whether particular marketing activities are ethical or non-ethical cannot produce a definitive code of ethical marketing behaviour. This view does not preclude the general standpoint that deceptive advertising, price fixing, witholding product test data, falsifying market research behaviour and other such practices are essentially unethical. However Ferrell and Gresham (1985) suggested that people's views of what was ethical was contingency based. They proposed that a more useful standpoint from which to judge ethical behaviour in marketing would be the establishment of a set of criteria or framework for recognising which factors determine ethical or unethical decisions in marketing. Whether the eventual marketing outcomes are thought to be ethical or otherwise is decided by the various publics or stakeholders, shareholders, marketers, suppliers, competitors, customers, and commentators.

Ferrell and Gresham (1985) propose three elements, each with attendant variables, that are likely to influence the ethical status of either or both of a) the marketer's intentions and b) the marketing output. These elements are:

(i)   individual factors: The marketer's knowledge, beliefs, values, attitudes and intentions, influenced by the moral standards transmitted by family, education and the cultural context.

(ii) significant others: The marketer's reference groups within the organisation. The extent of influence from such groups would be affected by the social distance the marketer experiences from those groups and by the organisational climate of ethical/unethical behaviour. If top management is visible, its inherent power will ensure it exerts greater influence; whereas peers will be more influential where management is remote.

(iii) opportunity: Increased opportunity for unethical marketing behaviour will positively affect occurrence. Companies and professions that promote and enforce ethical codes raise standards of ethical behaviour and conversely a diminution of punishment and higher rewards associated with unethical behaviour will tend to increase it.

The first and second elements agree with such well-established work as that of Engel, Blackwell and Kincaid (1993) on consumers, and of Hakansson (1983) on organisational buyers, and most marketers would expect to find the variables cited having an effect on people's behaviour. Support for the second and third elements comes from Hunt, Chonko and Wilcox (1984) and from Chonko and Hunt (1985) who found that a strong lead from top managers reduced their employees' perception of ethical problems or ambiguity. The Ferrell and Gresham (1985) model proposes that any particular marketing decision in the face of a given ethical dilemma will be the outcome of effect of the ethical issue mediated by the three areas of influencing factors. The evaluation of the behavioural outcome by society occurs independently of the marketer's internal consideration of the issue. Like many behaviour models it does not purport to provide a measurement in a general sense. It is a guide to the factors that observers may consider.

But if this has given some indication of where to look for clues as to the marketer's ethical intentions and directions in marketing decisions, what might motivate a company to take an ethical stance in its marketing decisions?

There is some evidence that a strong steer from top management on positive ethical policies not only creates a working climate with fewer conflicts for employees, it also elicits a higher level of organisational commitment from them. Hunt, Wood and Chonko (1989) found a positive association between corporate values and organisational commitment in a sample of more than 1,200 professional marketers comprising of marketing managers, marketing researchers and advertising agency managers.

Reinforcing the idea that value judgements on marketing ethics are contingent on circumstances, they found also that the marketers notions of corporate ethics were apparently related to their own marketing specialisms. Moreover, just as Ferrell and Gresham (1985) had suggested, they found that age, education, income and some occupational features affected their evaluation of the ethics of particular marketing decisions.

Perhaps a more persuasive idea to convince top management that adopting an ethical corporate policy is beneficial is the suggestion that it can have a positive effect on the company's success. Donaldson and Davis (1990) argue that such policies can have a beneficial effect on 'the bottom line'. Taking the view that management can only operate effectively on a system of shared values in terms of each functional area of the business, they propose the view that some sort of ethical standpoint, good or bad, is integral to those shared values. The argument to adopt ethical values that are 'consistent, justifiable and without need of further improvement' rests on the surmise that managerial decisions and actions will be seen more favourably, and that the organisational culture and relationships between people will be strengthened. These effects, they assert, will lead to higher quality in products, processes and services, and better output and achievements generally in the organisation.

Essentially these premises constitute the rationale for implementing internal marketing and TQM (total quality management). Alternatively they present the profit motive in ethical garb. Donaldson and Davis (1990) acknowledge that some people will respond with scepticism to this approach and, to counter this, cite examples of manufacturing and retailing companies with practices from both sides of the ethical/unethical divide to support their case.

3 Empirical Evidence

But how far do companies agree with this approach? Some studies of senior executives in companies show them claiming to hold relatively high ethical principles in relation to business. Burke, Maddock and Rose (1993) carried out a study examining the 'attitudes to business ethics' among a sample of top decision-makers and other professional groups. They obtained responses from 498 senior managers and 165 junior managers to their questionnaire on business ethics. The overwhelming majority of the senior managers had authority in functional, decision-making roles, where ethical judgements enter the considerations; 13.5% of the senior managers were in marketing. The other functional areas represented were company secretaries, 10.0%, personnel, 16.9%, finance, 18.6%, and other directors, 2.9%. The research was supported by *The* Co-operative Bank Ltd, an organisation that has publicly espoused a stringent ethical code and promulgated this theme in its advertising campaigns since 1992.

There were four areas under investigation – conduct of business, employee relations, social responsibility, and environmental concern. Of these, the first, conduct of business, focused on aspects that the researchers identified as being 'at the heart of business'. The constituent parts were defined as: marketing, pricing, and direct relations with competitors and customers.

The researchers concluded from the study that senior managers and professionals had a high level of concern for ethical issues in general, whilst maintaining awareness of the importance of 'a profit-oriented competitive position'. Their results indicated that more than three-quarters felt that ethical behaviour in business was feasible and disagreed with the idea that 'telling lies in business is plain common sense'. The vast majority claimed they thought 'it was always possible to tell the truth when promoting or selling products and services'; 77% disagreed that in business 'there was one rule – make as much as you can'; and 88% disagreed that tax evasion was a necessary or legitimate business tactic.

Nonetheless, the sample of respondents did not adopt an anti-competitive stance; free-market ideology and practice was supported. Two-thirds of those questioned were unconcerned about the destination of invested funds, believing this to be the company's concern only, and nearly a third believed a high interest rate on money lent for high risk ventures was usually defensible. Burke, Maddock and Rose (1993) concluded in their discussion of the survey cited above,

> When it comes to making money, individuals appear less ethically sensitive than they are when dealing with colleagues or considering issues such as the environment.

The expressed concern for ethical approaches in business by the senior managers in the survey was not related solely to high-quality, high-value products or services. The fundamental marketing notion of customer-focus was cited as the justification for selling low-quality goods; that is, the practice is quite acceptable if that is what the customer wants. This approach accords comfortably with the Institute of Marketing definition of marketing:

> Marketing is the management process which identifies, anticipates and supplies customer requirements efficiently and profitably.

4   Marketing Strategy

The scope of marketing decisions includes strategic marketing planning as well as operational marketing management. At the strategic level the company adopts a stance towards competitors. Most strategic marketing theory and terminology derives, as does corporate strategy, from a basis in military strategic thinking. So the language of such strategy is couched in terms of warfare, rivalry and aggression with recommendations to attack or defend, to surprise or outflank. The objectives have been to establish an invincible position, either as market dominator, entailing the eventual extinguishing of some other companies in the same market, or as a specialist market nicher, the main player in a specific market sector. Suppliers and buyers are characterised as part of the competition (Porter, 1980). The arguments in favour of this standpoint are persuasive. Successful national and international companies can be seen to be highly competent in these areas.

Such strategies reduce choice for the customer, maximise the cost–price gap initially, may reduce employment in the competitors as they lose market share or fail and, if adopted widely, perhaps adversely affect whole economies. The accompanying notion holds that many medium-size companies operating in the same market are adrift strategically. This overlooks stable markets where there is sufficient competition to stabilise prices, and where many firms have operated successfully over many years. It lacks the explanatory power to deal with the advantages of long-term buyer–supplier relationships, and with the need for these in the era of on-line, electronic data exchange between buyers and suppliers as a tool of quick response to the market. Moreover it does not explain the confidence generated in a market where customers perceive a substantial number of firms operating, such that they believe that they are able to compare market offerings and have real choice in what they buy. Blanchfield, Lea and Richards (1994) found that whilst customers had considerable dissatisfactions with the UK high street banks, the market concentration meant that they felt helpless to make their complaints heard and there was a lack of trust.

5   Market Research

Supporting the marketing effort may well be a programme of marketing research. To carry out a rigorously organised survey, of customers or internal employees, without sampling or respondent bias or error and with strictly appropriate statistical treatment and interpretation of results, is in itself a demanding exercise. The dangers of unintentional misrepresentation or mistaken analysis of results into market predictions are always there. Unfortunately there are possibilities too that results may be massaged to produce the predicted or desired outcomes.

The Market Research Society has high ethical standards for members to observe in all aspects of the market research process. There are organisations and individuals who attempt to pass themselves off as carrying out market research, when they are engaged in thinly isguised selling operations. To the public, accosted in shopping centres, over the telephone or on their doorstep with the initial claim that their interviewer is a market researcher, the apparent differences between these activities and genuine market research may be small. These activities contaminate the general image of the market research process as a respectable procedure.

6 The Marketing Mix

The marketing mix elements each offer complex opportunities for marketing decision-making and thereby contain the potential for ethical and unethical choices by marketing and business personnel. The marketing mix comprises McCarthy's 4 'P's' of product, price, promotion and place, applied most often to products available in the market, and the additional 3 'P's' of people, process and physical evidence (Booms and Bitner, 1981), which conveniently elaborates the distinction between the decision areas crucial to product and service offerings in the market, whilst extending the mix concept to explain the key issues in long-term transactions between buying and supplying organisations, that is, the notion of relationship marketing.

7 Product

Marketing decisions about products are not confined to quality and relative value. The corporate-level decisions of what business and markets to be in and therefore what product to offer may be seen as ethically loaded. The industries that produce for example, tobacco, infant milk supplement or nuclear fuels, attract interlinked ethical and environmental arguments which are marshalled to criticise both the effects of the products in general and the decisions to offer them in particular markets.

At a less controversial level, the range of products produced, the numbers of product features and their availability may be fine-tuned not just to existing customer demand but to influence and stimulate future demand. Offering new features without losing a product's identity is a familiar way of stimulating sales in the consumer market. The up-dating of many consumer products such as books, computer software, the restyling of cars, the seasonal cycle of garment fashions and related but slower movements of style in home furnishings, all meet a latent consumer desire for some aesthetic stimulation and change.

Some critics characterise this as manipulation of buyers, especially in consumer markets where discretionary income is more easily spent on impulse. Moreover, the investment required for the introduction of restyled products usually involves the withdrawal of the market offerings that are selling least well or making less profit, leaving perhaps a section of consumers no longer able to obtain the product they want and can afford, or unable to find parts and service for an existing consumer durable.

Nonetheless, the dissatisfactions associated with the need to withdraw a product, or product elimination, are not just a problem for the consumer. Harness and MacKay (1994) recounts how the major firms in the financial services industry are legally obliged to keep track of small numbers of customer accounts that the firm would prefer to close, for perhaps 25 years after the issue date. However, when banks and building societies fail to inform existing customers that new financial packages with more attractive terms have been launched, the media are often quick to report this. In these circumstances the financial companies are often castigated for *not* exercising product elimination. They are seen leaving their loyal customers in a less advantageous position in respect of either their savings or their liabilities than the newly recruited customers.

Conversely, the rise of environmental awareness on the part of the consumer, resulting in pressure to withdraw products from the market, may not always be to a company's disadvantage. Concern about depletion on the ozone layer has affected the market acceptability of many products. Amongst them has been the gas known as CFC, blamed as damaging to the ozone in the upper atmosphere of the earth and widely used in the manufacture of refrigerators and as the propellant in aerosol sprays. The development and commercial substitution of an alternative product became a priority in the early 1990s with a few major chemical companies rushing to satisfy the new consumer demand for a non-CFC aerosal propellant. In 1994, however, industry analysts pointed out that the patent on the original product was coming to an end which would have allowed a more competitive market to develop in its manufacture and supply. The substitute product is at an early stage in its patent life, and by responding quickly to the changing consumer demand and thereby supporting the aerosol market, the chemical companies involved have ensured their share of the profit.

8 Price

Setting the price element in the marketing mix is subject to frequent consumer and media speculation but evidence of the ethical direction of the marketing decisions is not always visible. Price is not the chief criteria for all consumers when making purchase decisions, and even those who do judge some products primarily by price do not apply the same criteria to everything they buy. The rise in consumer concern with healthy eating, which some UK dairy firms identified as a serious consumer market issue in the 1970s, has raised demand for food products which are low in fat. A report by Peta Cottee (1994) of the Food Commission, criticised food manufactures for exploiting the public's anxieties about fat content in food when surveys had revealed that low-fat products were priced at around 40% higher than their non-reduced-fat equivalents. Marks & Spencer and Ambrosia priced low-fat and regular versions the same.

When launching new products or entering new markets, marketers conventionally distinguish between pricing strategies of 'market skimming' – beginning with a relatively high price which will be affordable by relatively well-off opinion leaders and establish the product's perceived quality status before lowering the price later as sales volume builds – and of 'market penetration' – when a relatively lower price is set at the outset to build market share more quickly. Both these strategies may be successful in relation to particular market conditions and neither necessarily involve any unethical market behaviour where customers are unlikely to be dependent on new products.

Experienced buyers in both domestic and business markets hold an internal estimate of price bands within which they expect to pay for goods or services of particular quality levels which they purchase with varying degrees of frequency. The idea of a fair price for a given standard of quality is based on prior purchasing practice and is usually shared within the buyer's reference groups. Only the knowledgeable business-to-business purchaser may be in a position to be able to calculate the costs to the producer of bringing a product to market. For the small business buyer the relevant information is usually obscured by the size of the supplier or the supply chain, and the consumer has little chance of appreciating the gap between costs and price. The consensus about the right price to pay is therefore a key criterion in buying decisions.

Where market competition exists between many organisations of sufficiently equivalent power and size it would be anticipated that unethical pricing practices such as operating a cartel to keep the price artificially high to the buyer are less likely to survive, as any of the firms can bid for increased market share by cutting their margins and prices whilst maintaining their overall profit in an increased volume of sales. However, few markets exist in the economist's paradigm of perfect competition; some are highly fragmented with a lack of shared information, some highly concentrated. Power is frequently unequal between direct industry rivals and between suppliers and purchasers in the supply chain. Price wars are waged by large companies on small ones in order to gain market share. The small company may seek rescue from a 'white knight', or friendly larger company, or hostile takeovers sometimes occur where no rescuer can be found. The customer may benefit from reduced prices in the short term, as was the case in the newspaper price wars in the UK during 1994. When smaller firms are bought out and the market becomes more concentrated, however, customers may expect firms to attempt to maximise the cost–price gap. The existence of Anti-Trust legislation in the US and the requirement for the Department of Trade and Industry to investigate any threat to 'public interest' from proposed takeovers and mergers in already concentrated industries by referral to the Monopolies and Mergers Commission is a formal recognition of this tendency.

Well before this stage is reached, small and medium-sized firms may find themselves squeezed by the arrival of a large player in their market. During the autumn of 1993, publicity highlighted how the independent town-centre retailers in the toys market were experiencing tough price competition from a chain of toy superstores located on out-of-town sites. Offering very well-priced goods and wide choice in products, but accessible largely to car-owners, the toy supermarkets could force the small toyshops out of business. If this happens there will be reduced access and choice to lower-income families without cars whose contribution to market volume is too low to sustain the independent toyshops. The decision to adopt a market penetration strategy might be seen to pose a social dilemma if not an ethical one.

9   Place

By 'place', marketers refer to the sum of locations by which the product moves from the supplier to the customer, including means of the distribution, arriving finally at the point of delivery to the customer. For retailing, this comprises the whole supply chain up to and including the location of the retail outlet. With non-store retailing, the communications mode selected and the delivery service become part of the 'place'. For business-to-business marketing, the supply chain is again part of the place concept, as is the point at which the customer is able to access the information required about the goods or service they wish to buy. Frequent repeat purchases in business will be made by ordering from the supplier, perhaps electronically or from catalogues. Less regular business purchases requiring specification and negotiation may involve a personal visit from the supplier's sales staff.

Marketing decisions about the extent to which the goods will be available in locations to all who might wish to buy will naturally be tempered by the need to protect against losses if a particular channel of distribution is unprofitable. So business-to-business marketing properly includes the elimination of sales calls on customers deemed unprofitable, and retail location decisions will keep some suppliers out of reach of less-well-off consumers. Generally there are other suppliers who will step into those markets, sometimes with 'cheap and cheerful' operations.

Further away from the customer, the less visible decisions about distribution channels may brook the precept that there are more temptations to act unethically where there is more interaction with the public. Individual employees may be reluctant to admit operator error, although monitoring procedures should overcome this. Some domestic consumers are brand loyal to certain food retailers, precisely because they feel uncertain whether some companies have, for example, the integrity, the profit margins or the necessary insurance to jettison products which are marginally damaged in the supply chain. Where consumers fear that unobservable and unspecified contamination of products could occur, some companies adopt even stricter codes of practice than regulations demand, to safeguard their reputation and sales.

10   Promotion

Marketing promotions or communications are inevitably subjected to greater public scrutiny than other aspects of marketing. Perceived lapses in ethical standards in selling, public relations, and advertising attract media attention, quite rightly. The rise of consumerism and the protection of the consumer and small businesses have been stimulated through television and radio and some crusading sections of the press. Popular TV and radio programmes and press campaigns often highlight some pernicious practices that have succeeded in deceiving customers, not because they were exceptionally gullible, but because most firms with which they dealt could be trusted. An unfortunate side-effect of the publicity attached to the mendacity of the few has sometimes been to taint the reputation of marketing *per se*. That selling is an essential part of the supply chain, that public relations and advertising keep the customer informed, and that each part contributes to the viability of the economy, can be overlooked.

The selling practices which attract most adverse attention tend to be those of intrusive, 'hard' sales techniques where the customer finds themselves oppressed by the process. 'Soft' sales techniques, using the consumer's latent desires and emotions as outlined by Packard (1969), have been heavily satirised and have become familiar to most consumers and more transparent. Hard selling, such as pressure to sign a sales agreement on the spot with a positive inducement, such as a reduced price offer available at that time only, has led to a legal requirement for a short 'cooling off' period, post sales, during which consumers can rescind their decision, but it does not apply to all goods. Similar pressures applied to captive holiday makers to invest in holiday property whilst they are abroad are now well known, itself a protection for most of the public.

Firms which train their sales staff courteously to advise customers whose needs they cannot supply adequately, to go to another supplier, even sometimes providing details of such, may receive gratitude from the individual customer but rarely public recognition. A policy of honesty and politeness in sales may build customer loyalty and company reputation, but it is difficult to quantify such effects. This approach to selling is advocated as part of an overall 'customer care' strategy and attempts to combine an ethical stance with a measure of long-term self interest.

Potentially damaging for the public image of marketing is the practice previously known for 20 or 30 years as pyramid selling, relaunched in the late 1980s variously as network marketing and multi-level marketing. Consumers are recruited to a selling operation which relies on their each reselling goods in which they have invested, to a minimum number of people who must also resell the goods, and so on, along an ever-enlarging chain or network. Claims have been made that this approach is not only respectable but will account for an increasing percentage of retail sales nationally by the year 2000. Croft (1994) showed in the results of his careful and detailed research into this area that the practices of these so-called marketing operations are virtually indistinguishable from the original pyramid concept, for which a simple mathematical calculation demonstrates that the population of the UK could not sustain the predicted sales. The selling appeal at recruitment is often to people who have very limited financial resources, who could ill-afford to be left with unsold goods.

In advertising, the honesty, legality and fairness of the content and context of the message is protected in the UK by the Advertising Standards Authority. This body responds to complaints from the public, and after adjudication may require advertisers to withdraw material it believes to be offensive, misleading or to break the law. There are also published rules with which advertisers must comply and breaking these is sufficient to cause the ASA to intervene without external request. Statements overtly attacking competitors' products fall into the forbidden category. The ASA regularly advertises itself, reminding the public of its existence and how to contact the organisation to make a complaint.

Some of the most controversial advertisements on which the A.S.A. took action in the early 1990s were those for the Italian clothing franchise chain, Benetton, in which were shown not clothes, but arresting and disturbing images depicting contemporary life. A huge bill-board picture of a new-born infant was shown, but images of international terrorism and the death-bed scene of the family around an Aids sufferer were not allowed on advertising display in the UK.

An advertising campaign launched in May 1992 that has been intended to be not only ethical in itself but also to portray the ethical policies of the company, is that of *The* Co-operative Bank Ltd. The bank had not previously used television advertising extensively, so was not well known in areas of the country where they lacked a strong branch network. The advertising message expressed with clarity the bank's ethical stance on investment, i.e., on the ways that it would and would not use customers' money. The television campaign was complemented with press advertising. By implication only, the message contrasts *The* Co-operative Bank's actions with those of its far larger rivals. At the time of launch, as Blanchfield (1994) elsewhere says, 'the media interest was noticeable amidst reports of scandal and crises in the dealings of financial institutions'. Its impact was reflected in the national press immediately: 'After recent fiascos, it is difficult to believe that ethics and moral values can have anything to do with banking. The Co-op Bank has proved otherwise with the launch of its new ethical policy' (*The Guardian*, 1 May 1992).

The Co-operative Bank traces its antecedents back to its foundations, however, maintaining that they had retained an ethical approach to business since establishment in 1872. The mission statement of the bank consists of eight principles. Blanchfield (1994) notes that the eight principles not only set out commercial goals but also address the banks's social objectives. They refer to factors such as the quality and excellence of service, education and training, quality of life and freedom of association in social, political, racial and religious matters, and the bank places great emphasis on integrity. Its ethical stance has been widely recognised and commended and has received a number of national awards.

The very impact that this campaign makes, does rely on a contrast effect with the public perception of banks as somewhat lacking in their care for the customer. It is not a message free from risk since any failure to meet the claimed standards could rebound badly on the bank. This has not happened, and the campaign developed successfully into its third year with new advertising messages and copy.

11   People, Physical Evidence and Process

Lewis (1991) reports from her empirical findings how customers' expectations of service quality have risen over an extended period, creating greater potential for competition in the financial services. The three service aspects of the marketing mix, noted above, of people, physical evidence and process are involved in the five dimensions of service performance identified by Parasuraman, Zeithaml and Berry (1985). These are:

tangibles – physical facilities, equipment, appearance of personnel,
reliability – ability to perform the promised service dependability and accurately,
responsiveness – willingness to help customers and provide prompt service,
assurance – knowledge and courtesy of employees ansd their ability to inspire trust and confidence,
empathy – caring, individualized attention the company provides its customers.

The adoption of the customer care approach inherent in the above aspirations for a service has sound business objectives – customer retention through customer satisfaction and loyalty. Keeping existing customers makes sound marketing sense since the costs are higher in recruiting new customers. Variations of Customer Charters abound as companies and politicians recognise this. The ethical organisation will make the approaches above possible to operate by also adopting policies and practice towards its own staff that enable them to meet the stated objectives. When insufficient account is taken of the needs of the employees in training and resources to meet the exacting new standards set for interaction with their stakeholders, a greater customer dissatisfaction is aroused, with potentially dire consequences for public confidence in the service provider. In the specific area of financial services Gibbs (1993) says 'lack of confidence and the need for trust may form a vicious circle'.

Earlier, Lewis (1991) found both US and UK bank customers had very high expectations of service across most of the dimensions of service investigated. In general the UK customers were more satisfied than their US couterparts. The areas in which they had most confidence and satisfaction were related mainly to the personal qualities of the staff, possibly reflecting the banks' training exercises with staff. However, on issues of facilities and knowledge of personal needs of customers, they were were low in their perceptions and evaluations of service.

12 Conclusion

So how importantly does marketing feature in the health of a company's ethical stance in business? Fearnley (1993) found 'corporate reputation' to be a selling point but to be largely a 'wasted asset'. It comprises largely the sum of experiences of employees and external groups, hence its existence and nature is intimately associated with the elements of the marketing mix. Like a product brand, the corporate reputation is composed of several elements but is predominantly 'in the eye of the beholder'.

However, Fearnley (1993) also asserts that 'the most dominant factor in a good corporate reputation' is the quality of the product and/or service, for although the customer increasingly buys 'the company along with the offering', it is the offerings themselves that continue to be the main interest, concern and focus of the customer.

Hence marketing ethics cannot be divorced from the issues that concern business ethics as a whole. As with any less-than-scrupulous practice in whatever functional area of business, adopting a compromise in ethical standards in marketing may turn out to be a tactic of short-term value. The need for repeat business may be a guard against unethical behaviour, but the best protection lies in the company's overall ethical stance reflected throughout its policies on internal standards and organisation, and its commitment to its external stakeholders.

References

Blanchfield, C. (1994) 'Consumer Market Responses to Perceived Business Ethics of Financial Institutions', unpublished M. Phil. thesis, University of Huddersfield.

184   *Management and Ethics*

Blanchfield, C., Lea, E.C. and Richards, G. (1994) 'Business Ethics, Do Consumers Care?', Marketing Education Group, Annual Conference, University of Ulster, Coleraine, 4–6 July.
Booms, B. H. and Bitner, M. J. (1981) 'Marketing Strategies and Organization Structures for Service Firms', in J. H. Donnelly and W. R. George (eds), *Marketing of Services*, American Marketing Association, Chicago, p. 47–51.
Burke, T., Maddock, S. and Rose, A. (1993) 'How Ethical is British Business?', *Research Working Paper Series 2*, No. 1, University of Westminster, January.
Chonko, L. B. and Hunt, S. D. (1985) 'Ethics and Marketing Management: An Empirical Examination', *Journal of Business Research*, vol. 13 (August) pp. 339–59.
Cottee, P. (1994) Report of The Food Commission, in K. Knight, 'Healthy Profits on Low-fat Foods', *The Times*, Wednesday 19 October 1994.
Croft, R. (1994) 'Multi-level Marketing: Claims to Respectability under Scrutiny', Marketing Education Group, Proceedings of the 1994 Annual Conference, University of Ulster.
Donaldson, J. and Davis, P. (1990) 'Business Ethics? Yes, But What Can It Do for the Bottom Line?' *Management Decision*, vol. 28, no. 6, pp. 29–33.
Engel, J. F., Blackwell, R. D. and Kincaid, P. W. (1993) *Consumer Behaviour*, The Dryden Press, London.
Ennew, C., McGregor, A. and Diacon, S. (1993) 'Ethical Aspects of Savings and Investment Products', MEG, Proceedings of Annual Conference, vol. 1, pp. 297–307.
Fearnley, M. (1993) 'Corporate Reputation: The Wasted Asset', *Marketing Intelligence and Planning*, vol. 11, no. 11, pp. 4–8.
Ferrell, O. C. and Gresham, L. G. (1985) 'A Contingency Framework for Understanding Ethical Decision Making in Marketing', *Journal of Marketing*, vol. 49 (Summer) pp. 87–96.
Gibbs, P. T. (1993) 'Customer Care and Service: a Case for Business Ethics', *International Journal of Bank Marketing*, vol. 11, no. 1, pp. 26–33.
Hakansson, H. (ed.) (1983) *International Marketing and Purchasing of Industrial Goods: An Interaction Approach*, Wiley, Chichester.
Harness, D. and MacKay, S. (1994) 'Product Elimination Strategies of the Financial Services Sector', Marketing Education Group, Proceedings of the Annual Conference, University of Ulster.
Hunt, S. D., Chonko, L. B., and Wilcox, J. B. (1984) 'Ethical Problems of Marketing Researchers,' *Journal of Marketing Research*, vol. 21 (August) pp. 304–24.
Hunt, S. D., Wood, V. R. and Chonko, B. (1989) 'Corporate Ethical Values and Organisational Commitment in Marketing', *Journal of Marketing*, vol. 53, pp. 79–90.
Laczniak, G. R. (1983) 'Business Ethics: A Manager's Primer', *Business*, vol. 33 (January-March) pp. 23–9.
Lewis, B. R. (1991) 'Service Quality: An International Comparison of Bank Customers' Expectations and Perceptions', *Journal of Marketing Management*, vol. 7, pp. 47–62.
Packard, V. (1969) *The Hidden Persuaders*, Penguin, Harmondsworth.
Parasuraman, A., Zeithaml, V. and Berry, L. L. (1988) 'A Conceptual Model of Service Quality and its Implications for Future Research', *Journal of Marketing*, vol. 49 (Fall), pp. 41–50.
Porter, M. E. (1980) 'Competitive Strategy', Free Press, New York.
Ricklefs, R. (1983) 'Executives and General Public Say Ethical Behaviour is Declining in U.S.', *Wall Street Journal*, 31 October, p. 25.
Tendler, S. (1994) 'A nation of robbers, fiddlers and thieves', *The Times*, 21 Sept.

CHAPTER 12

Ethical Issues in Purchasing

1 Introduction

The purchasing function of modern organisations has changed from a relatively low-status, clerical role to that of a strategic business function. This has resulted from the increasing importance of material costs in the total production function and is allied to developments such as just-in-time (JIT) and total quality management (TQM) within production operations. These have led the way in changing the traditional adversarial relationship between supplier and buyer into one of partnership purchasing which works best when there is open communication and trust. Parallel to this change in the status of purchasing as a business function have been changes in the quality of those employed in purchasing. There has been a rise in the educational base of buyers and a greater willingness to seek professional qualifications as an aid to a more professional approach. Alongside this has gone increased attention to ethics, reflected in the growth in the number of codes of ethics in existence and company policies for ethical purchasing. However, there is evidence that unethical practices persist and continue to cause concern.

Purchasing managers occupy a boundary spanning role where, inevitably, they have to face situations where they must judge what is right (ethical) and wrong (unethical). Buyers can, by their actions, affect the company's profitability and reputation (Barr, 1993). Therefore, maintaining a strict ethical stance can be important in projecting the right image of the company. Other business functions remain sceptical of the honesty and independence of buyers whilst gift-giving and entertainment remain endemic in purchasing. Dubinsky and Gwin (1981) reveal how relatively little attention has been paid to the ethical standards, and the perceptions held of buyers by their peers. Many of the issues of ethical concern in business arise within the purchasing function: deception, bribery, price rigging, unsafe products and public safety. In many ways the purchasing function has been the forgotten function of business, unseen, disregarded and undervalued, and this has been reflected in the status and salaries, and perhaps the ethical standards, of the professionals involved. Furthermore there is a surprising dearth of published studies of purchasing ethics when compared to the much larger literature available, for instance, on marketing ethics (Murphy and Laczniak, 1981).

2 Ethical Issues in Purchasing

Forker and Janson (1990) argued that, though the evidence needed interpreting with care, their research indicated that purchasing personnel adopt high ethical standards. This reinforces the conclusions of Browning and Zabriskie's (1983) study that: (1) buyers are ethical in their dealing with salespeople, (2) buyers' actions are more ethical than their beliefs, and (3) younger, better-educated buyers were more ethical than their older, less-well-educated colleagues. Nonetheless, this study and that of Forker and Janson still uncovered evidence that buyers continued to accept gifts and entertainment. Sibley (1979) examined the image held of the purchasing department by themselves in comparison with the image held of it by other departments in one organisation. His study revealed the importance ethics can play in forming images of the professionalism of different groups. He argued that the continued practice of accepting gifts from vendors created an image among their colleagues that purchasing staff were vendor-loyal, though this was not part of the image purchasing personnel held of themselves. Rudelius and Buchholz (1979) reflect the concern of purchasing personnel themselves to adopt more ethical practices when they reported their desire for more top management guidance on ethical concerns. The purchasing managers they surveyed readily distinguished which of the scenarios raised ethical concerns. They also argued, dubiously, that only the acceptance of high-value gifts had ethical implications. Thus Rudelius and Buchholz (1979, p. 3) report that: 'a bottle of whisky at Christmas may be acceptable, but a case smacks of a bribe'.

Narayanam (1992), Ramsey (1989) and Barry (1992) all reflect this tendency amongst purchasing personnel to regard some favours as acceptable whilst others are clearly not.

The evidence that purchasing is still plagued with unethical buyers is readily available. Felch (1985), Dubinsky and Gwin (1981) and Rudelius and Buchholz (1979) all provide lists of the common unethical practices prevalent in purchasing. Most of the evidence comes from the USA though there are one or two articles published in the UK and a preliminary study conducted by Wood in 1994. Only Barry (1992) in a UK study strikes a dissenting note in observing that buyers are increasingly saying 'no' to lavish gifts and entertainment. Certainly he provides evidence that major companies such as Whitbread and Allied Dunbar are tightening their policies on the acceptance of gifts or entertainment by their buyers.

The offering of free gifts, free meals or free entertainment appears still to be widespread both in the USA (see Forker and Janson, 1992) and in the UK (see Ramsey, 1989, and Wood, 1994). It remains the most frequently cited issue of ethical concern in purchasing. Ramsey (1989) and Narayanam (1992) argue that gift-giving is endemic in purchasing. Narayanam (1992, p. 25) states boldly:

> There is no denying the fact that bribery is rampant among professionals and that not much is done to combat the evil.

Forker and Janson report on the 1987 study commissioned by Ernest & Whinney in the USA in which they compared replies to this survey with one taken in 1975. In 1987 no less than 97% of the respondents had accepted one or a small number of favours (gifts or entertainment) whereas only 79% had done so in 1975. The mean value of those favours was also higher (though that might be purely a reflection of inflation). However, the frequency with which offered favours were accepted was lower in 1987 than in 1975. Wood (1994) reported that 82% of the respondents who reported unethical practices mentioned gift-giving, free hospitality or free holidays.

Many of these gifts are of such low value that they do not appear to be designed to gain undue influence. Yet Ramsey (1989) argues for 'no bribes please' (in his article) and he describes gifts or offers of entertainment as *unprofessional characteristics* which the buyer considers in making the purchase decision compared with *professional characteristics* such as delivery, price or quality. He strongly emphasises that the professional buyer does not accept gifts of any value and stays firmly at what he calls the 'righteous' end of his spectrum of purchase characteristics. Supporting evidence on the continuance of the practice of offering sales inducements, or bribes as Ramsey calls them (1989, p. 33), is found in Barry (1992), Rudelius and Buchholz (1979), Dubinsky and Gwin (1981) and Wood (1994). The Chartered Institute of Purchasing and Supply (CIPS, 1977) allows its members to accept gifts of very low value such as pens and calendars which are primarily promotional materials. However, gifts of whisky or other forms of alcohol, and of chocolates, which are particularly prevalent at Christmas, are seen by Ramsey as bribes, even if ineffective ones. Gifts such as expensive holidays in exotic locations or even cars may be more blatant but should be seen as different in degree rather than kind from other gifts.

Why are buyers so reluctant to employ the word 'bribe'? Ramsey (1989, p. 33) argues it is because buyers recognise that using the word 'bribe' suggests a willingness to be influenced. They go to elaborate lengths to explain how the 'gifts' do not influence them, and refuse to see the gifts for what they are, which is a bribe according to Ramsey. The purpose of giving a gift to a buyer is to gain influence and the value of the gift is irrelevant to that intention. Gifts of low intrinsic value should be seen merely as inefficient means to achieve influence, but that does not alter their purpose. Ramsey calls on purchasing departments to come clean and call a bribe a bribe.

> If a company feels that it is acceptable for their purchasing staff to receive bribes, then that is their business, but at least let them have the guts to be honest about it. (1989, p. 33)

We may want to question whether it is entirely their own business, but the meaning of Ramsey's stricture is clear. He continues:

> They should give all their suppliers a break and put up a board in the company's reception area stating 'Our purchasing department accepts bribes'. This would simplify everything and cut out the need for all of the basic ritualistic behaviour that goes on around Christmas. (1989, p. 33)

However, many of the studies indicate (Rudelius and Buchholz, 1979; Forker and Janson, 1992) that the vast majority of purchasing managers are honest and ethical and in the survey by Wood (1994) many managers expressed their resentment at the offering of gifts, even those of low value. Ramsey (1989) and Sibley (1979) would retort that the image of purchasing managers held by their managerial peers is very much coloured by the prevalence of gift-giving.

The second major area of concern covers a number of practices which can be placed under the generic heading of deception. Purchasing personnel can and do exaggerate the difficulties their company is experiencing in order to place undue pressure on suppliers, either to cut prices or improve non-price factors. Dubinsky and Gwin (1981) and Rudelius and Buchholz (1979) report that this practice causes considerable concern to purchasing managers themselves. Those purchasing managers who adopt a professional approach to their work regard this practice as unethical, as they do the allied practice of inventing competition purely as a ruse to pressure suppliers on current price or quality and delivery. One purchasing manager described this as a pressure tactic to 'see what they will give' (Wood, 1994). Other deceptive practices include calling for quotations or even pre-sales services where there is no intention to offer orders subsequently, or even in some instances recompense for the pre-sales services. Suppliers find it difficult to object to such practices because proof is not readily available and objections now may sour relations for the future. The development of a partnership approach to purchasing (Clutterbuck *et al.*, 1992), where a fully open relationship is developed between suppliers and purchasers, helps to eliminate many of these deceptive practices.

A third major group of issues in purchasing ethics relates to discrimination, particularly in the form of showing favouritism toward certain suppliers. The basis of discrimination can vary: for instance, of favouring those suppliers who are also good customers; of favouring any supplier known to be favoured by senior management; of giving orders on the basis of personal preferences; to the practice of allowing suppliers to deal directly with other departments which do not adopt a strict professional approach to procurement. All these practices work against the development of a professional ethic by purchasing managers. These practices may prevent a company obtaining supplies on the most favourable terms available. It can make the choice of supplier arbitrary rather than the result of open and free competition. However, for the purchasing professional themselves, the practice which causes greatest concern is when other departments are allowed to deal directly with suppliers. In the survey by Wood (1994), 20% of respondents registered their resentment to this practice.

The final broad grouping of unethical practices in purchasing relate to the issue of information disclosure. There are a number of practices which breach confidentiality, which are reported in various studies (see Dubinsky and Gwin, 1981, and Felch, 1985, for instance). Some suppliers seek information on their competitors with the implied promise it will be of benefit to the purchaser. Purchasing managers themselves divulge information to favoured suppliers for which they have not obtained permission to release in this form. Companies openly reveal the price of the current supplier to create a 'Dutch auction' in which other suppliers compete to offer the lowest price. Finally some companies operate a tendering system in which the criteria for selection are released to some suppliers but not others.

The growth of the corporate hospitality industry over the last ten to fifteen years is further evidence that the practice of sales inducements is not necessarily dying out, merely changing its form. Corporate hospitality is a highly effective marketing tool, and Robson reports on a survey by Business Marketing Services which indicated it is more effective in attracting business and influencing customers than advertising, direct mail, brochures or exhibitions (Robson, 1992, p. 28). Robson also quotes the marketing manager of Keith Prowse Hospitality as saying that the targeting of corporate hospitality is impeccable. The whole issue of corporate hospitality, whatever its effectiveness, is fraught with ethical problems. The whole tenor of the approach suggests that it is a 'hard sell in a soft package', where half the purpose is to get customers to drop their objectivity in viewing products or services. If the case against the unethical nature of corporate hospitality is not already clear, then Business Marketing Services note that some companies do not use it with new clients because 'they feel it is too direct and perhaps too close to bribery' (Robson, 1992, p. 28). Given the foregoing it is hardly surprising that Barry is able to report David Sheridan (former purchasing chief at Whitbread) as saying, 'it is almost impossible not to suffer some softening up as a result' of accepting a supplier's goodwill (Barry, 1992, p. 24).

Buyers must remember that there is no such thing as a free gift, for the cost of them or any entertainment is ultimately borne by their employers in the price of the goods they buy. Corporate hospitality is expensive, but it is also a normal marketing expense for the companies who provide it for customers and clients, and therefore it will be reflected in the price.

3   Codes of Ethics

Browning and Zabriskie (1980) report that 90% of their respondents stated that their companies had a policy on ethics. Forker and Janson (1990) reported that 72% of companies in the Ernest & Whinney survey had company ethics policies, though this was a reduction on the 78% reported in the 1975 survey. Bradley (1989) reported that 72% of the companies in his survey had formal ethics policies or codes. Barry (1992) gives specific examples of codes in action in leading UK companies.

Further, both professional bodies for purchasing professionals in the UK and USA have had formal codes of ethics or practice for a considerable time; in the case of the Chartered Institute of Purchasing & Supply (CIPS) in the UK their codes dates from 1977. Browning and Zabriskie (1980) recorded that a majority of the respondents to their survey were aware of the code of the National Association of Purchasing Management, the American professional body. Similar evidence about the awareness of the CIPS' code amongst purchasing personnel is not available for the UK. Nonetheless evidence is given in Barry (1992) and Clutterbuck *et al.* (1992) that public and private organisations are attempting to tackle some of the more common problems of unethical practices in purchasing – for instance, on the acceptance of gifts and entertainment. Bradley (1989) found that only 35% of the companies he surveyed had specific ethics policies for purchasing, which might suggest the need for a more tailored policy to deal with the specific problem of ethics in this area. Rudelius and Buchholz (1979) and Sibley (1979) offer some support to this observation when they reported their respondents as pleading for much more policy guidance on ethical issues in purchasing from their organisation's top management.

4   Vignettes

Gary Brown was a newly appointed purchasing manager at Culcutt Engineering reporting to Alan Fitzgerald the general manager. The company operated a system of first line suppliers who enjoyed stock orders, and a number of second line suppliers to fill in shortages. Gary was given complete discretion on the selection of second line vendors and the volumes which were to be given to them. After a number of months it became clear that Fitzgerald took an interest in the second line spend and offered Gary favourable comments on the price and service of one particular supplier. Shortly afterwards, a representative of this company called and commented that the figures were a little low and unlikely to qualify for the holiday this year: it would be a shame if your general manager missed it this year. What should Gary do?

Bill Lancaster was the purchasing officer of Denver Components Ltd. During an average week he received calls from up to twelve representatives, though he did not always grant them a hearing. Bill was a member of CIPS and prided himself on the professional standards he set in his work. He was therefore taken aback when one representative he had known for a number of years, Gerald Aspey of Deakin Steel Stockholders, suggested that Bill reveal information he had on the prices of other steel suppliers to enable Deakin to undercut them. In return they would offer Bill's company information on their competitors. Gerald and Bill had a cordial working relationship which up to this time was strictly professional, with only gifts of minor value having been offered and accepted before. Deakins was a good competitive supplier who received the bulk of Denver's order for steel. However, Bill had heard that their new owners were aggressively pushing for increased sales. What should Bill do?

Both these vignettes illustrate situations very common in purchasing. The first is based upon a specific case but the second is a compilation of a number of examples collected by the author. Both explain the ways in which purchasing personnel are often pressurised to act unprofessionally and unethically.

Gary Brown faces a dilemma which many purchasing managers strongly resent, whilst that faced by Bill Lancaster tends to be regarded as more of a nuisance by purchasing managers. Brown would want to be loyal to his general manager but would not want to take unprofessional characteristics into account in his decisions on second line suppliers. He could discuss the situation with Alan Fitzgerald setting out his objections to the approach from the supplier but would probably feel inhibited from doing so. This is a situation where a company code of ethics, with specific provisions for purchasing, would assist a manager in resolving his difficulties. In the real case the supplier was highly competitive so they obtained many orders as of right, but Brown decided not to artificially engineer orders just to allow the general manager to win the holiday.

For Bill Lancaster his already cordial relationship with Gerald Aspey should allow him to explain his objections to giving any information on other suppliers because it is unethical. Again a company code would offer good support here to a manager in this situation. Clearly Lancaster, as a member of the CIPS, has recourse to their code which specifically forbids this sort of trading of information. Deakin Steel and Gerald Aspey must be told that orders are given on the basis of price, quality, delivery and other relevant factors, but no others.

5 Ethical Principles in Purchasing

A cursory knowledge of the major ethical theories is sufficient to be able to conclude that most of the practices described in this chapter are unethical, even if they are legal. Most of the practices involve some form of bribery, or corruption or deception, all unethical. There is, perhaps, one exception to this assertion, in that managerial egoism generally allows any form of behaviour if it is in the actor's self-interests. This can be interpreted as the individual's or the organisation's interests, but it should be readily apparent to the reader now, that such a view is not conducive to the conduct of business. It would be impossible to trust anyone if managerial egoism were allowed free reign.

Utilitarianism is an ethical theory with which business feels comfortable. The utilitarian approach of measuring the net benefits of actions intuitively appeals to managers whose daily lives are preoccupied with similar decision-making methodologies. Clearly it may be possible to demonstrate that some of the practices we have described, such as exaggerating company difficulties or inventing competition in order to induce suppliers to lower their prices, or to improve delivery and quality, may be shown to produce an overall net benefit to society, though there is no clear reason why this should necessarily follow. Utilitarianism is often seen as the philosophical underpinning for free-market economics in which the rationale of the maximisation of economic welfare is seen to result from the free interplay of market forces rather than from any system of planning or control. Many of the unethical practices in purchasing which have been described in this chapter, for example showing favouritism to particular suppliers or allowing the offering of gifts or hospitality, are not likely to lead to the maximisation of economic welfare which results when free competition forces economic efficiency to the highest possible levels. Where, because of the unethical behaviour of the purchasing manager, an organisation does not gain its supplies from the most efficient supplier, having taken all factors into account, then society's economic welfare cannot be maximised. A failure to disclose necessary information to some potential suppliers, but not to others, would also be seen by utilitarians as being unethical. In the end most of the unethical practices identified would lead to a retreat from the maximisation of economic welfare which utilitarianism argues should be used to test the justness of any action.

Unethical purchasing personnel are likely to find even less support for their actions in any of the duty-based theories than they did in the theory of utilitarianism. These duty-based theories, which argue that actions are best judged without regard to consequences, contend that moral laws take the form of categorical imperatives, in Kant's phrase, and these should be followed by all as a matter of duty. Kant's categorical imperative: Act in such a way that the action taken could be a universal rule of behaviour for everyone, is unlikely to be acceptable to those who themselves are happy to engage in bribery and corruption. If such an action were to operate against their interests they are unlikely to want to see it universalised, for if it were, then the advantage they had gained by their unethical actions would disappear. However, discussions with purchasing personnel reveal that the majority of them regard the offering of gifts as widespread, and as almost part of normal practice. Nonetheless it is unlikely purchasing personnel would argue that it should become a universal behaviour. Clearly deception of any form, for instance the showing of favouritism and the selective use of information, are all designed to gain the individual or their organisation some advantage which if it were universalised, would disappear. Kant would be astounded if such behaviour were not felt to breach his categorical imperative.

Consideration of the unethical practices which this chapter has detailed in terms of Ross's *prima facie* duties (Ross, 1938) leads us to conclude that several of his duties will be breached. The duties of fidelity, gratitude, justice, and nonmaleficence are breached by the acceptance of gifts; by engaging in deception, for example by inventing competition or by showing favouritism to those suppliers favoured by senior managers; or by revealing confidential and commercially valuable information. Ross's *prima facie* duties propose the primacy of honesty in all actions, in equality and fairness, and in acting so that we respect the special obligations we have to other actors such as employers. Garrett (1966) supports this approach and adds that we must examine the intentions behind the act, not simply the act itself. Ends, for Garrett, are only properly evaluated if we examine the intrinsic nature of the acts rather than simply their consequences. Many of the actions that are viewed as unethical in purchasing, are so viewed because intrinsically they are designed to give an unfair advantage to an individual or to an organisation.

Rawls's theory of justice (Rawls, 1972) with its two principles, of liberty and difference, offers no support to any of the actions which this chapter has detailed. Under his liberty principle Rawls is arguing for maximum liberty, freedom of information and action. Further, under the difference principle of Rawls, actions are acceptable only if they do not increase inequalities and do not operate to worsen the position of the least advantaged. Both of these principles (Rawls, 1972) are likely to be breached whenever bribery, corruption, deception and other such practices are present.

Another approach which derives partly from the Aristotelian school might be described as virtue ethics (see McIntyre, 1981), where virtue is about the development of good habits, amongst which Aristotle suggested truthfulness, justice, generosity. None of Aristotle's virtues result from the unethical practices found in purchasing.

It would seem that purchasing personnel can find, at best, only minimal support among ethical theorists for the practices which have been explored in this chapter. Many purchasing personnel recognise this, and so in surveys they always claim that they themselves are not in favour of such practices. The puzzle is, then, why do such practices persist?

Further Reading

There are no books on purchasing ethics though most textbooks such as Baily and Farmer (1990) include a section, or in a small number of cases a chapter, on ethics in purchasing. Therefore readers wishing to read more need to select from the references given for this chapter, though even there the amount of material available is limited.

References

Baily, P. and Farmer, D. (1990) *Purchasing Principles and Management*, 6th edn, Pitman, London.

Barr, C. (1993) 'A Code of Ethics: Good, Bad or Indifferent?', Proceedings of 2nd PSERG Conference, University of Bath, pp. 19–26.

Barry, A. (1992) 'Days of Wine and Roses', *Purchasing and Supply Management*, October, pp. 22–5.

Bradley, P. (1989) 'Purchasing Ethics? The Rest of Business Should Be So Strict', *Purchasing*, 4th May, pp. 24–5.

Browning, J. M. and Zabriskie, N. B. (1980) 'Professionalism in Purchasing: A Status Report', *Journal of Purchasing and Materials Management*, Fall, pp. 2–10.

Browning, J. M. and Zabriskie, N. B. (1983) 'How Ethical are Industrial Buyers?', *Industrial Marketing Management*, vol. 12, pp. 219–24.

CIPS (1977) *The Ethical Code of the Chartered Institute of Purchasing and Supply*, CIPS, Stamford.

Clutterbuck, D., Dearlove, D. and Snow, D. (1992) *Actions Speak Louder: A Management Guide to Corporate Social Responsibility*, Kogan Page, London.

Dubinsky, A. J. and Gwin, J. M. (1981) 'Business Ethics: Buyers and Sellers', *Journal of Purchasing and Materials Management*, Winter, pp. 9–16.

Felch, R. I. 1985) 'Standards of Conduct: The Key to Supplier Relations', *Journal of Purchasing and Materials Management*, Fall, pp. 16–18.

Forker, L. B. and Janson, R. L. (1992) 'Ethical Practices in Purchasing', *Journal of Purchasing and Materials Management*, Winter, pp. 19–26.

Garrett, T. (1966) *Business Ethics*, Prentice-Hall, Englewood Cliffs, N.J.

McIntyre, A. (1981) *After Virtue: A Study of Moral Theory*, Duckworth, London.

Murphy, P. E. and Laczniak, G. R. (1981) 'Marketing Ethics: A Review with Implications for Managers, Educators and Researchers', in B. Enis and K. Roering (eds), *Review of Marketing 1981*, American Marketing Association, Chicago, pp. 251–66.

Narayanam, D. (1992) 'The Right Stuff', *Purchasing and Supply Management*, October, pp. 25–6.

Ramsey, J. (1989) 'No Bribes Please, We're Professionals', *Purchasing and Supply Management*, December, pp. 31–3.

Rawls, J. (1972) *A Theory of Justice*, Oxford University Press, Oxford.

Robson, P. (1992) 'A Day at the Races, a Night at the Opera', *Purchasing and Supply Management*, Octobe, pp. 27–9.

Ross, W. D. (1938) *The Right and the Good*, Clarendon Press, Oxford.

Rudelius, W. and Buchholz, R. A. (1979) 'What Industrial Purchasers See as Key Ethical Dilemmas', *Journal of Purchasing and Materials Management*, Winter, pp. 2–10.

Sibley, S. D. (1979) 'Images of the Purchasing Department', *Journal of Purchasing and Materials Management*, Fall, pp. 19–23.

Wood, G. (1994) 'Ethical Issues at the Marketing/Purchasing Interface: The Practitioner's Experience', Proceedings of the British Academy of Management Conference, University of Lancaster.

CHAPTER 13

Ethical Issues in Operations Management

1 Introduction

There is an interesting trade-off between the desirability of a high standard of ethical behaviour, both in principle and in operation, and the necessity for cost-cutting and aggressive competition. The drawing up of a corporate ethical policy is a comparatively straightforward affair compared with the multi-faceted possibilities for dysfunction at the operational level. It is a classical application of the differences between 'Whats' and 'Hows'. It is often not a particularly demanding exercise to generate a list of 'Whats' – politicians do it all the time. It is in the transformation process and at the delivery point that greater traumas occur in terms of ethical consideration.

Evers (1994) suggests that ethics should be top priority for every manager, but putting business ethics in practice can be a difficult task in today's cut-throat world of business. She states:

> It is all too easy to assume that ethics and good practice are being swept under the carpet everywhere when the unscrupulous are brought to book. Our consultations show that managers are very conscious of the dilemmas they face. From the chair to the most junior executive, we all have a responsibility to our customers, staff, shareholders and the public. Managers see excellence, quality and basic trust as necessary core values. They are calling for open, and early discussion of ethical conflicts as part of everyday decision making.

These ethical considerations have been present in embryonic form from the dawn of civilisation and have been continually refined throughout the ages. It was within the boundaries of the discipline known by the modern functional title of Operations Management that many ethical issues have been, and will continue to be explored.

In the thirteenth century, Walter of Henley in England wrote a treatise to his son advising him on how to select suitable ploughmen, train them and set output targets per day (Currie, 1977). Ethical considerations about what was realistic relative to the resources provided were included. In Italy in the middle ages, the genius of Leonardo Da Vinci was called upon by a friend who was an employer of labour to determine how much loose earth a labourer could shovel in a summer's day. Investigating in his usual methodical and scientific way, Da Vinci gave precise output information to the employer. He spoke of one optimal method – which would undoubtedly achieve more – 'there are some who do this, but they do not last' (Currie).

2   Definition of Operations Management

Operations Management is concerned with the efficient transformation of the resources of an organisation into goods and/or services which it has been set up to provide. In order to consider issues of an ethical nature within this functional area, it will be necessary to constrain the wide ambit of resources, roles and activities embraced by the term 'operations management'; an approach which takes account of ethical behaviour on the part of operations managers in both the production and service sectors is required. Such managers often carry between them a wide range of job titles with little or no reference to 'operations management'. Scrutiny, however, of their job specifications and daily duties, will quickly identify whether they are 'operations managers' or not. Someone continually dealing with the efficient balancing of input resources to achieve planned output levels of goods and/or services with the right timing, quantity and quality levels, would qualify.

In order to appreciate ethical behaviour principles which occur in operations management the following model job descriptions are useful. Model 1 is associated with the manufacturing sector and Model 2 with the service sector.

Model 1: Operations manager (production)

The job specification for this type of manager includes on-going responsibility for the:

- reception of incoming raw materials and bought-out components
- safe and secure storage of materials
- movement of materials within the plant
- production scheduling of orders
- maintenance of quality specifications
- negotiations with suppliers/customers on Just-In-time issues
- packaging and palletisation of product
- distribution of product using in-house or contract carriers

- direction of employees engaged in these operational areas
- general manufacturing productivity levels
- standard time values used for the manufacturing processes
- employee suggestion schemes
- layout and design of the work areas
- health and safety at work for employees
- staff payment systems including bonus schemes
- efficient maintenance of the machinery or plant
- record keeping, scheduling and control of orders
- decision-making on operational issues
- management of quality

Model 2: Operations manager (administrative/service)

The job specification for this type of manager includes on-going responsibility for the:

- reception of incoming mail, faxes, computer printouts, telephone calls and bought-out materials
- secure storage of documents and computer files
- movement of information/data within the work area
- prioritising of jobs to be done
- maintenance of a quality staff performance
- negotiations with suppliers/customers
- dealing with enquiries
- decision-making on policies
- despatch of information using appropriate modes of delivery
- direction of staff
- general productivity levels
- training and development of staff
- layout and design of the work areas
- health and safety at work for staff
- staff work systems including flexible and part-time work methods
- maintenance of the computers and office equipment
- record keeping: scheduling and control
- decision-making on operational issues
- management of quality

Comparison of the lists associated with each model shows similarity and difference. Much of the responsibility of the Model 1 manager is associated with a tangible outcome from the process, which can be checked and verified by objective methods. The Model 2 manager will tend to preside over operations in which there is a greater degree of subjective decision making and the associated potential communication problems.

Research undertaken in the USA in 1990 led to the listing of 26 ethical issues (see Table 13.1).

TABLE 13.1   Ethical Issues

Rank	Issue
1	Drug & alcohol abuse
2	Employee theft
3	Conflicts of interest
4	Quality control
5	Discrimination
6	Misuse of propriety information
7	Fiddling of expense accounts
8	Plant closures and lay-offs
9	Misuse of company assets
10	Environmental pollution
11	Misuse of others' information
12	Industrial espionage
13	Inaccuracies in documents and records
14	Receiving excessive gifts and entertainment
15	False or misleading advertising
16	Giving excessive gifts or entertainment
17	Receiving 'backhanders'
18	Insider (information) trading
19	Relations with local communities
20	Antitrust issues (e.g. price-rings)
21	Bribery
22	Political contributions and activities
23	Improper relationships with local government personnel
24	Improper relationships with national government personnel
25	Inaccurate charging to government bodies
26	Improper relationships with foreign government personnel

Source: *Ethics, Policies and Programs in American Business: Report of a Landmark Survey of US Corporations*, Ethics Resource Centre. (Adapted to UK terminology.) (Quoted in Hellriegel, Slocum, and Woodman, 1993.)

Both Model 1 and Model 2 managers would need to take account of the effects of drug or alcohol abuse on his/her own work performance. They would also need to be concerned about the safety of staff at the workplace where either their own, or the judgements of colleagues were impaired by alcohol or drugs. The requirements of the law, the job security, the personal shame aspects, and the opportunities to get help can all be traded off unethically against the overall well-being and productivity of the firm.

Significant employee theft levels from the premises can be controlled to some extent by the introduction of increasingly sophisticated security and budgetary control procedures. These however could outweigh the loss itself and cause annoyance to the decent and honest staff.

An ethical dilemma for the Model 1 manager is the balancing of freedom with responsibility and at which point to introduce greater accountability. The Model 2 manager could be concerned about computer fraud, which could ultimately, in the worst scenario, ruin the firm. Solving such problems involves not only specialised technical expertise – possibly having to be imported into the firm on a contract basis – but also a lot of painstaking detective work. The ethical dilemma here is one of relationship and trust and the likelihood of an ensuing 'witch hunt' once any real evidence is unearthed. The passing on of confidential files and trade secrets would flow from this kind of situation.

3 Quality

Quality Control issues will continually present ethical difficulties for Operations Managers. In production terms, the saving of cost by putting fewer nuts into each bar of chocolate – knowing that the firm can probably 'get away with it' because of generally apathetic and undiscriminating customers – is always a temptation in difficult trading conditions, for at least short-term gain.

The Operations Manager controlling hospital ward admittances and discharges could be tempted to cut a day off each patient's hospital stay, knowing this would be popular with the patient. The ethical issues go under scrutiny, however, when a totally unfit patient is discharged and there is a serious relapse, or there is disclosure that five days' charges were levied on four days' of treatment.

The greater degree of prominence being given to quality issues today in a difficult economic climate is providing a wealth of difficult ethical issues which involve Operations Managers.

Although writing primarily about supervisors employed in the automotive industry, Lowe (1993) explains how from the 1920s there was a proliferation of specialist departments being formed, which narrowed the width of the job. Since the 1980s however, the search for so-called 'Lean Production' systems has now greatly widened the manufacturing supervisor's role – probably to an even wider span than sixty years before. They have become the central focus for integrating strategic goals like total quality and continuous improvement with concerns such as scheduling and manning levels, which were previously the domain of higher managers. In the drive to optimise resources and achieve targets, ethical dilemmas continually arise for the Operations Manager.

4 Managerial Roles

With the widening range of responsibilities, planning has become rather more important than traditional decision-making on outcomes. A planning cocktail which ensures there is no discrimination, uses optimal work methods ensuring health and safety, generates high productivity levels, meets quality and quantity criteria, enables detailed scheduling and financial control procedures to operate, maintains privacy and confidentiality, and ultimately satisfies the customer, is difficult to construct – particularly under the severe time constraints imposed by the pace of modern business.

Stevenson (1993) argues that the Operations Manager is the key figure in a system, with the ultimate responsibility for the creation of goods and services.

Managing a banking operation requires a different kind of expertise to managing a steel-making operation. Nevertheless they are both essentially managerial. The same can be said of any Operations Manager who has to coordinate the use of resources by planning, organising, staffing, directing and controlling within an ethical framework.

The planning process involves future courses of action and responding to questions such as:

- What are we making?
- What will be the effects on staff, the environment, the customer?
- Where shall we make it?
- How shall we provide the service?
- What quantities and quality standards will apply?
- What will be the effects of growth/decline on the staff and locality?
- What profit will accrue if we exploit the market?

Organising refers to the administrative structure – a working system in itself. Ethical decision-making involves the *who?*, *what?*, *where?*, *when?*, *how?* and sometimes *why?* of a situation:

- Where is power vested?
- How secure must the manufacturing specifications be kept?
- What safety measures are incorporated for staff?
- How accurate must the record keeping be?

Staffing deals with the most unpredictable and volatile resource issue, the human factor:

- Who is employed?
- What training and skills are really necessary?
- What working system is required?
- What kind of pay systems are appropriate and fair?
- Which types of formal procedure are necessary?

Ethics deals with right and wrong in the actions and decisions of individuals and institutions of which they are a part. Ethical issues in business are both pervasive and complex. Daily decision-making within a functional area, such as Operations Management, involves 'right and wrong', 'good or bad' conclusions. In addition to managers, most ordinary employees experience ethical dilemmas in the performance of their duties.

5 Examples of Ethical Problems

- The Operations Manager of a haulage company is considering placing a £400,000 order for new 38-tonne lorries with a European manufacturer after visiting their plant for a couple of hours. The all-expenses-paid trip for the manager, who was accompanied by his wife, lasted several days. The specifications of the equivalent British-made truck are better.
- The Operations Director of a technology-based company in a fast-moving industry is under pressure from his Board to try to secretly 'head-hunt' an employee of a rival company. This employee has advanced R&D information and could be expected to bring with him specialised manufacturing knowledge of product and materials. The Board recognises that it has under-resourced its R&D effort for some years, and fallen well behind its competitors. The future of the company has become uncertain.
- Operations Managers in the construction industry are being encouraged to form an illegal 'price-ring' to give identical price quotations, which include high profit margins, for an extensive government motorway-building project. There is an unwritten understanding that whichever company lands the contract, it will sub-contract the appropriate portions of the work to the unsuccessful companies.

6 An Analytical Framework

The three examples can be analysed using the framework below.

1. *Magnitude of Consequences*
   - A decision on food quality which causes illness to 1,000 diners is of greater magnitude than a decision causing the same illness to 10 people.
   - A decision regarding machine safety which causes death to an operator is of greater magnitude than one that causes a cut finger.
2. *Probability of the Effect*
   - Manufacturing a car which is dangerous to occupants during normal driving routine has a greater probability of harm than the manufacture of a car which is dangerous in high-speed cornering.

- Selling a gun to a known armed robber has a greater probability of harm than selling a gun to a law-abiding citizen.
3. *Social Consensus*

   This is the degree of social agreement that exists to define something as good or evil. Obviously cultural awareness is essential.
   - The evil involved in positively discriminating against minority-group job applicants has greater social consensus than not acting positively on behalf of such applicants.
   - The evil involved in trying to bribe a well-paid customs officer in the UK has greater social consensus than bribing a poorly paid guard at a border crossing into an Eastern European country.
4. *Temporal Immediacy*

   This is the length of time between the present and the start of the impact of the decision. A shorter time implies immediacy, with less time available for the generation of alternatives, or taking advice.
   - Producing a new pharmaceutical product which will give bad side effects immediately to 1% of the people taking it, has greater temporal immediacy than a product which might produce those side-effects in people after 30 years.
   - Cutting the company retirement pensions for existing pensioners has a greater temporal immediacy than announcing changes which will affect employees with another possible 20 years of service.
5. *Proximity*

   This is the feeling of nearness (social, cultural, psychological or physical) that the decision-maker has for those affected by the decision.
   - Enforced redundancy announcements where one is based has greater ethical proximity than in a remote plant.
   - The use in agricultural operations of noxious chemicals in fields adjacent to one's own urban area has greater ethical proximity than the use of the same chemicals in a remote desert area.
6. *Concentration of Effect*

   This is the inverse function of the number of people affected by a decision of given magnitude.
   - A change in acceptance of claims under a product quality guarantee which denies 10 people each claiming £10,000 compensation, has more concentrated effect than a change which denies claims made by 10,000 people of £10 each.
   - Delayed payment to an individual or small business of £1,000 has a more concentrated effect than non-payment of the same sum to government tax inspectors.

Not all of the six factors are present in each ethical decision. Where there is more than one present, the ethical intensity increases. Ethical intensity refers to the degree of importance given to an ethical issue.

7 Vignette

Production workers at British Depa Crepes Ltd, nylon processors in Oldham, were required to submit a daily timesheet from which bonus payments were calculated on a weekly basis. Many workers were simultaneously performing similar jobs in the same department on adjacent machinery. An individual sometimes came under peer pressure to claim excessive extra allowances against poor input materials or difficult ambient conditions, to generate higher bonus payments, just before the annual or Christmas holiday period, when domestic finances were stretched. The thinking employee, knowing that all additional manufacturing costs had to be funded out of a very slim profit margin, felt the ethical dilemma of short-term financial gain and peer popularity, against personal honesty and integrity and possible longer-term unemployment. The Operations Manager concerned with the authorisation of the submitted time-sheet was also caught up with ethical issues. Whilst the question of peer pressure does not apply, popularity as a boss does. This, however, had to be traded off against accountability to agreed operating budgets, possible reprimand by senior managers who might have a potential promotion in mind, the creation of precedents and the problem of defending a decision if queried by technologists.

The analysis of this situation in ethical terms can be undertaken in a number of ways. Two approaches are particularly useful. The first is advocated by Premeaux and Mundy (1993) and the second is adapted from the work of Hellriegel, Slocum and Woodman (1992).

Analysis 1

Rights: the entitlements of the individual

of workers:	to act as an individual; to act honestly; not be discriminated against either by peers or management.
of the Operations Manager:	to authorise correct claims; to reject excessive claims; to amend erroneous claims; to manage without threats from above or below; to act professionally at all times.

Justice: the equity and distributive fairness of the situation

for workers:	is the bonus scheme itself 'fair'? is the time-sheet booking system for extra allowance 'fair'? does it pay to be honest?

for the Operations Manager: can a really fair decision be made?
                                what is best for all parties?
                                are there precedents, custom and practice?
                                how can I maintain credibility?

Act Utilitarian: the decision giving the greatest social benefit
The Operations Manager must weigh up the full range of short and long-term effects of the final decision. The likelihood is that most will find the temporal immediacy of the short-term implications rather more compelling than the longer-term considerations. The achievement of being a popular manager leading a better-paid, more stable, happier workforce is an attractive objective. In the back of the mind can also be the hope that any excesses will be lost in the morass of data produced by the company information system. Even if questions were asked some weeks later, it has all become rather remote, subject to personal interpretation and a fallible memory.

Rule Utilitarian: the evaluation of the rules governing the decision
The Operations Manager will need to consider whether there are rules in existence, written or otherwise, to cover the decision-making process. If there are rules, when were they designed and by whom? Have the operating conditions changed since the rules were drawn up, and if so, have amendments been made? Are there past records to evaluate how particular decisions worked out? What room for personal discretion is there for the manager.

An analysis of this type generates a considerable number of ethical issues which the Operations Manager, and the company itself, needs to address.

Analysis 2

Some examples are given of the possible thoughts and motivations of personnel involved in the vignette.

1. *Hedonist Principle*:
   The worker wants as much reward as possible, for as little effort as possible, for as much of the working life as possible.
   The Operations Manager may be guided by his/her own interests and personal objectives, rather than what is best for the firm.
2. *Might equals Right Principle*:
   The workers may feel strong in the collective sense as trade unionists with the ability to use local, even national muscle to achieve objectives. The Operations Manager could have considerable latitude in terms of what his/her managerial authority allows them to do with time-sheet claims.
3. *Conventionalist Principle*:
   The workers may have come to believe that it is customary and acceptable to the firm, for them to overclaim just before a holiday.

4. *Intuition Principle*:
   In the absence of clear rules, the organisation may be trusting the Operations Manager with making whatever decision seems to be right, even if different decisions had been made previously.

5. *Organisational Ethic Principle*:
   This would occur if the managers had been trained (or cajoled) into always automatically thinking of the company first. In the UK it would not be a principle uppermost in workers minds. In the vignette scenario, workers had a 'them and us' mindset. Operations Managers working for a charity, for example, may so believe in its aims that personal concerns always take second place.

6. *Means-to-an-End Principle*:
   The Operations Manager faced with making a rapid decision has to square his/her conscience on any sanctioned irregularity with the expectation that all will work out well in the long run.

7. *Utilitarian Principle*:
   The Operations Manager will need to weigh up perceived good effects of the decision against his/her own accountability and career prospects.

8 *Professional Ethic Principle*:
   The workers, if unionised, may well have agreements of either a local, district or national level with employers which need to be adhered to in order to establish credibility. The Operations Manager belonging to a professional body, will probably be a signatory to guidelines of the type shown in Section 8 (below). In some professions, loss of professional membership, accreditation and qualifications, results in unemployment.

9. *Disclosure Principle*:
   The Operations Manager has already built up a relationship with staff. He/she must decide how much information on the actions taken and the underlying rationale, should be communicated to those affected. The timing of disclosure may also be highly significant.

10. *Distributive Justice Principle*:
    The workers will want to feel that equal treatment is being given with no discrimination based on arbitrary criteria. This is one of the reasons that workers join trade unions.

11. *Categorical Imperative Principle*:
    The workers may believe that excessive extra allowance claims at times are justifiable and should be formalised. An unreasonable Operations Manager may refuse all extra allowance claims and advise staff that the norm is to only pay the standard time value for units produced.

12. *Golden Rule Principle*:
    This requires almost a 'world-view' of the scenario to be constructed. This would be akin to the system's *weltanschaung*, a viewpoint conditioned by environment, background, beliefs, and upbringing. Such a position is more easily attained when time is available for communication and discussion.

8 Guidelines for Ethical Decision-Making in Operations Management

Pagano and Verdin (1988) offer a list of guidelines that you can apply to difficult social problems and ethical dilemmas. These guidelines will not tell you exactly what to do, but they will help you evaluate the situation more clearly by examining your own values and those of your organisation.

1. Is the problem/dilemma really what it appears to be? If you are not sure, find out.
2. Is the action you are considering legal? Ethical? If you are not sure, find out.
3. Do you understand the position of those who oppose the action you are considering? Is it reasonable?
4. Whom does this action benefit? Harm? How much? How long?
5. Would you be willing to allow everyone to do what you are considering doing?
6. Have you sought the opinion of others who are more knowledgeable on the subject and who would be objective?
7. Would your action be embarrassing to you if it were made known to your family, friends, co-workers or superiors? Would you be comfortable defending your actions to an investigative reporter on the evening news?

Code of Professional Ethics
The Institute of Management Services, a leading professional body in the Operations Management field, has produced a code of ethics for its members.

Members shall:

1. Conduct themselves in a manner which will merit the respect of the community for persons engaged in the profession.
2. Uphold the reputation of the Institute and the dignity of the profession.
3. Carry out their professional duties responsibly and with integrity.
4. Collect and marshall facts without bias, and not allow their personal views or the views of others to influence their professional judgement, interpretation, analysis and presentation of those facts.
5. Not discuss with, or disclose to, any persons not authorised to receive such information by their employer or their employer's delegated representative, whether within or outside their employer's organisation, the data, results, reports or proposals arising from their work; nor shall they cause such confidential information to be misused or to be published without permission.
6. Not use information acquired during a previous employment in any way which could be detrimental to their former employer.

7. Not receive any undisclosed material benefits other than their normal emoluments consequent upon any recommendation they may make in the course of their duties.

In addition there is a guide to good practice which stipulates that members 'must always attempt to use their professional skills with integrity and objectivity. In the event of commitments conflicting, they should stress their professional accountability. . . and that their skills be used impartially and responsibly.'

References and Bibliography

Bedeian, A. G. (1993) *Management*, Harcourt Brace Jovanovich, New York.

Currie, R. M. (1977) *Work Study*, 4th edn, Pitman, London.

Dart, R. L. (1991) *Management*, 2nd edn, The Dryden Press, London.

Evers, S. (1994) 'The Manager as a Professional', Institute of Management, reviewed in *Management Services*, vol. 38, no. 3 (March).

Gaither, N. (1992) *Production and Operations Management*, 5th edn, Dryden Press, London.

Hellriegel, D., Slocum, J. W. and Woodman, R. W. (1993) *Organisational Behaviour*, 6th edn, West Publishing, St Paul, Minnesota.

Lee, S. M. and Schnieder, M. J. (1994) *Operations Management*, Houghton Mifflin, Boston, Mass.

Lowe, J. (1993) 'Manufacturing Reform and the Changing Role of the Production Supervisor', *Journal of Management Studies*, vol. 30, no. 5 (Sept).

Pagano, A. M. and Verdin, J. A. (1988) *The External Environment of Business*, ch. 5, Wiley, Chichester. (Quoted by Dart, 1991.)

Premeaux, S. R. and Mundy, R. W. (1993) 'Linking Management Behaviour and Ethical Philosophy', *Journal of Business Ethics*, vol. 12, no. 5 (May).

Stevenson, W. J. (1993) *Production/Operations Management*, 4th edn, Irwin, New York, p. 17.

CHAPTER 14

Ethical Issues in Human Resource Management

1 Introduction

There is little mention of ethics in the current literature in the United Kingdom relating to either human resource management or personnel management. The term 'ethics' is hardly referred to in the most popular HRM/Personnel Management texts (Sisson, 1989 and 1994; Torrington and Hall, 1987; Towers, 1992); the word does not appear in any of the indexes. A recent United Kingdom text by Beardwell and Holden (1994) titled *Human Resource Management: A Contemporary Perspective* does explicitly refer to ethics in relation to management, learning and development and job design, but devotes no more than part of four pages (out of 687) to the issue. As far as business ethics textbooks are concerned human resource management is treated only narrowly (see Chryssides and Kaler, 1993; Donaldson, 1989). There is the occasional chapter on the workplace but where this is the case the discussion usually focuses on employee rights in general or on some novel situation such as an employer's use of polygraph tests to access employee honesty (Beauchamp, 1989).

A different picture emerges when textbooks from the United States are surveyed, and where ethics and ethical issues feature prominently (Mathis and Jackson, 1994; Schuler and Huber, 1993). Schuler and Huber state that

> increasingly, human resource management professionals are becoming involved in more ethical issues. Some of the most serious involve differences in the way people are treated based on favoritism or relationship to top management.

As supporting evidence they quote a survey carried out in 1991 (see appendix) by the Society for Human Resource Management (SHRM) and the Commerce

Case Clearing House (CCCH). The survey involved over 1,000 Human Resource professionals who 'identified more than forty ethical incidents, events, and situations relevant to HR activities' (Schuler and Huber, p. 24).

Providing some answers to the question as to why interest in ethics among management and business academics would seem to be more developed in the United States than in the United Kingdom is not the main purpose of this chapter, but the political context within which business operates in each of the two countries concerned may have some bearing on the matter. In the United Kingdom, the political context can be summed up by what Colin Crouch calls 'the rejection of compromise' (1990). There are three aspects to this. Firstly, there has been a rejection by the government of the search for compromise in industrial relations. Secondly, there has been the installation of a tough legal framework for trade union action. Thirdly, the company has emerged as the most important level for industrial relations activity 'replacing the branch, shop-floor and state levels that had previously competed for importance within the British system' (Crouch, p. 327). The combination of economic, political and legal changes in the United Kingdom over the past fifteen years inspired by the 'rejection of compromise' has led to Line Managers becoming more influential than Personnel Managers. Increased competition has resulted in managers having to tightly control labour costs on the one hand and to maximise employees' contributions on the other, thus finding themselves able to take more initiatives in the management of their organisation, and increasingly carrying out responsibilities traditionally undertaken by Personnel Managers.

Whether one holds the view that Personnel Management is more concerned with mediation and problem-solving and is short-term and reactive, whilst Human Resource Management driven by Line Management is long-term and integrated into business policy and planning, there is a case to be made which suggests that Personnel Management is likely to be more ethical than Human Resource Management. This is, quite simply, because Line Managers who are nearer to the 'coal face' tend to be motivated by the need to achieve operational targets and are less concerned with the 'soft' moral issues. Personnel Managers see themselves as personnel specialists first and as company managers second. Furthermore many Personnel Managers are members of the Institute of Personnel Management. According to Keith Sisson, personnel management activities

> have come to be associated with a group of specialist managers, above all in Britain, where they have had their own professional organisation, the Institute of Personnel Management (IPM), an examination scheme covering membership, and codes of practice. (1989, p. 3)

The Institute of Management, a general professional body which is more attractive to Line Managers, also has its own Code of Conduct and Guides to

Professional Management Practice. This states that one of the manager's duties

> involves the acceptance and habitual exercise of ethical values, among which a high place should be accorded to integrity, honesty, loyalty and fairness.

Added to such abstract and potentially meaningless notions the Institute falls short of describing an external code of ethics. It does this on the grounds that

> it is usual for managers to encounter circumstances or situations in which various values, principles, rules and interests appear to conflict.

and, therefore, no ready answer can be provided.

In contrast to the Institute of Management Code and Guides, the IPM Codes of Practice addresses what constitutes ethical approaches to precise areas such as continuous development, employee data, equal opportunities, employee involvement and participation, redundancy, psychological testing, harassment and counselling. Although there is no compulsion, legal or otherwise, for IPM members to adhere to the guidelines laid down, they are supposed to represent good practice. These codes provide guidelines for more than mere minimum legal standards. For example, The IPM Code on Equal Opportunities includes recommendations to overcome discrimination in the areas of age and disability which go beyond legislative requirements. In the case of age discrimination it recommends that 'as a general rule age should not be used as a primary discriminator in recruitment, selection, promotion and training decisions'. It is ironical that the IPM journal, *Personnel Management*, frequently contains job advertisements which discriminate on grounds of age.

In the United States the professional organisation for human resource specialists, the Society for Human Resource Management (SHRM), has a code of practice which emphasises 'a high standard of personal honesty and integrity at every phase of daily practice', 'thoughtful consideration to the personal interest, welfare, and dignity of all employees', a 'high regard and respect for the public interest' and that human resource professionals must never 'overlook the importance of the personal interests and dignity of employees' (Schuler and Huber, 1993). It is in this 'respect for individuals' as the basis of their policies, codes of conduct and practices that companies in the United States may claim to be ethical in their relationships with their employees and potential employees. This is in marked contrast to the legalistic and formal approach adopted by the British IPM and the highly abstract notions coupled with an abdication of responsibility demonstrated by the Institute of Management. It is also to be noted that neither of these British institutions emphasise the notion of 'public interest', thus clearly reflecting the absence of the notion of social responsibility or accountability on the part of companies towards society or the community at large.

And yet almost every human resource decision and issue can pose ethical questions. To what degree should managers consult with employees over issues which effect their everyday lives? What support should organisations give to employees who are now excess to requirements or who no longer can carry out their job? What degree of assistance should an employer offer to an employee who is suffering a personal crisis? Should employees be forced to work overtime? How should employers deal with job applicants? Should organisations operate affirmative action policies with regard to selection, training and promotion? To what degree should jobs be made safe? How much information should be given to employees regarding the organisation? Each of these questions, if one was to adopt the concept of 'respect for individuals' as the founding principle of an ethical code of conduct for Human Resource Management, would demand far clearer policies and practical answers than those outlined by the Institute of Management or the IPM.

One of the most problematic aspects of Human Resource Management concerns recruitment and selection. The following part of this chapter will discuss two case studies which will enable us to focus on some of the ethical issues encountered in this area. Although simple cases, they are typical of the type of recruitment and selection situations which occur in the United Kingdom today. According to Maclagan most ethical situations faced by managers 'are not the headline-hitting issues one reads about in the press; research has shown that most managers never face such dramatic situations, but do continually experience small, everyday, matters which nevertheless have an ethical dimension' (1993, p. 3). The case of Smallhouse School and Tiphill County Council are real ones but the names are fictitious. They demonstrate different issues and it is, therefore, not the intention that they can be directly compared.

2 Vignette – Smallhouse School

Smallhouse School is a private girls' grammar school which takes in pupils from the age of four and which provides education up to and including A-levels. It is a fairly large school and has a good reputation in the area of examination success. The following advertisement appeared in a national newspaper on 17 May 1994:

SMALLHOUSE SCHOOL – GIRLS' DIVISION
Small Lane, Small Town, OP3 5RT
Tel 002–245–555
Required for September 1994, to assist
with the teaching of
FRENCH

in the Junior School age range 4/11 years. This is a part-time appointment.
Applications from native speakers preferred.
A letter of application with full curriculum vitae
and names of two referees should be sent to the Headmistress immediately.

Looking more closely, what does the advertisement tell us about the job? We know that it entails assisting with the teaching of French to children in the age range of 4 to 11 and that a French native speaker is preferred. We do not know how many hours are required or what the rate of pay is. Nor is there any information relating to qualifications and experience. The phrase 'assist with the teaching of' is not explained. It is not clear whether this person would be a teacher or merely an *assistant.* The method of application, which seeks a letter of application as well as a full curriculum vitae with names of two referees, is quite clear. There is, however, no closing date for applications. Even though the job does not commence for another four months applicants are asked to apply 'immediately'.

The advertisement does not encourage candidates to telephone and seek more information. Those who did telephone to seek extra information were told 'you must be a qualified teacher', 'it will be for approximately 4 or 5 hours per week' and 'we have not decided what the rate of pay will be'. So what Smallhouse School actually want is a qualified French native teacher for four or five hours per week.

Smallhouse School can certainly be accused of being inefficient. Key aspects of the person specification are missing from the advertisement. They have still not decided what the rate of pay will be and this has created some degree of inconvenience to some applicants. There are several ways, therefore, in which this advertisement falls short of what one would expect if respect for individuals had been demonstrated.

Since anyone seeing the advertisement would have inadequate information to decide whether to apply or not, many who telephoned to seek clarification would realise the job was not suitable and they would feel they had wasted their time as well the price of a telephone call. There could be others who would have completed the application process ignorant of the fact that they would fail at the first hurdle by not being qualified teachers. These people would have spent a considerable amount of time in completing their application. There would be others for whom the four or five hours would have been totally inadequate. The manner in which the school handled this stage of the recruitment process can be described as incompetent and failing to show respect for individuals. The failure to disclose an accurate description of the job and the qualities required for the position as well as the absence of information relating to the hours required and pay, would almost certainly result in many applicants merely wasting time and effort for a job which they do not qualify for or one which is unsuitable for them. It is probably not the case that the school deliberately demonstrated a lack of respect for the applicants but more likely that they just did not think of the effect of their actions. Had the school followed good recruitment practice, for example as laid down in the IPM Code, then not only would it have been more ethical in its dealings with potential and actual applicants but it would have been more efficient to themselves. It would have received fewer telephone queries and the applications would have been more likely to be from suitable candidates. In this case it could be claimed, therefore, that the school was not only inefficient but that in showing a lack of respect for individuals they were also unethical.

3   Vignette – Tiphill County Council

Compared with Smallhouse, Tiphill County Council is well organised with regard to recruitment and selection. It has a clear recruitment and selection policy which includes the need for a clear job description and personnel specification which is sent to all potential candidates. The personnel specification itemises those aspects which are essential and those which are desirable. The job advertisement describes the job adequately, clarifies the closing date for applications, provides full details of salary and makes it clear how candidates can seek additional information and how they can apply for the position. The person specification, which was drawn up by the members of the interviewing panel, was as follows:

Essential:
The person appointed to this post must:

(a) Have some experience in educationally based group work with adults and/or young people.
(b) Have a range of effective communication and listening skills as well as the ability to work with a range of people on their terms.
(c) Have an understanding of the current issues affecting women's lives.
(d) Have experience of working with groups of people in a personal/collective development context.
(e) Have a clean driving licence and be prepared to drive the District minibus (after taking the appropriate preparation and test).
(f) Have an ability to plan and work in a systematic way.

There was also a list of desirable criteria but this will not be presented here because it is not central to the case.

Tiphill also organises its interviews well and keeps all candidates informed. The short-listing is carried out by all members of the interview panel. Candidates who are not short-listed are informed of this. Some, but not all, of the interview panel members are trained. At the interview the questions are free from bias and appear to be fair. Indeed Tiphill take considerable pride in the fact that the selection process is fair.

All questions relate directly to the person specification. Any other questions would break equal opportunities policies and allow the interviewee the right of appeal,

stated the interview chairman. The questions are generally open-ended and candidates are given opportunities to explain their strengths. The interview organiser is prepared to spend time with unsuccessful candidates to explain why they had not obtained the job. So is this the ethical company as far as recruitment and selection is concerned? It would be had it not been for several aspects of their policy.

Tiphill's Recruitment and Selection policy requires that all jobs must be advertised and that at least three candidates must be short-listed and interviewed for each vacancy. This is based on a notion of fair competition. For example, if there was only one candidate then the selection panel would have nothing to compare the candidate with. This aspect will be discussed later. Given all of the apparent concern and effort which is paid to recruitment and selection at Tiphill can it be described as ethical? In order to answer it is necessary to examine what happens is practice. The example below refers to a vacancy for a Community Worker.

The job was advertised in a local newspaper. Three candidates were short-listed. One was an 'internal candidate' already doing the job in a part-time capacity with the same authority. One was an ex-teacher who had considerable experience with working in the community but not in an official capacity and certainly not as a community worker. The other, who eventually was offered the position, was an experienced Community Worker who was currently working for another authority. As stated in Tiphill's policy the short-listing was carried out by the interview panel. The interview panel comprised a trained chairman and five people representing the community of whom two had received formal interview training. The training involved mainly matters relating to the avoidance of discrimination. All three candidates were said to meet the criteria laid down in the person specification.

The selection event, which lasted all day, was organised as follows: an informal tour of the premises with the opportunity to meet existing staff, lunch, a thirty-minute period where the three candidates could talk among themselves and a forty-five minute individual interview. The interview was described by the candidates as a 'grilling'. The overall impression given to the candidates was that the interview panel was fairly well organised although the interview concerning the ex-teacher did give rise to one problem. This candidate had made it clear on her application that she did not have direct experience of doing this type of work but had made out a case that she possessed the necessary skills to do it. During the interview the candidate was asked 'What experience do you actually have in doing this type of work'? The candidate replied that she did not have any direct experience of community work in an official capacity and that she had made this clear on the application form. She then proceeded to explain that she had dealt with community matters on a voluntary basis, and gave examples. Several members of the panel returned to this question later and persisted in drawing attention to this. The candidate felt irritated by this since she had made her position clear right at the start. Later on the same day the candidate was told over the telephone by the chairman that although she had interviewed well she did not get the job because of her lack of experience in this area. So the panel had decided that the candidate's lack of professional experience was the deciding factor despite the fact that they were fully aware of this before the interview and still decided to short-list this person.

Furthermore this factor was not a requirement listed in either the essential or desirable criteria. During the session where the three candidates were left on their own it became obvious to all of them that the ultimately successful candidate was the best person for the job. What was irritating for the others, particularly the ex-teacher, was that she felt that she had been invited to the interview to make up the numbers. For an appointment to be made the organisation's policy stated that at least three candidates were required. In this case the ideal candidate was obvious from the application forms. On the basis of this case one may ask how ethical is it to invite people for a full day's interview when they have virtually no chance of being successful?

The organisation's policy of insisting on at least three candidates should be questioned. The policy, aimed at ensuring 'fair competition', could be seen as flawed because what the panel ought to be doing is comparing candidates with the personnel specification and not against each other. If candidates had been rated against the personnel specification then not only would the interviews have been more likely to be fair but the information obtained would have led to better decision-making. If only one applicant met the initial selection criteria would it have been less ethical or more ethical to interview that one candidate and appoint her rather than to interview the two other candidates on false pretence? We would submit that although the Tiphill policy in this case was fair it remained unethical because it was based on formal notions of fairness and not 'respect for individuals'.

4   Towards Ethical Recruitment and Selection

The two case studies discussed above focused on matters of recruitment and selection and demonstrated how a lack of care and respect for the individual, whether it be in not providing enough information or in misleading interviewees as to the actual job specification in order to be seen to adhere to company procedures that are 'seen to be fair', can lead to unethical behaviours on the part of the employer.

In the UK, selection is usually considered as a one-way process where the applicant's needs are almost ignored. In discussing selection practice, Anderson (1991, p. 183) claimed that 'there may still be a tendency to focus exclusively on the organisation's perspective in making decisions and to neglect the increasingly important aspects of how candidates make decisions, in deciding whether to accept job offers or not'. He also identified the absence of candidates' rights in the UK whilst giving an example from Sweden where employee representatives are present when psychologists' reports are considered and candidates are informed of the results before the potential employing organisation. The candidate can also have the results destroyed if he or she wishes to withdraw.

Other countries have practices which protect applicants in various, and sometimes novel, ways. In France, for example, 'candidates have the right to withhold information or give *incorrect* answers, if they feel that an employer is asking inappropriate questions, without prejudice to their subsequent employment rights' (Income Data Services, 1990). In the United Kingdom the only safeguards which exist for applicants regarding interview questioning relate to discrimination on sex and race. If a successful candidate gives false information and the employer discovers this sometime in the future then this may result in the employee's dismissal. An example of this could be where the applicant had previously left their employment because of ill-health but had now fully recovered. In a subsequent application they might be expected to disclose reasons for leaving the previous job. The candidate may be unwilling to disclose the real reasons for leaving because their experience tells them that it would end their chances of being selected. Equally, if they give incorrect information they are then vulnerable should this be ultimately discovered. Irrelevant and inappropriate questions can sometimes, therefore, lead the candidates to resort to being 'economical with the truth' so as not to disqualify themselves from the selection. A recruitment and selection policy which is very much one-way, and where the needs and rights of candidates are not respected (in this case, invasion of personal privacy and confidentiality), can leave the door wide open for abuse of power, disrespect and generally unethical behaviour on the part of recruitment and selection personnel.

In the UK, ethical recruitment and selection as key aspects of Human Resource Management will start to materialise if respect for individuals becomes a priority. However, for this to come about a change in the political climate generally will be required, as ethical behaviour and attitudes towards individuals do not sit comfortably with notions of 'rejection of compromise', a market-driven economy, and the idea that there is no such thing as society, or communities. An incoming Labour government, currently a distinct possibility, might produce 'radical' changes which revolutionise social relations at work. Indeed Tony Blair, Labour's likely future Prime Minister, has introduced the concept of ethics as the principle underpinning his policies and is referring to his ideology as being 'ethical' socialism. If Works' Councils, along the lines that operate in Germany or France, could be legislated for and given 'rights' to oversee recruitment and selection practices then some improvements are likely. The notion of 'candidates' rights' could materialise which would result in organisations having to adopt practices along the lines expressed in the next paragraph.

Ethical recruitment and selection practice might include the following: job descriptions and personnel specifications to be drawn up for all positions; these should accurately reflect the realities of the job; advertisements should contain all essential information including pay, conditions, job details and qualities and experience required; no candidate should be invited to an interview unless they meet the essential qualities laid down in the personnel specification; unsuccessful applicants should have their applications returned to them along with the selectors reasons for their decision; and applicants should be given the results of any assessment made about them including referee's comments. This list is not exhaustive but could provide a starting point for ethical recruitment and selection. If companies adopt such practices and extend this type of thinking to other workplace issues, such as communication and consultation, then we will see the start of real ethical human resource management.

There is much written about trust, commitment, cooperation and loyalty in current management literature. Most of the impetus for this comes from capital not labour. It is claimed that some success has already been achieved in this direction but much of this is due to high levels of unemployment, the recession and the government's anti-union laws. Given these factors, employees are, in general, settling for a quiet time and making little in terms of demands. Whether this will last in the light of the possibility of the end of the recession and the resulting expected shortage of labour remains to be seen. What is likely is that those companies who adopt ethical human resource management will reap higher rewards in terms of the ideals of employee commitment, trust and loyalty than those organisations who merely adopt a strong line in rhetoric. For this to happen, British business must undergo a substantial shift in structure, finance and attitudes. Meanwhile ethics is just starting to emerge on the agenda of Human Resource Management, an example being a forthcoming conference at Nottingham Business School which has 'values, ethics and human resource management' as one of its themes.

Appendix: Ethical Issues

Situation	Percent*
Hiring, training or promotion based on favouritism (friendships or relationships)	30.7
Allowing differences in pay, discipline, promotion, etc. because of friendships with top management	30.7
Sexual harassment	28.4
Sex discrimination in promotion	26.9
Using discipline for managerial and non-managerial personnel inconsistently	26.9
Not maintaining confidentiality	26.4
Sex discrimination in compensation	25.8
Non-performance factors used in appraisals	23.5
Arrangements with vendors or consulting agencies leading to personal gain	23.1
Sex discrimination in recruitment or hiring	22.6

* These percentages refer to those who responded with a 4 or 5 on a five point scale measuring 'degree of seriousness'. Number of respondents = 1,078.

Source: 1991 SHRM/CCH Survey quoted in Schuler and Huber, 1993.

Further Reading

There is little written from what might be described as an ethical human resource management approach. The Institute of Personnel Management and Incomes Data Services (1990) have jointly produced a series titled *European Management Guides*. Specifically one of these provides a guide to recruitment in Belgium, Denmark, France, Germany, Greece, Irish Republic, Italy, Netherlands, Portugal and Spain. Watson (1994) provided a useful overview of recruitment and selection practice in Britain. Watson makes a case for improvements in recruitment and selection and claims that the pressures on British management to produce 'procedures that are sound and defensible, as well as job related, appear to have grown considerably in recent years' (1994, p. 215). A fairly thorough description of recruitment and selection practice appears in Langtry (1994). On a wider front, Townley (1994) has produced an interesting book which reconceptualises the field of human resource management and explores an alternative politics and ethics at work. For a general critique of human resource management, see Blyton and Turnbull's *Reassessing Human Resource Management*. There are many interesting chapters in this book not least the one by Blyton and Morris which concludes by stating 'that a high quality, flexible and committed workforce can only be achieved and sustained over a significant period if the overall employment relationship is based on a more equitable reciprocity' (1992, p. 128).

Business and managerial ethics as academic subjects are on the increase in the UK, reflecting a growing interest in society at large, and amongst the younger generation in particular, about questions of morality in personal relationships as well as in the relationships between corporations and the individual. However, discussing the underlying philosophical considerations and principles which govern ethical concepts has never been of any great particular concern in the UK outside the confines of university philosophy departments. Nevertheless, students of Human Resource Management, who appreciate the need to develop a comprehensive philosophical understanding of the notion of ethics, will find an introduction to the subject in the works of Kant (1948), Kohlberg (1981), and Wittgenstein (1980). Finally, and challenging all male notions of impartiality or objectivity, in her book titled *In a Different Voice: Psychological Theory and Women's Development* (1982), Carol Gilligan suggests an alternative (feminine) morality of care as opposed to a (masculine) morality of justice.

References

Anderson, G. (1991) 'Selection', in B. Towers (ed.), *The Handbook of Human Resource Management*, Blackwell, Oxford.
Beauchamp, T. L. (1989) *Case Studies in Business, Society, and Ethics*, Prentice-Hall, New Jersey.
Beardwell, I. and Holden, L. (1994) *Human Resource Management: A Contemporary Perspective*, Pitman, London.
Blyton, P. and Morris, J. (1992) 'HRM and the Limits of Flexibility' in Blyton and Turnbull (eds) (1992).
Blyton, P. and Turnbull, P. (eds) (1992) *Reassessing Human Resource Management*, Sage.
Chryssides, G. D. and Kaler, J. H. (1993) *An Introduction to Business Ethics*, Chapman & Hall, London.
Crouch, C. (1990) 'United Kingdom: The Rejection of Compromise', in G. Baglioni and C. Crouch, *European Industrial Relations: the Challenge of Flexibility*, Sage.
Donaldson, J. (1989) *Key Issues in Business Ethics*, Academic Press, London.
Gilligan, C. (1982) *In a Different Voice: Psychological Theory and Women's Development*, Harvard University Press.
Incomes Data Services (1990) *European Management Guides: Recruitment*, Income Data Services/Institute of Personnel Management.
IPM (1994) *The IPM Code of Professional Conduct: The IPM Codes of Practice.*
IRS (1991) *IRS Recruitment and Development Report*, 'The State of Selection 2', May.
Kant, I. (1948) *Groundwork to the Metaphysics of Morals* (trans. H. J. PatonJ), Hutchinson, London.
Kohlberg, L. (1981) *Essays on Moral Development, Vol. One: The Philosophy of Moral Development*, Harper & Row, New York.
Langtry, R. (1994) 'Selection', in I. Beardwell and L. Holden (eds), *Human Resource Management*, Pitman, London.
Maclagan, P. (1993) *Issues Concerning the Moral Development of People in Organisations*, Working Paper Series No. HUS/PWM/20, The University of Hull.
Mathis, R. L. and Jackson, J. H. (1994) *Human Resource Management*, West Publishing, St Paul, Minnesota.
Schuler, R. S. and Huber, V. L. (1993) *Personnel and Human Resource Management*, West Publishing, St Paul, Minnesota.
Sisson, K. (1989) *Personnel Management in Britain*, Blackwell, Oxford.
Sisson, K. (1994) *Personnel Management: A Comprehensive Guide to Theory and Practice in Britain*, Blackwell, Oxford.
Torrington, D. and Hall, L. (1987) *Personnel Management: A New Approach*, Prentice-Hall, New Jersey.
Towers, B. (ed.) (1992) *The Handbook of Human Resource Management*, Blackwell, Oxford.

Townley, B. (1994) *Reframing Human Resource Management: Power, Ethics and the Subject of Work*, Sage, New York.
Watson, T. (1994) 'Recruitment and Selection', in Sisson (1994).
Wittgenstein, L. (1980) *Culture and Value*, Blackwell, Oxford.

CHAPTER 15

Ethical Issues in Accounting

1 Introduction

Accountants are employed in many types of organisations – public, private and charitable. All the ethical issues faced by accountants which result from the type of organisation they are employed by cannot be examined in this chapter. From here onwards, therefore, the relevant issues will be examined in the context, primarily, of limited liability companies in the United Kingdom (UK).

The chapter is divided into two sections. The first begins by providing an overview of the UK accounting profession, considering its role and distinguishing between professional accountants employed by business organisations (preparers of accounting information), and independent professional accountants (auditors). This distinction is used to facilitate the discussion of the rules governing the professional conduct of accountants which follows.

Section 2 contains four vignettes which illustrate the kind of ethical dilemmas commonly facing accountants in the different facets of their working lives. Each case is followed by an analysis of the influences prevailing upon the individual practitioner attempting to make ethical decisions.

2 The Accounting Profession

The modern accounting profession originated as a result of the creation of the limited liability company during the Industrial Revolution. The accounting profession grew out of the statutory accounting and auditing requirements of the various Companies Acts, culminating in the Companies Act 1967, which gave the accounting profession an exclusive right to audit the accounts of limited companies in the UK. These requirements were developed to protect the interests of the large number of new investors who had no knowledge of, or influence on, the day-to-day management of the companies in which they had invested. In addition, the accounting profession itself gradually developed a consensus on the treatment of transactions, to avoid inconsistencies between the financial statements of different companies.

In the 1990s, the accounting profession continues to influence both the framing and interpretation of legislation, and remains strong and independent. Currently the profession is made up of six accounting bodies[1] which have formed a joint representative body, the Consultative Committee of Accounting Bodies (CCAB). The CCAB has provided an effective mechanism for producing a coordinated approach from these bodies.

3   Accountants – A Variety of Roles

It is useful to distinguish between the role of a professional accountant employed by a business organisation and an independent professional accountant.

Accountants employed within organisations

The role of the accountant within organisations has developed in two broad directions:

The management accountant

According to the Chartered Institute of Management Accoutants (CIMA) (1991), the role of management accounting is to provide:

> information required by management for such purposes as: formulation of policies; planning and controlling the activities of the enterprise; decision taking on alternative courses of action; disclosures to those external to the entity (shareholders and others); disclosure to employees; and safeguarding assets.

If a business chooses to employ a management accountant, their role is to provide financial information which can be used by managers to help them achieve the objectives of the enterprise.

The financial accountant

The role of the financial accountant is to provide economic information (in the form of financial statements) about the performance and financial adaptability of an organisation to users in the 'outside world'. The Accounting Standards Board (ASB)'s Statement of Principles (1991), defines the users of financial statements as: investors; employees; lenders; suppliers and other trade creditors; customers; government agencies; and the public.

The directors of a company are responsible for preparing financial statements which comply with statutory requirements (embodied in the

Companies Act 1985), and which give a 'true and fair view' of the company's position and performance. The financial accountant, acting on behalf of the directors, advises on which items should be selected for inclusion in the financial statements, and how they should be measured and presented.

Accountants in professional practice

Accountants in professional practice offer a variety of accounting services which fall into two categories:

The auditor

Audits are undertaken by independent professional accountants appointed by the shareholders. Under the Companies Act 1985 (as amended by the Companies Act 1989), the auditor has three main duties: to report to the members whether, in the auditor's opinion, the financial statements give a true and fair view of the state of affairs of the company and comply with the Companies Act 1985; to fulfil their obligations under the Companies Acts and under the Articles of Association of the company; and to exercise reasonable care and skill.

The auditors' role, therefore, is to express an independent opinion on the fairness and reliability of the company's financial statements and thus on the directors' stewardship of the owners' funds.

Related services

Accountants in professional practice offer a variety of accounting services including tax services, management consultancy, insolvency services, advice on acquisitions and mergers, and, recently, environmental audits.

4 The Rules Regulating the Professional Conduct of Accountants

The professional conduct of members of the accounting bodies is governed by rules and standards, both technical and ethical:

Technical rules (accounting regulations)

Governing the preparation of management accounting information

An 'official terminology' of Management Accounting has been issued by CIMA (1991) which attempts to standardise the definitions of a range of commonly used concepts, techniques and methods. Its application, however, is not mandatory. Information which is to be made available outside the organisation should comply with the technical rules governing the preparation of financial statements.

Governing the preparation of financial statements

In the UK[2] the predominant sources of accounting regulations are to be found in the form of legislation and accounting standards. Broadly speaking, the Companies Acts 1985 regulates the preparation, form and content of company financial statements, while accounting standards support the legal requirements by giving detailed guidance.

Accounting standards are formulated by a private-sector, self-regulatory body, the Financial Reporting Council (FRC).[3] The FRC is responsible for setting and issuing accounting standards, through the FRC's two main subsidiary organisations, the Accounting Standards Board (ASB) and the Review Panel. The FRC has a chairman appointed jointly by the Secretary of State for Trade and Industry and the Governor of the Bank of England. Membership of the FRC is comprised of members of the accounting profession, together with others who are concerned with the use, audit, or preparation of accounting information, for example representatives from industry and commerce, stockbrokers and analysts, banks, trade unions and the Department of Trade and Industry. Finance comes from the government, the professional bodies, and private-sector contributions.

Some legal recognition, though not enforceability, has now been given to accounting standards by the amended Companies Act 1985, which requires large companies to comply with accounting standards of explain departures in the notes to the accounts.

Governing the conduct of audits

The conduct of audits is regulated by the Auditing Standards and Guidelines published by the Auditing Practices Board (APB), which was established by the CCAB in 1991.

Professional ethics

In its Guide to Professional Ethics, the ICAEW[4] states that:

> In addition to the duties owed to the public and to his or her client or employer a member of the Institute is bound to observe high standards of conduct which may sometimes be contrary to his personal self-interest.

Guidance, which applies to members both in practice in business, is given in the form of fundamental principles and statements. The fundamental principles are framed in broad and general terms, and give basic advice on professional behaviour. Statements elaborate on what is expected of members in particular circumstances.

The fundamental principles are:

- A member should behave with integrity in all professional and business relationships. Integrity implies not merely honesty but fair dealing and truthfulness.
- A member should strive for objectivity in all professional and business judgements. Objectivity is the state of mind which has regard to all considerations relevant to the task in hand but no other.
- A member should not accept or perform work which he or she is not competent to undertake unless he obtains such advice and assistance as will enable him competently to carry out the work.
- A member should carry out his or her professional work with due skill, care, diligence and expedition and with proper regard for the technical and professional standards expected of him as a member.
- A member should conduct himself or herself with courtesy and consideration towards all with whom he comes into contact during the course of producing his work.

The statements identify areas of risk which may bring into question the independence of members. For members in practice, the areas of risk identified are: undue dependence on an audit client; significant overdue fees from a client; actual or threatened litigation; influences outside the practice; family and other personal relationships; interests in shares and other investments; beneficial interests in trusts; trustee investments; voting on audit appointments; loans; goods, services and hospitality; and the provision of other services to audit clients.

The code of professional ethics (and accounting regulations) is enforced through the Joint Disciplinary Scheme (JDS) which was formed in 1979, and is run jointly by the ICAW, the ICAS, and the ACCA. These professional bodies can discipline members for misconduct, incompetence, and efficiency. The punishments available range from suspension from membership, to fines, reprimands, serious reprimands, and withdrawal of practising certificates.

5 Vignettes

Background information

All the facts of this case are fictitious, and they are not intended to resemble any companies, persons or ships.

RBSC Limited is a company registered in the UK, and is a wholly owned subsidiary of the UK Shipping Consortium Limited. RBSC Limited's ultimate holding company is registered overseas, and is owned by a family with worldwide shipping interests. The principal activity of RBSC Limited is the chartering of the supertanker RBII, which carries a cargo of crude oil. The ship is registered in Hong Kong and employs a British crew.

The RBII is due to sail to Portsmouth in March 19X5 for dry-docking and a five-yearly overhaul of the hull. The company's next financial year end is 31 December 19X4.

Case 1 – The management accountant

The management accountant, Angela, has been employed by RBSC Limited for several years and now holds a senior position in the company.

In March 19X4, the management team identified four possible ports (in different parts of the world) with dry-docking facilities which could carry out the overhaul of the hull. Angela was asked to quantify each alternative, in order to determine the most cost-effective port. The costs relevant to the decision included estimates for each port of: the costs of sailing to the port; charter fees lost due to the ship being out of service; dry-docking fees; and repair costs. Where possible, Angela obtained estimates from suppliers; however, a number of assumptions had to be made about the future exchange rates and the number of days the ship would be out of service.

At the end of the exercise, it was clear that the highest-cost port, at an estimated £7m, would be Portsmouth. The managing director (MD), who has a financial interest in the Portsmouth shipyard, persuaded Angela to change a number of the assumptions on which the calculations were based in order to make Portsmouth appear to be the lowest-cost port at an estimated £6m.

Case 2 – The financial accountant

The financial accountant, Frank, who was appointed in June 19X4, has experience of auditing and is recently qualified. Being in a relatively high-profile, high-risk business, Frank had been pleased to be able to negotiate a salary substantially above the market rate for an equivalent position in other sectors, together with an annual bonus based on performance.

Frank is currently preparing the financial statements for the year ended 31 December 19X4. The published, audited accounts for the year ended 31 December 19X3 included a cumulative provision for dry-docking charges of £1m. Frank is aware that a costing exercise has been carried out, but is unable to obtain a copy, and is being stonewalled by Angela and the managing director. The receptionist, who opens the post, has informed him that 'everyone knows' that the dry-docking charge is likely to be in the region of £6m.

The managing director is putting Frank under considerable pressure to include a cumulative provision of only £3m, and has suggested that any concerns about the likely level of dry-docking charges need not be disclosed to the auditors. The managing director is currently negotiating a substantial loan from the bank.

Case 3 – The auditor

(1)   The Audit Manager

After reviewing the financial statements (prepared by the financial accountant) for the year ended 31 December 19X4, the audit manager, Clare, identified the provision of £3m for dry-docking charges as an item carrying significant audit risk. On investigation, the audit team was unable to obtain documentary evidence to substantiate the provision and has also been made aware of the rumour that the actual figure is likely to be £6m.

The managing director is refusing to discuss the subject and threatening to appoint alternative auditors, unless the accounts are finalised before the meeting with the bank.

(2)   The Audit Partner

The audit partner, Mike, is a junior partner in a medium-sized firm of chartered accountants. The audit fee from RBSC Limited represents a significant proportion of his fee income, but a small proportion of the fee income of the partnership as a whole. Mike has also advised RBSC Limited on the appointment of the financial accountant, and has given general advice on various sources of finance.

The managing director and Mike eventually compromised, and agreed on a provision of £4m for dry-docking charges. The accounts were duly signed by the partnership as presenting a true and fair view, and were used by the company to obtain a bank loan. In March 1995, the actual dry-docking charges amounted to £7m.

6   Discussion

Case 1

In order to behave ethically Angela must strive for objectivity and behave with integrity.

In this situation Angela must make a judgement as to who exactly she owes these duties to. Although the managing director is her immediate superior, the primary duty is owed to the company itself, which is managed by the board of directors as a whole. Angela is, therefore, under a duty to ensure that the board has accurate information on which to base its decisions, e.g. in relation to dry-docking. Further, as the managing director is seeking to influence Angela in this decision, she must take a decision as to whether or not she should inform the board of his attempts to 'persuade' her to alter her assumptions. In other words, does her ethical duty only extend to ensuring accurate information is provided or does it extend to reporting the surrounding circumstances?

Question: If the Board decide to go along with the managing director's decision after the assumptions in favour of Portsmouth, does Angela's duty extend to trying to inform the company's shareholders/auditors of her misgivings?

Case 2

Frank is clearly a well-paid, highly valued member of the management team. However, he must not allow these factors to affect his professional judgement.

Frank has a clear duty to 'users' of financial information, which group includes lenders. Therefore, if the dry-docking costs would be a relevant factor in the bank's decision to lend, the financial accountant should ensure that accurate information is available. As in Case 1, the financial accountant should report his findings direct to the board, whom he should also remind that they have a duty to ensure that the company's audited accounts present a 'true and fair view' of the company's affairs.

Question: If the board take the same position as the managing director, should Frank inform the auditors of his concerns?

Case 3

1. The audit firm has a statutory duty to ensure that the company's accounts give a 'true and fair view' of the company's affairs. In a situation such as this, Clare should have insisted that documentary evidence of the dry-docking estimates be made available.

   However, if this request had been denied Clare's ethical position becomes less clear. She clearly has a duty to the company's shareholders but would she be fulfilling her duty by simply passing the problem on to the audit partner. The answer to the question is probably 'yes'. The partner is working within the same code of ethics as Clare but has greater experience on which to make the appropriate decision and, with his partners, will have the ultimate responsibility for signing off the accounts as presenting a 'true and fair view'.

   Question: What if the audit partner comes to a decision which Clare believes to be unethical, and potentially breaching the auditor's statutory duties?

2. It seems that Mike put himself in a difficult position, even before this situation arose. Clearly, from a personal perspective, he may be relying too heavily on the fees from one audit client, even though the relevant provision of the professional code refers to the audit fee income of the practice as a whole. In addition, by providing related services, other than auditing, he has placed a further strain on his independence, or at least his apparent independence. In relation to these matters he should consider his position for the future, following discussions with his partners.

None of these factors should have affected Mike's judgement in this situation; his duties here are both statutory and ethical. If he could not justify the relevant dry-docking provision in the accounts, and felt the item was material, he should not have signed the accounts, and he should, indeed, have sought the advice of his partners. This is particularly important as his partners will be jointly and severally liable with Mike should action be taken against the firm in relation to the inaccurate accounts.

Question: Would the partner's position be any difference if the actual dry-docking charges amounted to £4.2m?

Notes

1. The six accounting bodies are:
   The Institute of Chartered Accountants of England and Wales (ICAEW)
   The Institute of Chartered Accountants in Ireland (ICAS)
   The Institute of Chartered Accountants of Scotland (ICAS)
   The Chartered Association of Certified Accountants (ACCA)
   The Chartered Association of Management Accountants (CIMA)
   The Chartered Institute of Public Finance and Accountancy (CIPFA)
2. The extent to which accounting requirements are embodied in legislation or private sector regulations varies between countries.
3. The FRC replaced the Accounting Standards Committee (ASC) in 1990. Prior to 1990, the accounting bodies had direct responsibility for setting and issuing accounting standards, through the ASC.
4. The ICAEW's Guide to Professional Ethics is used to illustrate the fundamental principles guiding professional conduct, on which there is broad consensus among the six accounting bodies.

References and Bibliography

Accounting Standard Board (1991) *The Objective of Financial Statements and the Qualitative Characteristics of Financial Information*, The ASB Limited.
Ang, J. S. (1993) 'On Financial Ethics', *Financial Management*, Autumn, pp. 32–59.

Brown, K.M. (1994) 'Using Role Play to Integrate Ethics into the Curriculum: A Financial Management Example', *Journal of Business Ethics*, Feb., pp. 105–10.

Chartered Institute of Management Accountants (1991) *Management Accounting: Official Terminology*.

Claypool, G. A., Fetyko, D. F. and Pearson, A. (1990) 'Reactions to Ethical Dilemmas: A Study Pertaining to Certified Public Accountants', *Journal of Business Ethics*, Sept., pp. 699–706.

Cohen, J. R. and Pant, L. W. (1991) 'Beyond Bean Counting: Establishing High Ethical Standards', *Journal of Business Ethics*, Jan., pp. 45–56.

Gunz, S. and McCutcheon, J. (1991) 'Some Unresolved Ethical Issues in Auditing', *Journal of Business Ethics*, Oct., pp.777–85.

Hawley, D. (1991) 'Business Ethics and Social Responsibility in Finance', *Journal of Business Ethics*, Sept., pp. 711–21.

Hiltebeitel, K.M. and Jones, S. K. (1992) 'An Assessment of Ethics Instruction in Accounting Education', *Journal of Business Ethics*, Jan., pp. 37–46.

Huss, H. F. and Patterson, D. M. (1993) 'Ethics in Accounting: Values Education without Indoctrination', *Journal of Business Ethics*, Mar., pp. 235–43.

Jennings, M. (1991) 'Ethics, Excellence and Accountants', *Accountancy*, Jan., pp. 23–4.

Kullberg, D. R. (1990) 'Business Ethics: Not a Luxury; Standards of Ethical Conduct for Management Accountants', *Management Accounting*, Feb., pp. 20–1.

Loeb, S. E. and Rockness, J. (1992) 'Accounting Ethics and Education: A Response', *Journal of Business Ethics*, July, pp. 485–90.

Martens, S. and Stevens, K. (1994) 'The FASB's Cost/Benefit Constraint in Theory and Practice', *Journal of Business Ethics*, Mar., pp. 171–9.

McNair, F. and Milam, E. E. (1993) 'Ethics in Accounting Education: What is Really Being Done', *Journal of Business Ethics*, Oct., pp. 797–809.

Mitchell, A., Puxty, T. and Sikka, P. (1994) 'Ethical Statements as Smokescreens for Sectional Interests: The Case of the UK Accountancy', *Journal of Business Ethics*, Jan., pp. 39–51.

Patten, D. M. (1990) 'The Differential Perception of Accountants to Maccoby's Head/Heart Traits', *Journal of Business Ethics*, Oct., pp. 791–8.

Peek, L. E., Peek, G. S. and Horras, M. (1994) 'Enhancing Arthur Business Ethics Vignettes', *Journal of Business Ethics*, Mar., pp. 189–96.

Schlachter, P. J. (1990) 'Organisational Influences on Individual Ethical Behaviour', *Journal of Business Ethics*, Nov., pp. 389–853.

Stanga, K. G. and Turpen, R. A. (1991) 'Ethical Judgements on Selected Accounting Issues: An Empirical Study', *Journal of Business Ethics*, Oct., pp. 739–47.

Waples, E. and Shaub, M. K. (1991) 'Establishing an Ethic of Accounting: A Response to Westra's Call for Government Employment of Auditors', *Journal of Business Ethics*, May, pp. 385–93.

Ward, S. P., Ward, D. R. and Deck, A. B. (1993) 'Certified Public Accountants: Ethical Perception Skills', *Journal of Business Ethics*, Aug., pp. 601–10.

CHAPTER 16

Ethical Dilemmas at Work

1 The Individual at Work

How are the ethical problems facing the individual at work any different from those to be faced anywhere else? Surely here, if nowhere else, the argument that business ethics is no more than ethics applied to business has some application. Certainly it is true that many of the difficult moral decisions faced in the workplace are raised by issues that are not peculiar to work but are to do with one's treatment of other people and theirs of you. Must one keep this promise? Was that indeed a promise or merely a vague statement of intent? How far should should one go in taking decisions that affect others without consulting or, at least, informing them? And so on. But it is also true that an individual who works in or for an organisation is in a position which is complicated by factors that do not apply to a person acting in a private capacity.

We all have rights, duties, responsibilities, powers, interests, etc. which accrue to us as people within a society. We have the right to vote, to apply for a passport, to join a political party; we have a duty of care towards our dependent children and, perhaps, to others such as elderly relatives; we have ties of affection and obligation that bind us to friends and acquaintances; we might belong to churches, clubs, building societies and so on. All of these contribute to defining us as moral individuals surrounded by a network of reciprocal relationships with others to whom we owe and from whom we expect loyalty, respect, esteem, friendship, duty and obligation in different proportions and to a greater or lesser extent.

We do not lose these moral relationships once we enter the workplace. Obviously we gain new ones. Some of these will arise, as before, because of our status as a private person, the moral individual which we are. Some of them, however, will be contingent not on our being whom we are but on our holding the post that we do within the organisation. We acquire new powers and responsibilities which, strictly speaking, are not ours at all, but those of the position we fill or the function we perform. And not only will these new powers, responsibilities, duties, interests, concerns, etc. be different from the ones we had before, they may even conflict with them.

2   Power, Authority and Trust

For example, in a private capacity it is accepted that, whatever we may feel to be the nature and extent of the care and concern we should owe to everyone, we owe a special degree of consideration to those closest to us. We should look after them and help them whenever we can and to the best of our abilities. But should the personnel manager of a large industrial company show special consideration to friends and relatives who apply for jobs within that company? Should a financial journalist use knowledge gained from doing the job to tip off people she knows have risky investments? Should someone with a large investment in a company warn close relatives who also have shares that he is about to unload his and that the values of those shares is therefore likely to go down substantially? Should the purchasing manager give a lucrative contract to a cousin who is in the right line of business but happens to be in financial difficulties at the moment and needs the business badly?

The fact that in such cases the person is no longer acting solely on her or his own account clearly makes a difference. What would be permitted, even laudable, behaviour for a private person becomes suspect once that person is acting in trust for a third party, the organisation. It is even more suspect if what makes it *possible* for that person to act in that way is that power and authority lent by the organisation itself. But though this is clear enough in principle, in practice drawing the lines between the private and the public is not easy. Consider the following:

(a) An executive of a financial services company is also the treasurer of a local charity. She is punctilious about not using company stationary or reprographic facilities for this work, but she does use a company computer for the work, because the software is too expensive for the charity to fund for the very occasional use it would make of it.
(b) The manager of a large city-centre store uses personal influence to obtain a relatively low-paid job for an old friend who has been out of work for a very long time. The friend is more than adequately qualified for the job, but the competition for it was fierce.
(c) An estate agent arranges to sell a house which the owners wish to put on the market at a ridiculously low price because they want to move quickly. Before making the details public the agent rings his sister-in-law whom he knows is looking for just such a house as this, and the deal is concluded privately.

(d) As in (c), except that the agent realises that the price suggested is lower than it need be even for a quick sale, but says nothing. 'The customer is always right.'
(e) As in (d), except that the sister-in-law does not want the house at all, but sells it on immediately and splits her profit with the agent.
(f) The purchasing manager of a medium-sized company receives quotations for office stationary from a number of suppliers including one run by a cousin. In terms of cost the differences between them are marginal. The decision is taken to place the order with the cousin.

In Case (e), the actions of the estate agent may not be illegal, but hardly anyone would have any problem in deciding that they were morally indefensible. In all the other cases a moral conclusion is not so easy to draw. Case (a) may well be defensible, even praiseworthy, provided only that the executive does what she does openly and with the consent, tacit or explicit, of the company for which she works. All the cases show, at the least, a potential for an abuse of power which can arise from a failure to distinguish what is appropriate behaviour in one role as opposed to another.

3 Secrecy, Confidentiality and Loyalty

Problems raised by the protection of confidential information and the circumstances under which it may or should be disclosed are not peculiar to business ethics, nor are they generated solely by role conflict. They arise in all circumstances, both public and private. The duty to tell the truth is always qualified by the need to ask whether the person you are telling it to is entitled to know it. The simplest, most widespread and, usually, most trivial example of this is gossip. The word has two meanings, its most familiar being idle or groundless rumour, tittle-tattle, malicious or spiteful untruth. But the second is related to its origin as godparent (OE *godsibb*, person related to one in God, *Concise Oxford Dictionary*), where it means the easy or unconstrained smalltalk which goes on between close friends and relations. Both senses matter, for gossip need not be a source for moral concern and, in the second sense, is important in building and maintaining the intimacy necessary between those who work or live closely together. It also has a vital function in its role as grapevine where it is an extremely efficient communications network and acts to preserve the common knowledge base without which concerted cooperative action (at any level, from that of the family, through the institutional to the cultural) would be all but impossible. It cannot, therefore, nor should it be, proscribed. But in its first sense it is clearly dangerous. Those who engage in gossip must walk a thin line between passing on what justifiably is in the public domain (the weather, last night's episode of *Eastenders*, the new policy on allocating spaces in the company car park) and what one may know but ought not to casually and promiscuously disclose (X's marital problems, Y's alcoholism or the state of Z's health). It is not that such things always ought to be kept secret, but disclosing them risks harming others, and that risk, together with its avoidability and defensibility, must always be considered. (Perhaps the information is already public knowledge – Y is proud of being an ex-alcoholic and boasts of it – or perhaps there is a public interest in disclosure – Z persists in driving a car despite dizzy spells and in the teeth of doctor's advice.)

It also matters how one came to be in possession of such information, and here issues of trust are raised again. Many social positions and occupations require one to be entrusted with information which one may not deal with as if one had learned it in a private capacity. One may, indeed, have strong contractual, professional or moral obligations not to disclose such information at all, or only to specific individuals in specific circumstances. The confidentiality of medical records is, for example, if not quite absolute, then very nearly so. Without the consent of the patient such records may only be disclosed to other health care professionals who may need to see them or by court order or to the police in the investigation of serious crime (see Brazier, 1987, ch. 3). Medicine is special, however only in the fact that the law treats virtually all of what goes on between doctor and patient as confidential, not in the degree of protection it offers such confidential information. Disclosure of *any* information given in confidence is an offence (though a civil rather than a criminal one) when protecting that confidentiality is in the public interest and is recognised as grounds for dismissal in English law (Selwyn, 1993). This may apply even after an employee has left an organisation, which raises problems of its own.

An organisation clearly has a right to protect information whose disclosure, to competitors, say, would threaten its prosperity or survival. This might include client lists, industrial processes, management structures or procedures – any form of information which might plausibly be considered the intellectual property of the organisation rather than of individual employees and not in the public domain. It is normally held that an contract of employment creates a duty of fidelity, i.e. that an employee owes a loyalty to an employer which divulging information likely to damage that employer would violate (Smith and Wood, 1993). So, for example, someone who, just before he left a business in order to set up in competition with it, copied out a list of its clients for future use, would be in breach of contract (*Robb* v. *Green* [1895–9] All ER 1053). Two areas are less clear than this, however. The first concerns the extent to which someone may use the skills and knowledge they gained in one employment when they take up a new job or, even, make those those skills and that knowledge the basis on which they obtain the new job. The Inland Revenue has long had the problem that expensively trained tax inspectors frequently find employment with businesses of the kind they were trained to inspect – gamekeepers become poachers. In television, too, it is well known that BBC-trained technicians are highly valued by independent production companies whose size means that they do very little training of their own and whose competitiveness often depends on just that fact. The law distinguishes between confidential information which is, in effect, the property of the original employer and may not be passed on even when the employee is in a new job, and the skills and knowledge which form part of an employee's ability and which he or she is entitled to use in order to gain new employment (*Faccenda Chicken Ltd* v. *Fowler* [1986] ICR 297). The moral issue is not so straightforward (though even the law finds it easier to make the distinction than to apply it). Are you justified in allowing an organisation to spend a lot of money in training and developing your skills so that you can immediately leave and find a better job somewhere else?

The second area concerns whistle-blowing. This problem has been given extensive treatment elsewhere (see, for example, Bok, 1982, ch. xiv; Shaw and Barry, 1989, ch. 7; Donaldson, 1987, ch. 7), and so we do not intend to discuss it in full. It does need to be mentioned, however, because it also poses the question of whether one may pass on material which would otherwise be confidential. The law is perfectly clear on this; the duty to respect confidentiality does not extend to cover breaches of the law or other wrongful actions – 'there is no confidence as to the disclosure of an iniquity' (Selwyn, 1993) – nor does it release an employee from a legal obligation to disclose information, for example, to the Health & Safety Inspectorate or FIMBRA. The law in the UK does (as it does not in the US, or only imperfectly so) protect an employee against dismissal for justifiably blowing the whistle, both at common law and by statute. But it does not, and probably cannot, protect an employee against loss of promotion, non-renewal of contract or other forms of victimisation. Nor is it even clear how far the whistle-blower will be protected against dismissal to the extent that what is disclosed is not criminal but merely immoral or in some other way dubious. Certainly Sarah Tisdall was not protected from the consequences of her breach of the Official Secrets Act in virtue of her disclosure that a government minister allegedly misled the House of Commons about the placement of Trident missiles.

4   Resolving Dilemmas

How can managers cope with the ethical dilemmas that they face at work? Are there any useful guidelines which they can be given?

The answers to these questions are not straightforward and the first essential step is to look further into the questions themselves. In relation to the first question, would our answer differ if we rephrased the question to ask 'How can people cope with the ethical dilemmas they face?'. Why do we use the label 'manager' when dealing with the sub-set of ethical dilemmas faced by people at work? Again, would our answer differ if we asked 'How can people cope with the ethical dilemmas they face as a supporter at a football match?' Does the context of the ethical dilemma make a difference?

The use of a special label to describe a person – manager, shop-floor worker, football supporter – implies a role, as we have seen. As a manager you are expected to carry out the role of manager, however that is defined in your particular context. Roles carry expectations. Your superiors at work will define their expectations of your behaviour in your role in formal ways, through a job description, or in informal ways, by demonstrating in their own behaviour how they expect managers to behave. Coping with the differences between formal and informal expectations is a skill which adults acquire, to varying levels of competence through experience. However, life is made more complicated by fact that you probably have several roles at work. Managers may have to act as spokesperson for their section, chair of a selection panel, contributor to a discussion or policy paper, receiver of complaints, peacemaker, leader, coordinator and so on. Informally, they may organise the five-a-side football team or collect in the tea money.

Switching from role to role with skill and aplomb is a difficult art. However, assuming you can do it, would you expect your ethical standards to differ between these roles? There is a widespread acceptance that differing roles demand differing ethical standards. This general acceptance lies beneath the first question. Is it legitimate to ask this question? Some commentators argue that it is not. Campbell and Drummond (1989), for example, state:

> It is time to stop feeling helpless and to see that there are ways in which you can bring together the kind of citizen you want to be in your private life and the kind of citizen you want your company to be in its public life.

They argue that the ethical standards of a person should not be changed or ignored just because the context changes.

However, it is the case that many managers do indeed make unethical decisions in their work role with a readiness which they may find inacceptable in their private lives. Why is this the case?

Gellerman (1986) argues that there are four major rationalisations used by managers to justify unethical behaviour. These are:

- a belief that the activity is within reasonable ethical and legal limits – that it is not really illegal or immoral;
- a belief that the activity is in the individual's or corporation's best interests so that the individual would somehow be expected to undertake the activity;
- a belief that the activity is 'safe' because it will never be found out or publicised; the classic crime and punishment issue of discovery;
- a belief that because the activity helps the company the company will condone it and even protect the person who engages in it.

The use of the term 'rationalisations' implies that there may be other more fundamental reasons which lie behind the manager's unethical behaviour. What is it about organisational life which provides the fertile ground for such rationalisations? In choosing not to behave ethically, and consequently using a rationalisation to justify their behaviour, are managers telling us more about their personal moral development than about their organisation?

When people enter into work for an organisation, they usually sign a contract and there is often a job description which indicates their tasks. They receive payment and possibly other rewards in return for their fulfilment of their tasks. No contract or job description will require the person to act illegally or unethically. However, the sale of one's labour power to another often carries with it assumptions and expectations. People quickly get to know what is really expected of them. Organisational culture has a deep influence on employees.

The strength of the organisational culture is reinforced at times when jobs are scarce. When unemployment is high, people are more willing to bend the rules in order to keep their job.

Social and organisational influences, therefore, do have a significant influence on behaviour at work and, consequently, on ethical behaviour.

5 Advising Managers

Several influential management books end with a paean to ethics, for example, Tom Peters in *Thriving on Chaos* – 'Set absurdly high standards for integrity – and then live with them with no fuzzy margins.'

Nash's (1981) view is that 'Such advice fails to help the already well minded manager who nevertheless finds the ethical aspects of business sometimes painful frequently confusing and occasionally a matter for personal disappointment in oneself or in one's company.'

It is also the case that such advice will not be well received by those managers who have decided to act unethically, even if they are able to offer a rationalisation of their action. Preaching will do no good in this context for either the well-minded manager or for those who have decided to act unethically.

Trying to undertand the reasons why normal moral values of private life seem to break down or become ineffectual in a business context is the challenge. Nash offers five reasons:

- the analytical frameworks which managers use;
- the goals they set;
- the organisational structures they adopt;
- the language they use to motivate others;
- their personal assumptions about the intrinsic worth of other people.

If ethical issues and concerns do not figure in any of these areas, then it is unlikely that the organisation will be fostering a climate in which ethical behaviour becomes the norm. The need to produce rationalisations to justify unethical behaviour is diminished in organisations which pay attention to the ethical dimensions of their corporate life.

Assuming that managers do not wish to behave unethically and that the ethical dilemmas they face may sometimes not be amenable to simplistic, formulaic solutions, then managers need to develop skill and experience in coping with ethical dilemmas. Nash (1981) offers the following list of questions to act as guidance for managers. Such an approach is helpful for managers who are predisposed to behave ethically and who work within organisations which require or encourage ethical behaviour. The questions are:

1. Have you defined the problem accurately?
2. How would you define the problem if you stood on the other side of the fence?
3. How did the situation occur in the first place?
4. To whom and to what do you give your loyalty as a person and as a member of the corporation?
5. What is your intention in making this decision?
6. How does this intention compare with the probable result?
7. Whom would your decision or action injure?
8. Can you discuss the problem with the affected parties before you make your decision?
9. Are you confident that your decision will be as valid over a long period of time as it is now?
10. Could you discuss without qualm your decision with your boss, your chief executive officer, the board of directors, your family, society as a whole?
11. What is the symbolic potential of your action if understood, if misunderstood?
12. Under what circumstances would you allow exceptions to your stand?

This modelling of an approach to ethical dilemmas may appear cumbersome at first sight, and for managers who have not been able to clarify their own values or who work in an unsympathetic climate it may seem to be quite irksome. However, this kind of approach has been found to be useful in practice and it does become easier with practice – like any other skill.

Behaving ethically is based partly on the strength of commitment to a value system, fortitude in adversity and skill in analysing ethical issues – and the skill level can be improved with practice (see, for example, Delaney and Sockell, 1992; and Kavathatzopoulos, 1993)

References

Bok, S. (1982) *Secrets: Concealment and Revelations,* Oxford University Press, Oxford.

Brazier, M. (1987) *Medicine, Patients and the Law,* Penguin, Harmondsworth.

Campbell, D. and Drummond, J. (1989) *Good Business: Case Studies in Corporate Social Responsibilities,* SAVS, Bristol.

Delaney, J. T. and Sockell, D. (1992) 'Do Company Ethics Training Programmes Make a Difference? An Empirical Analysis', *Journal of Business Ethics,* vol. 11, pp. 719–27.

Donaldson, J. (1989) *Key Issues in Business Ethics,* Academic Press, London.

Gellerman, S. W. (1986) 'Why Good Managers Make Bad Ethical Choices', *Harvard Business Review,* July/August.

Kavathatzopoulos, I. (1993) 'Development of a Cognitive Skill in Solving Business Ethics Problems: The Effect of Instruction', *Journal of Business Ethics,* vol. 12, pp. 379–86.

Nash, L. (1981) 'Ethics without the Sermon', *Harvard Business Review,* Nov/Dec.

Shaw, W. and Barry, V. (1989) *Moral Issues in Business,* 4th edn, Wadsworth Pub. Co., Belmont, Ca.

Selwyn, N. M. (1993) *Selwyn's Law of Employment,* Butterworth, London.

Peters, T. (1987) *Thriving on Chaos: Handbook for a Management Revolution,* Knopf, New York.

Smith, I. T. and Wood, J. C. (1993) *Industrial Law,* Pitman, London.

Bibliography

1 Books

Adams, R., Carruthers, J. and Hamill, S. (1992) *Changing Corporate Values*, Kogan Page, London.

Allinson, R. E. (1993) *Global Disasters: Inquiries into Management Ethics*, Prentice-Hall, New Jersey.

Aristotle (1947) *Metaphysics*, W. D. Ross (trans).

Baily, P. and Farmer, D. (1990) *Purchasing Principles and Management*, 6th edn, Pitman, London.

Baumol, W. J. and Batey Blackman, S. A. (1991) *Perfect Markets and Easy Virtue*, Blackwell, Oxford.

Beauchamp, T. L. (1989) *Case Studies in Business, Society, and Ethics*, Prentice-Hall, New Jersey.

Beardwell, I. and Holden, L. (1994) *Human Resource Management: A Contemporary Perspective*, Pitman, London.

Bedeian, A. G. (1993) *Management*, Harcourt Brace Jovanovich, New York.

Bentham, J. (1789) *Introduction to the Principles of Morals and Legislation*, in M. Warnock (ed.), 1962, *Utilitarianism*, Fontana, London..

Blanchfield, C. (1994) 'Consumer Market Responses to Perceived Business Ethics of Financial Institutions', unpublished M.Phil. thesis, University of Huddersfield.

Blyton, P. and Turnbull, P. (eds) (1992) *Reassessing Human Resource Management*, Sage.

Bok, S. (1982) *Secrets: Concealment and Revelation*, Oxford University Press, Oxford.

Bradley, I. C. (1987) *Enlightened Entrepreneurs*, Weidenfeld & Nicolson, London.

Brazier, M. (1987) *Medicine, Patients and the Law*, Penguin, Harmondsworth.

Brech, E. F. L. (1953) *The Principles and Practice of Management*, Longmans, London.

Burke, T. (1992) *The Co-operative Bank Survey of Business Ethics in the UK*, University of Westminster, London.

Burnham, J. (1945) *The Managerial Revolution*, Penguin, Harmondsworth.

Cadbury, A. (1992) *The Financial Aspects of Corporate Governance*, Stock Exchange.

Campbell, A. and Tawadey, K. (1992) *Mission and Business Philosophy*, Butterworth Heinemann, Oxford.

Campbell, D. and Drummond, J. (1989) *Good Business: Case Studies in Corporate Social Responsibility*, SAUS, Bristol.

Cannon, T. (1994) *Corporate Responsibility: A Textbook on Business Ethics, Governance, Environment: Roles and Responsibilities*, Pitman, London.

Chryssides, G. D. and Kaler, J. H. (1993) *An Introduction to Business Ethics*, Chapman & Hall, London.

Clutterbuck, D., Dearlove, D. and Snow, D. (1992) *Actions Speak Louder: A Management Guide to Corporate Social Responsibility*, Kogan Page, London.

Crouch, C. and Marquand, D. (eds) (1993) *Cooperation and Competition Within Capitalist Economies*, Blackwell, Oxford.

Currie, R. M. (1977) *Work Study*, 4th edn, Pitman, London.

Dart, R. L. (1991) *Management*, 2nd edn, The Dryden Press, London.

David, F. R. (1991) *Strategic Management*, 3rd edn, Macmillan, Basingstoke.

Davies, P. W. F. (1992) 'The Contribution of the Philosophy of Technology to the Management of Technology', Ph.D. thesis, Brunel University with Henley Management College.

Deal, T. and Kennedy, A. (1982) *Corporate Cultures*, Addison-Wesley, New York.

Dewit, B. and Meyer, R. (eds) (1994) *Strategy: Process, Content, Context (An International Perspective)*, West Publishing Company, St. Paul, Minnesota.

Donaldson, J. (1989) *Key Issues in Business Ethics*, Academic Press, London.

Donaldson, J. (1992) *Business Ethics: A European Casebook*, Academic Press, London.

Donaldson, T. (1982) *Corporations & Morality*, Prentice-Hall, New Jersey.

Donaldson, T. (1989) *The Ethics of International Business*, OUP, New York.

Engel, J. F., Blackwell, R. D. and Kincaid, P. W. (1993) *Consumer Behaviour*, The Dryden Press, London.

Etzioni, A. (1988) *The Moral Dimension Toward a New Economics*, The Free Press, New York.

Ferrell, O. C. and Fraedrich, J. (1994) *Business Ethics. Ethical Decision Making and Cases*, 2nd edn, Houghton Mifflin, Boston, Mass.

Freeman, R. E. (1984) *Strategic Management – A Stakeholder Approach*, Pitman, London.

Friedman, M. and R. (1962) *Capitalism and Freedom*, University of Chicago Press.

Friedman, M. and R. (1980) *Free To Choose*, Avon Books, New York.

Gaither, N. (1992) *Production and Operations Management*, 5th edn, Dryden Press, London.

Garrett, T. (1966) *Business Ethics*, Prentice-Hall, Englewood Cliffs, NJ.

Gilligan, C. (1982) *In a Different Voice: Psychological Theory and Women's Development*, Harvard University Press.

Goyder, G. (1993) *The Just Enterprise*, Adamantine Press, London (first published in 1987 by Andre Deutsch).

Hakansson, H. (ed.) (1983) *International Marketing and Purchasing of Industrial Goods: An Interaction Approach*, Wiley, Chichester.

Handy, C. (1978) *Understanding Organisations*, Penguin, Harmondsworth.

Harris, N. (1989) *Professional Codes of Conduct in the U.K.: A Directory*, Mansell, London.

Hayek, Fv. (1982) *Law, Legislation and Liberty, Vol 2, The Mirage of Social Justice*, Routledge & Kegan Paul (first published 1976).

Hellriegel, D., Slocum, J. W. and Woodman, R. W. (1993) *Organisational Behaviour*, 6th edn, West Publishing, St Paul, Minnesota.

Hirsch, F. (1977) *Social Limits to Growth*, Routledge & Kegan Paul, London.

Hobbes, T. (1962) *Leviathan, or The Matter, Form and Power of A Commonwealth Ecclesiasical and Civil*, Collier Books, New York [1651].

Hosmer, L. T. (1987) *The Ethics of Management*, Irwin, New York.

Jay, A. (1967) *Management and Machiavelli*, Penguin, Harmondsworth.

Johnson, D. G. (ed) (1991) *Ethical Issues in Engineering*, Prentice-Hall, Englewood-Cliffs, NJ.

Kant, I. (1948) *The Moral Law*, ed. and trans. H. J. Paton, Hutchinson (first published 1785).

Kohlberg, L. (1981) *Essays on Moral Development, Vol. One: The Philosophy of Moral Development*, Harper & Row, New York.

Lee, S. M. and Schnieder, M. J. (1994) *Operations Management*, Houghton Mifflin, Boston, Mass.

Lynch, D. and Kordis, P. L. (1990) *Strategy of the Dolphin (Winning Elegantly by Coping Powerfully in a World of Turbulent Change)*, Arrow, London (first published by Hutchinson in 1989).

Lyons, J. (1965), *The Forms and Limits of Utilitarianism*, Oxford University Press, Oxford.

MacIntyre, A. (1981) *After Virture: A Study of Moral Theory*, Duckworth, London.

MacIntyre, A. (1967) *A Short History of Ethics*, Routledge, London.

Madsen, P. and Shafritz, J. M. (eds) (1990) *Essentials of Business Ethics*, Meridian, New York.

Mahoney, J. and Vallance, E. (eds) (1992) *Business Ethics in a New Europe*, Kluwer, Dordrecht.

Manley, W. W. (1992) *The Handbook of Good Business Practice*, Routledge, London.

Mathis, R. L. and Jackson, J. H. (1994) *Human Resource Management*, West Publishing, St Paul, Minnesota.

Mathews, J. B. (1994) *Policies and Persons: A Casebook in Business Ethics*, 2nd edn, McGraw-Hill, New York,

Mill, J. S. (1861) *Utilitarianism*, in M. Warnock (ed.), 1962, *Utilitarianism*, Fontana, London.

Mintzberg, H. (1994) *The Rise and Fall of Strategic Planning*, Prentice-Hall International, Hemel Hempstead.

Packard, V. (1969) *The Hidden Persuaders*, Penguin, Harmondsworth.

Pagano, A. M. and Verdin, J. A. (1988) *The External Environment of Business*, Wiley, Chichester.

Parfitt, D. (1984) *Reasons and Persons*, Oxford University Press, Oxford.

Peters, T. (1987) *Thriving on Chaos: Handbook for a Managerial Revolution*, Knopf, New York.

Peters, T. J. and Waterman, R. H. (1982) *In Search of Excellence: Lessons from America's Best-Run Companies*, Harper & Row, New York.

Raven, W. (1994) *Considering Stakeholders' Interests*, Corporate Social Responsibility Consultants.

Rawls, J. (1972) *A Theory of Justice*, Oxford University Press, Oxford.

Regan, D. (1980) *Utilitarianism and Cooperation*, Oxford University Press, Oxford.

Ross, W. D. (1938) *The Right and the Good*, Clarendon Press, Oxford.

Rowe, A. J. *et al.* (1994) *Strategic Management: A Methodological Approach*, 4th edn, Addison Wesley, New York.

Schuler, R. S. and Huber, V. L. (1993) *Personnel and Human Resource Management*, West Publishing, St Paul, Minnesota.

Selwyn, N. M. (1993) *Selwyn's Law of Employment*, Butterworth, London.

Sen, A. (1987) *On Ethics and Economics*, Blackwell, Oxford.

Shaw, W. and Barry, V. (1989) *Moral Issues in Business*, 4th edn, Wadsworth, Belmont, Calif.

Simon, H. A. (1947) *Administrative Behaviour: A Study of Decision-Making Processes in Administrative Organisations*, Macmillan, New York.

Sisson, K. (1989) *Personnel Management in Britain*, Basil Blackwell, Oxford.

Sisson, K. (1994) *Personnel Management: A Comprehensive Guide to theory and Practice in Britain*, Blackwell, Oxford.

Smith, A. (1976) An Inquiry into the Nature and Causes of the Wealth of Nations, Oxford University Press, Oxford (first published 1776).

Smith, I. T. and Wood, J. C. (1993) *Industrial Law*, Butterworth, London.

Soloman, R. (1992) *Ethics and Excellence: Cooperation and Integrity in Business*, Oxford University Press,Oxford.

Sorell, T. and Hendry, J. (1994) *Business Ethics*, Butterworth Heinemann, Oxford.

Stacey, R. D. (1993) *Strategic Management and Organisational Dynamics*, Pitman, London.
Stevenson, W. J. (1993) *Production/Operations Management*, 4th edn, Irwin, New York.
Toffler, A. (1970) *Future Shock*, Bodley Head, London.
Torrington, D. and Hall, L. (1987) *Personnel Management: A New Approach*, Prentice-Hall, New Jersey.
Towers, B. (ed.) (1992) *The Handbook of Human Resoyrce Management*, Blackwell, Oxford.
Townley, B. (1994) *Reframing Human Resource Management: Power, Ethics and the Subject of Work*, Sage, New York.
Warnock, M. (ed.) (1962) *Utilitarianism*, Fontana, London.
Webley, S. (1988) *Company Philosophies and Codes of Business Ethics: A Guide to Their Drafting and Use*, Institute of Business Ethics, London.
Webley, S. (1992) *Business Ethics and Company Codes*, Institute of Business Ethics, London.
Whittington, R. (1993) *What is Strategy – And Does it Matter?*, Routledge, London.
Williamson, O. (1985) *The Economic Institutions of Capitalism*, The Free Press, New York.
Winkler, E. R. and Coombs, J. R. (1993) *Applied Ethics: A Reader*, Blackwell, Oxford.
Wittgenstein, L. (1980) *Culture and Value*, Blackwell, Oxford.

2 Articles

Anderson, G. (1991) 'Selection' in B. Towers (ed.), *The Handbook of Human Resource Management*, Blackwell, Oxford.
Ang, J. S. (1993) 'On Financial Ethics', *Financial Management*, Autumn, pp. 32–59.
Anon (1993) 'Corporate Governance Reform Hit by QMH Affair', *Accounting Age*, 11 Nov.
Arrow, K. J. (1973) 'Social Responsibility and Economic Efficiency', *Public Policy*, vol. 21.
Bader, G. E. S. (1988) 'New Frontiers in Planning – Strategic Issues for the 1990's', *Long Range Planning*, vol. 19, no. 6, pp. 66–74.
Baron, M. (1991) 'The Moral Status of Loyalty', in Johnson (1991) pp. 225–40.
Barr, C. (1993) 'A Code of Ethics: Good, Bad or Indifferent?', *Proceedings of 2nd PSERG Conference*, University of Bath, pp. 19–26.
Barry, A. (1992) 'Days of Wine and Roses', *Purchasing and Supply Management*, October, pp. 22–5.
Blanchfield, C., Lea, E. C. and Richards, G. (1994) 'Business Ethics, Do Consumers Care?', Marketing Education Group, Annual Conference, University of Ulster, Coleraine, July 4–6.
Blyton, P. and Morris, J. (1992) 'HRM and the Limits of Flexibility', in Blyton and Turnbull (1992).
Booms, B. H. and Bitner, M. J. (1981) 'Marketing Strategies and Organization Structures for Service Firms' in *Marketing of Services*, eds J. H. Donnelly and W. R. George, Chicago, American Marketing Association, pp. 47–51.
Bowie, N. (1986) 'Business Ethics', in J. DeMarco and R. Fox (eds), *New Directions in Ethics*, Routledge, London.
Bowie, N. (1990) 'Business Ethics and Cultural Relativism', in Madsen and Shafritz (1990) pp. 366–82.
Bowles, S. and Gintis, H. (1993) 'The Revenge of Homo Economicus: Contested Exchange and the Revival of Political Economy', *Journal of Economic Perspectives*, vol. 7, pp. 83–102.
Bradley, P. (1989) 'Purchasing Ethics? The Rest of Business Should Be So Strict', *Purchasing*, 4th May, pp. 24–5.

Brown, K. M. (1994) 'Using Role Play to Integrate Ethics into the Curriculum: A Financial Management Example', *Journal of Business Ethics*, Feb., pp. 105–10.

Browning, J. M. and Zabriskie, N. B. (1980) 'Professionalism in Purchasing: A Status Report', *Journal of Purchasing and Materials Management*, Fall, pp. 2–10.

Browning, J. M. and Zabriskie, N. B. (1983) 'How Ethical are Industrial Buyers?', *Industrial Marketing Management*, vol. 12, pp. 219–24.

Bruce, M. (1987) 'Managing People First – Bringing the Service Concept to British Airways', *Industrial & Commercial Training*, Mar/April.

Burke, T., Maddock, S. and Rose, A. (1993) 'How Ethical is British Business?', *Research Working Paper Series 2*, No. 1, University of Westminster, Jan.

Camenisch, P. F. (1981) 'Business Ethics: On Getting to the Hearth of the Matter', *Business & Professional Ethics Journal*, vol. 1, pp. 59–69.

Campbell, A. and Yeung, S. (1994) 'Creating a Sense of Mission', in Dewit and Meyer (1994) pp. 147–56.

Carr, A. Z. (1968) 'Is Business Bluffing Ethical?', in *Managing Business Ethics*, ed. J. Drummond and B. Bain (1994) Butterworth Heinemann, Oxford, pp. 28–38. Reprinted from *Harvard Business Review*, vol. 46, 1968, pp. 162–9.

Carroll, A. B. (1991) 'The Pyramid of Corporate Social Responsibility: Toward the Moral Management of Organizational Stakeholders', *Business Horizons*.

Cavell, S. (1969) 'Music Discomposed', in Cavell, *Must We Mean What We Say?*, Cambridge University Press, Cambridge.

Chadwick, R. (1993) 'Codes and Ethics – An Unhappy Alliance?', Conference on Professional and Business Ethics, University of Central Lancashire (unpublished).

Chonko, L. B. and Hunt, S. D. (1985) 'Ethics and Marketing Management: An Empirical Examination', *Journal of Business Research*, vol. 13 (August) pp. 339–59.

Claypool, G. A., Fetyko, D. F. and Pearson, A. (1990) 'Reactions to Ethical Dilemmas: A Study Pertaining Certified Public Accountants', *Journal of Business Ethics*, Sept, pp. 699–706.

Cohen, J. R., Pant, L. W. (1991) 'Beyond Bean Counting: Establishing High Ethical Standards', *Journal of Business Ethics*, Jan., pp. 45–56.

Cohen, J. R., Pant, L. W. and Sharp, D. (1993) 'A Validation and Extension of a Multidimensional Ethics Scale', *Journal of Business Ethics*, vol. 1, pp. 13–26.

Cooke, R. A. and Young, E. (1990) 'The Ethical Side of Takeovers and Mergers', in Madsen and Shafritz (1990) pp. 254–69.

Croft, R. (1994) 'Multi-level Marketing: Claims to Respectability under Scrutiny', *Marketing Education Group, Proceedings of the 1994 Annual Conference*, University of Ulster.

Crouch, C. (1990) 'United Kingdom: The Rejection of Compromise', in G. Baglioni and C. Crouch, *European Industrial Relations: The Challenge of Flexibility*, Sage.

Danley, J. (1993) 'Corporate Moral Agency: The Case for Anthropological Bigotry', in Chryssides and Kaler (1993) pp. 279–86.

Davis, P. and Worthington, S. (1993) 'Cooperative Values: Change and Continuity in Capital Accumulation. The Case of the British Cooperative Bank', *Journal of Business Ethics*, vol. 12, pp. 849–59.

Delaney, J. T. and Sockell, D. (1992) 'Do Company Ethics Programmes make a Difference? An Empirical Analysis', *Journal of Business Ethics*, vol. 11, pp. 719–27.

Donaldson, J. and Davis, P. (1990) 'Business Ethics? Yes, But What Can It Do for the Bottom Line?' *Management Decision*, vol. 28, no. 6, pp. 29–33.

Donaldson, T. (1985) 'Multinational Decision-Making: Reconciling International Norms', in *Managing Business Ethics*, eds Drummond and Bain (1994) Butterworth Heinemann, Oxford, pp. 136–48. Reprinted from *Journal of Business Ethics*, vol. 4, pp. 357–66.

Dore, R. (1993) 'What Makes the Japanese Different?', in *Ethics and Markets. Co-operation and Competition within Capitalist Economies*, ed. Colin Crouch and David Marquand, Blackwell, Oxford, pp. 66–79.

Drucker, P. F. (1981) 'What is Business Ethics?', *The Public Interest*, Spring.

Dubinsky, A. J. and Gwin, J. M. (1981) 'Business Ethics: Buyers and Sellers', *Journal of Purchasing and Materials Management*, Winter, pp. 9–16.

Ennew, C., McGregor, A. and Diacon, S. (1993) 'Ethical Aspects of Savings and Investment Products' MEG, Proceedings of Annual Conference, vol 1, pp. 297–307.

Evans, R. (1991) 'Business Ethics and Changes in Society', *Journal of Business Ethics*, vol. 1011, pp. 871–6.

Evers, S. (1994) 'The Manager as a Professional', Institute of Management reviewed in *Management Services*, March 1994, vol. 38, no. 3.

Fearnley, M. (1993) 'Corporate Reputation: The Wasted Asset', *Marketing Intelligence and Planning*, vol. 11, no. 11, pp. 4–8.

Felch, R. I. (1985) 'Standards of Conduct: The Key to Supplier Relations', *Journal of Purchasing and Materials Management*, Fall, pp. 16–18.

Ferrell, O. C. and Gresham, L. G. (1985) 'A Contingency Framework for Understanding Ethical Decision Making in Marketing', *Journal of Marketing*, vol. 49 (Summer) pp. 87–96.

Flyvbjorg, B. (1993) 'Science, Ethics and Rationality', in Winkler and Coombs.

Forker, L. B. and Janson, R. L. (1990) 'Ethical Practices in Purchasing', *Journal of Purchasing and Materials Management*, Winter, pp. 19–26.

Forsyth, D. R. (1992) 'Judging the Morality of Business Practice: The Influence of Personal Moral Philosophies', *Journal of Business Ethics*, vol. 11.

Friedman, M. (1970) 'The Social Responsibility of Business is to Increase its Profits', *The New York Times Magazine*, 13 September 1970. Reprinted in Chryssides and Kaler (1993) pp. 249–54.

Fritzsche, D. J. and Becker, H. (1984) 'Linking Management Behaviour to Ethical Philosophy – An Empirical Investigation', *Journal of Business Ethics*, vol. 27, no. 1, pp. 166–75.

Gellerman, S. W. (1986) 'Why Good Managers Make Bad Ethical Choices', *Harvard Business Review*, July/August.

Genfan, H. (1987) 'Formalizing Business Ethics', *Training and Development Journal*, November.

Gibbs, P. T. (1993) 'Customer Care and Service: A Case for Business Ethics', *International Journal of Bank Marketing*, vol. 11, no. 1, pp. 26–33.

Goodpaster, K. E. (1983) 'The Concept of Corporate Responsibility', *Journal of Business Ethics*, vol. 2, pp. 1–22.

Goodpaster, K. E. (1983) 'Some Avenues for Ethical Analysis in General Management', Harvard Business School, case 9–383–007.

Gunz, S. and McCutcheon, J. (1991) 'Some Unresolved Ethical Issues in Auditing', *Journal of Business Ethics*, Oct., pp. 777–85.

Hamilton, K. (1993) 'Queens Calls in Valuers Again', *The Times*, 27 Nov. 93.

Harness, D. and MacKay, S. (1994) 'Product Elimination Strategies of the Financial Services Sector', Marketing Education Group, Proceedings of the Annual Conference, University of Ulster.

Harvey, B. (1992) 'Market Morality', *Times Higher Education Supplement*, 11 Sept. 92.

Hausman, D. M. and McPhearson, M. S. (1993) 'Taking Ethics Seriously; Economics and Contemporary Moral Philosophy', *Journal of Economic Literature*, vol. 31, pp. 671–731.

Hawley, D. (1991) 'Business Ethics and Social Responsibility in Finance', *Journal of Business Ethics*, Sept., pp. 711–21.

Hiltebeitel, K. M. and Jones, S. K. (1992) 'An Assessment of Ethics Instruction in Accounting Education', *Journal of Business Ethics*, Jan., pp. 37–46.

Hoffman, W. M. (1986) 'What is Necessary for Corporate Moral Excellence', *Journal of Business Ethics*, vol. 5, pp. 232–42

Höpfl, H., Smith, S. and Spencer, S. (1992) 'Values and Valuations: The Conflicts between Culture Change and Job Cuts', *Personnel Review*, vol. 21, no. 1, pp. 24–38.

Hosmer, L. T. (1991) 'Managerial Responsibilities on the Micro Level', *Business Horizons*, July/August, pp. 49–55.

Hunt, S. D., Chonko, L. B. and Wilcox, J. B. (1984) 'Ethical Problems of Marketing Researchers', *Journal of Marketing Research*, vol. 21 (August) pp. 304–24.

Hunt, S. D., Wood, V. R. and Chonko, B. (1989) 'Corporate Ethical Values and Organisational Commitment in Marketing', Journal of Marketing, vol. 53, pp. 79–90.

Huss, H. F. and Patterson, D. M. (1993) 'Ethics in Accounting: Values Education Without Indoctrination', *Journal of Business Ethics*, Mar., pp. 235–43.

Jennings, M. (1991) 'Ethics, Excellence and Accountants', *Accountancy*, Jan., pp. 23–4.

Kavathatzopoulos, I. (1993) 'Development of a Cognitive Skill in Solving Business Ethics Problems: The Effect of Instruction', *Journal of Business Ethics*, vol. 12, pp. 379–86.

Keat, R. (1993) 'The Moral Boundaries of the Market', in Crouch and Marquand (1993) pp. 6–20.

Kitson, A. (1994) 'Managing Ethics: The Case of The Cooperative Bank', *European Case Clearing House*, no. 494–009–1.

Kullberg, D. R. (1990) 'Business Ethics: Not a Luxury; Standards of Ethical Conduct for Management Accountants', *Management Accounting*, Feb., pp. 20–1.

Ladd, J. (1982) 'Collective and Individual Moral Responsibility in Engineering: Some Questions', *IEEE Technology & Society Magazine*, vol. 12 (June) pp. 3–10.

Langlois, C. C. and Schlegelmilch, B. B. (1990) 'Do Corporate Codes of Ethics Reflect National Characteristics? Evidence from Europe and the United States', *Journal of International Business Studies*, vol. 12, no.3, pp. 519–39.

Langtry, R. (1994) 'Selection' in I. Beardwell and L. Holden (eds), *Human Resource Management*, Pitman, London.

Laczniak, G. R. (1983) 'Business Ethics: A Managers's Primer', *Business*, vol. 33, January-March, pp. 23–9.

Levitt, T. (1958) 'The Dangers of Social Responsibility', *Harvard Business Review*, vol. 3, no. 6, 1958.

Lewis, B. R. (1991) 'Service Quality: An International Comparison of Bank Customers' Expectations and Perceptions', *Journal of Marketing Management*, vol. 7, pp. 47–62.

Lickona, T. (1987) 'What Does Moral Psychology Have to Say to the Teacher of Ethics?', in D. Callahan and S. Bok (eds), *Ethics Teaching in Higher Education*, Plenum Press, New York.

Locke, D. (1976) 'Why the Utilitarians Shot President Kennedy', *Analysis*, vol. 36.

Loeb, S. E. and Rockness, J. (1992) 'Accounting Ethics and Education: A Response', *Journal of Business Ethics*, July, pp. 485–90.

Lowe, J. (1993) 'Manufacturing Reform and the Changing Role of the Production Supervisor', *Journal of Management Studies*, vol. 30, no. 5, Sept.

Lynn, M. (1993) 'Terry Thomas', *Management Today*, July, pp. 44–6.

MacIntyre, A. (1977) 'Why are the Problems of Business Ethics Insoluble?', Conference proceedings from Bentley College, Mass, pp.99–107.

Mahoney, J. (1993) 'Teaching Business Ethics', *Professional Manager*, March.

Mahoney, J. (1989) 'Morality at the Boardroom Level', *Times Higher Education Supplement*, 5 May 89.

Malloy, D. C. and Lang, D. L. (1993) 'An Aristotelian Approach to Case Study Analysis', *Journal of Business Ethics*, vol. 12, pp. 511–16.

Marckus, M. (1993a) 'Time for QMH to Publish Assets in Wonderland', *The Times*, 6 Nov. 93.

Marckus, M. (1993b) 'QMH Chiefs Face a Gale of Criticism', *The Times*, 29 Nov. 93.

Martens, S. and Stevens, K. (1994) 'The FASB's Cost/Benefit Constraint in Theory and Practice', *Journal of Business Ethics*, Mar., pp. 171–9.

McDonald, G. M. and Zepp, R. A. (1989) 'Business Ethics – Practical Proposals', *Journal of Management Development*, vol. 8, no. 1, pp. 55–66.

McNair, F. and Milam, E. E. (1993) 'Ethics in Accounting Education: What is Really Being Done', *Journal of Business Ethics*, Oct., pp. 797–809.

Miles, G. (1993) 'In Search of Ethical Profits: Insights from Strategic Management', *Journal of Business Ethics*, vol. 123, pp. 219–25.

Miliband, D. (1993) 'The New Politics of Economics', in *Ethics and Markets. Co-operation and Competition within Capitalist Economies*, ed. Colin Crouch and David Marquand, Blackwell, Oxford, pp. 21–30.

Mitchell, A., Puxty, T. and Sikka, P. (1994) 'Ethical Statements as Smokescreens for Sectional Interests: The Case of the UK Accountancy', *Journal of Business Ethics*, Jan, pp. 39–51.

Mulgan, G. (1993) 'Reticulated Organisations: The Birth and Death of the Mixed Economy', in *Ethics and Markets. Co-operation and Competition within Capitalist Economies*, ed. Colin Crouch and David Marquand, Blackwell, Oxford, pp. 31–47.

Murphy, P. E. (1988) 'Implementing Business Ethics', *Journal of Business Ethics*, vol. 7, pp. 907–15.

Murphy, P. E. and Laczniak, G. R. (1981) 'Marketing Ethics: A Review with Implications for Managers, Educators and Researchers' in Enis and Roering (1981) pp. 251–66.

Narayanam, D. (1992) 'The Right Stuff', *Purchasing and Supply Management*, October, pp. 25–6.

Nash, L. (1981) 'Ethics without the Sermon', *Harvard Business Review*, Nov/Dec.

Nash, L. (1992) 'American and European Corporate Ethics Practices: A 1991 Survey', in Mahoney and Vallance (1992).

Pangalos, P. (1993) 'QMH investor issue petition', *Sunday Times*, 28 Nov. 93.

Parasuraman, A., Zeithaml, V. and Berry, L. L. (1985) 'A Conceptual Model of Service Quality and its Implications for Future Research', *Journal of Marketing*, vol. 49 (Fall) pp. 41–50.

Patten, D. M. (1990) 'The Differential Perception of Accountants to Maccoby's, Head/ Heart Traits', *Journal of Business Ethics*, Oct., pp. 791–8.

Peek, L. E., Peek, G. S. and Horras, M. (1994) 'Enhancing Arthur Business Ethics Vignettes: Group', *Journal of Business Ethics*, Mar., pp. 189–96.

Premeux, S. and Mundy, R. W. (1993) 'Linking Managerial Behaviour to Ethical Philosophy', *Journal of Business Ethics*, vol. 5, pp. 349–57.

Ramsey, J. (1989) 'No Bribes Please, We're Professionals', *Purchasing and Supply Management*, December, pp. 31–3.

Randall, J. (1993) 'Queens Moat: now you see it, now you don't', *Sunday Times*, 31 Oct. 93.

Randall, J. and Olins, R. (1993) 'Queens Moat: City anger turns on Howell as new horrors emerge', *Sunday Times*, 31 Oct. 93.

Ricklefs, R. (1983) 'Executives and General Public Say Ethical Behaviour is Declining in U.S.', *Wall Street Journal*, October 31, p. 25.

Robson, P. (1992) 'A Day at the Races, a Night at the Opera', *Purchasing and Supply Management*, October, pp. 27–9.

Rudelius, P. W. and Buchholz, R. A. (1979) 'What Industrial Purchasers See as Key Ethical Dilemmas', *Journal of Purchasing and Materials Management*, Winter, pp. 2–10.

Ryan, L. (1994) 'Ethics Codes in British Companies', *Business Ethics*, vol. 3, no. 1 (January).

Schlachter, P. J. (1990) 'Organisational Influences on Individual Ethical Behaviour', *Journal of Business Ethics*, Nov., pp. 389–853.

Schoenfeldt, L.F. *et al.* (1991) 'The Teaching Of Business Ethics: A Survey of AACSB Member Schools', *Journal of Business Ethics*, vol. 10, pp. 237–41.

Sibley, S. D. (1979) 'Images of the Purchasing Department', *Journal of Purchasing and Materials Management*, Fall, pp. 19–23.

Sinclair, A. (1993) 'Approaches to Organisational Culture and Ethics', *Journal of Business Education*, vol. 12, pp. 63–73

Singer, A. E. (1994) 'Strategy as Moral Philosophy', *Strategic Management Journal*, vol. 15, pp. 191–213.

Skapinker, M. (1993) 'Queens moat shareholders establish fighting fund', *Financial Times* 16 Nov. 93.

Smart, J. J. C. (1986) 'Utilitarianism and Its Applications', in J. P. Demarco and R. M. Fox (eds), *New Directions in Ethics*, Routledge & Kegan Paul, London.

Snoeyenbos, M. and Jewell, D. (1989) 'Morals, Management and Codes', in Snoeyenbos *et al.*, *Business Ethics*, Prometheus Books, New York.

Soloman, R. (1993) 'Corporate Roles, Personal Virtues: An Aristotelian Approach to Business Ethics', in Winkler and Coombs (1993).

Stanga, K. G. and Turpen, R. A. (1991) 'Ethical Judgements on Selected Accounting Issues: An Empirical Study', *Journal of Business Ethics*, Oct., pp. 739–47.

Stead, W. E., Worrel, D. L. and Stead, G. S. (1990) 'An Integrative Model for Understanding and Managing Ethical Behaviour in Organisations', *Journal of Business Ethics*, vol. 9, pp. 215–26.

Stiglitz, J. (1993) 'Post Walrasian and Post Marxian Economics', *Journal of Economic Perspective*, vol. 7, pp. 109–14.

Stuttard, G. (1992) 'Robert Owen, 1771–1858; A 19th Century Pilgrim's Progress in the World of European Business Ethics', in Mahoney and Vallance (1992) pp. 49–58.

Tendler, S. (1994) 'A nation of robbers, fiddlers and thieves', *The Times*, 21 Sept. 1994.

Thomas, T. (1993) 'The Banker as Ethical Businessman', *Banking World*, March.

Vallance, E. (1993) 'Good at Work: The Ethics of Modern Business', *Banking World*, March.

Waples, E. and Shaub, M. K. (1991) 'Establishing an Ethic of Accounting: A Response to Westra's Call for Government Employment of Auditors', *Journal of Business Ethics*, May, pp. 385–93.

Ward, S. P., Ward, D. R. and Deck, A. B. (1993) 'Certified Public Accountants: Ethical Perception Skills', *Journal of Business Ethics*, Aug., pp. 601–10.

Watson, T. (1994) 'Recruitment and Selection' in K. Sisson (ed.), *Personnel Management: A Comprehensive Guide to Theory and Practice in Britain*, Blackwell, Oxford.

Weaver, G. R. (1993) 'Corporate Codes of Ethics: Purpose, Process and Content Issues', *Business and Society*, vol. 33, no. 1, p. 46.

Williams, J. G. (1993) 'Management Buyouts: Technical Problems or Ethical Dilemmas?', Conference on Professional and Business Ethics, October (1993) University of Central Lancashire (unpublished).

Wood, G. (1994) 'Ethical Issues at the Marketing/Purchasing Interface: The Practitioner's Experience', Proceedings of the British Academy of Management Conference, University of Lancaster.

Young, D. (1989) 'British Airways – Putting the Customer First', for Ashridge Strategic Management Centre, July,

3 Institutional Reports, etc.

Accounting Standard Board (1991) *The Objective of Financial Statements and the Qualitative Characteristics of Financial Information.*

British Airways (1992) *Report & Accounts, 1991–92.*

Burke, T. (1992) *The Co-operative Bank Survey of Business Ethics in the UK*, University of Westminster, London.

Cadbury, A. (1992) *The Financial Aspects of Corporate Governance*, Stock Exchange.

Chartered Institute of Management Accountants (1991) *Management Accounting: Official Terminology.*

CIPS (1977) *The Ethical Code of the Chartered Institute of Purchasing and Supply*, Stamford, CIPS.

Cooperative Bank plc., The (1992) *Annual Report and Accounts.*

Cooperative Bank plc., The (1993) Performance Management Appraisal.

Enis, B. and Roering, K. (eds) (1981) *Review of Marketing (1981)* Chicago, American Marketing Association.

Friends of the Earth (1991) 'Brazil – "Sustainability" and the Trade in Tropical Timbers', Briefing sheet, November.

Friends of the Earth (1991) 'Sustainability and the Trade in Tropical Rainforest Timber', Special Briefing, August.

Income Data Services (1990) *European Management Guides: Recruitment*, Income Data Services/Institute of Personnel Management.

IPM (1994) *The IPM Code of Professional Conduct: The IPM Codes of Practice.*

IRS (1991) *IRS Recruitment and Development Report*, 'The State of Selection 2', May.

Index

252   *Index*